Refrains for Moving Bodies

EXPERIENCE AND EXPERIMENT IN AFFECTIVE SPACES

Refrains for Moving Bodies

Derek P. McCormack

Duke University Press   Durham and London   2013

Printed in the United States of America on acid-free paper ∞
Designed by Courtney Leigh Baker and typeset in Whitman
by Copperline Book Services, Inc.

Library of Congress Cataloging-in-Publication Data
McCormack, Derek P.
Refrains for moving bodies : experience and experiment in affective spaces /
Derek P. McCormack.
pages cm
Includes bibliographical references and index.
ISBN 978-0-8223-5489-5 (cloth : alk. paper)
ISBN 978-0-8223-5505-2 (pbk. : alk. paper)
1. Cultural geography. 2. Movement, Psychology of. 3. Affect (Psychology) I. Title.
GF41.M395 2013
304.2 — dc23   2013025656

In the pulse of inner life immediately present now in each of us is a little past, a little future, a little awareness of our own body, of each other's persons, of these sublimities we are trying to talk about, of the earth's geography and the direction of history, of truth and error, of good and bad, and of who knows how much more?

—WILLIAM JAMES, *A Pluralistic Universe*

CONTENTS

PREFACE

In this book I explore the qualities of affective spaces generated for and by moving bodies through a process of participating in the possibilities these spaces afford for experimenting with experience. Like many in the social sciences and humanities, human geographers do not acknowledge often enough the influence of these spaces on the shape and substance of thinking. Perhaps this is because such influence resists individualization, registering and persisting as a vague set of swirling affects rather than as a discrete personality. *Refrains for Moving Bodies* is about how these spaces and their affective influence matter: it explores the potential of these spaces — or more precisely these spacetimes — to make a difference to the sensibilities through which thinking takes place. This difference cannot be tracked and traced with any degree of calculable precision. Yet as this book demonstrates, there are concepts and techniques through which, by encouraging a modest experimental empiricism, the play of this difference in the processual field of experience can be rendered palpable, even if only in passing.

Often, of course, the influence of affective spaces for moving bodies becomes discernible only in retrospect. For instance, in early 1991 I needed to make a decision: to continue working for a major multinational semiconductor manufacturer or to return to university to study geography after a break of over a year following an unsuccessful stint as a student of analytical chemistry. By chance, on the evening before that decision was made, I attended the Abbey Theatre in Dublin to see a production of Brian Friel's *Dancing at Lughnasa*.[1] Set in Donegal in 1936, the play centers on the lives of a family of sisters, one of whom has a young son, who, in middle age, serves as the narrator of the events. Friel's play articulates all kinds of tensions and tendencies in Irish popular culture, particularly those centering on the body as a site of expression, celebration, and social control. Perhaps unsurprisingly, *Dancing at Lughnasa* has been subject to a range of critical readings exploring how the text figures and performs the relation between place, gender, and identity.[2] To be sure, these readings have some purchase. Such readings were beyond me, however, as I sat and witnessed that particular performance: certainly, the habits of thinking on which they are based had yet to be cultivated. And even now when I think of it, aware as I am of the bleak futures that haunt the lives performed in the play, what I remember of that performance are moving bodies: bodies "moving rhythmically"; bodies responding more to the "mood of the music than to its beat"; bodies moving in but also generating a kind of space of experience "in which atmosphere is more real than incident and everything is simultaneously actual and illusory."[3]

It would be tempting to imagine that attending the Abbey production of *Dancing at Lughnasa* was a decisive moment: to think that a clear arc of influence could somehow be traced between that moment and any subsequent course of action or line of interest. What can be said, however, is that those moving bodies, in concert with props, lights, and sound, worked to create an affective context shaping, however briefly, the sensibility through which thinking, as an orientation toward futures, took place. And for my part, what can be said is that the next day I decided to return to university to study geography. That the geographies in which I would eventually become interested might involve moving bodies was certainly not obvious at that point. And when a concern with the relation between bodies and geography did first emerge on my horizon of interest, it was framed largely in terms of representation: bodies were maps of signification (and power) whose meaning could be challenged and contested through critical readings. Viewed in this way, the characters and the spaces in Friel's play could be understood in terms of how they represented wider cultural themes. While it offers a great deal of critical purchase on the cultural geographies of bodies, this approach clearly leaves something out: a concern with the experiential — and more precisely the affective — dimensions of geographies that are excessive of a practice of cultural-critical reading that attends to the codification of corporeality. Fortunately my own growing interest in the spaces of moving bodies coincided with the emergence within human geography and beyond of a sustained engagement with what Nigel Thrift has called nonrepresentational theory.[4] This diverse body of work has many features, but central to it is the claim that spaces, and our sense of their extent and intensity, cannot be reduced to questions of representation, where representation is either an internal (cognitive) or an external symbol. Nonrepresentational theories, in contrast, encourage us to think of spaces and places in terms of their enactive composition through practice. They encourage us to find ways of making more of the affective qualities of these spaces: precisely those qualities exemplified through the processual enactment of Friel's play in the Abbey Theatre that night. And they do so not at the expense of attention to lived experience, nor, indeed, to critique as naive any appeal to experience: rather, for nonrepresentational theories the important question is how to cautiously reaffirm experience as a source — however modest — of conceptual, empirical, and ethico-political experiment.

Written over the course of a decade or so of engagement with nonrepresentational theories, the chapters in this book explore how the affective spaces generated by and for moving bodies offer opportunities for experimenting with experience. Two interrelated questions motivate these chapters. The first question is a conceptual-empirical one: how to make sense of the peculiarly affective qualities of the spaces produced by and for moving bodies? *Refrains for Moving Bodies* develops answers to this question through pursuing a radical empiricism in which concepts participate in the felt process of being drawn into, and drawing out, the affective qualities of worldly experience rather than distancing thinking from that experience.[5] That is, concepts provide important ways of experimentally amplifying and modulating the felt qualities of the affects that move across and between bodies in encounters that are variously staged and contingent. In the process, *Refrains for Moving Bodies* affirms concepts as lived abstractions that sensitize thinking both to the affective qualities of spaces and to the myriad techniques and technologies through which these spaces are generated. What emerges in the process is an account of affective spaces — or more accurately spacetimes — as they are generated and modulated, and as they circulate across many different domains of practice and life.

The second question motivating this book follows on from the first, and can be formulated thus: what kinds of ethico-political experiments might be facilitated by conceptual-empirical participation in ecologies of practices organized around moving bodies? This question is particularly pressing in a world where the issue of what counts as a good life is more and more bound up in the capacities of bodies to affect and be affected through movement. Equally, its importance arises also from the problem of how best to grasp the value of forms of affective life that are always potentially in excess of the economic, geopolitical, and biopolitical formations in which they are implicated.[6] In this book, affective spacetimes are understood as relation-specific milieus in which the value of this excess might be explored through experiments with moving bodies.[7] A central claim underpinning what follows, therefore, is that exploring the ethico-political potential of these spacetimes is best pursued through the cultivation of an affirmative critique: that is, through a style of critique that does not let some of the problems and difficulties associated with the object of critique foreclose opportunities for making more of and valuing the excessive qualities of this object through forms of modest experiment.[8]

Refrains for Moving Bodies takes place precisely as a series of modest relation-specific experiments. Linking all these experiments, in what follows, is a commitment to stretching out the affective qualities of empirical moments, events, and encounters in order to sense what might emerge. Put another way, the moments of affective excess emerging from these contexts are affirmed here as generative intervals of potential from which new refrains for thinking, feeling, and moving, however minor, might emerge and be sustained within and across forms of life and the movements of thought of which they are composed.

ACKNOWLEDGMENTS

Movements of thought emerge and are sustained by a multiplicity of formative encounters within and beyond institutions. During the three years I spent studying geography and sociology at NUI Maynooth, Reamonn Fealy, Brendan Bartley, Paddy Duffy, Fran Walsh, Eamon Slater, and Michael McGreil, among many others, moved me to ask better questions of the world. At Virginia Tech, conversations with Rebekah Burgess, Carl Dahlman, Gail Hunger, Ivan Jadric, Paul Knox, Tim Luke, Gerard Toal, and Stephen White enormously expanded my sense of the promise of doing geography. Gerard Toal, in particular, was a critically formative mentor, and I learned so much from him about the practice and craft of scholarship and teaching. I was also tremendously fortunate to have had Nigel Thrift as a PhD supervisor — this book owes a great deal to the ongoing influence of his work and advice, and engages with just some of the many questions his thinking continues to open up. Like so many others, I benefited greatly from the remarkable atmosphere of conceptual and empirical experiment at Bristol encouraged by Nigel, Paul Cloke, Sarah Whatmore, and others — an atmosphere sustained and developed in all kinds of interesting ways by Sean Carter, J. D. Dewsbury, Shaun French, Billy Harris, Paul Harrison, Julian Holloway, Mark Paterson, Claire Pearson, Emma Roe, Sergei Shubin, and John Wylie. Thanks in particular to J. D., Paul, John, and Mitch Rose for having the foresight to organize that wonderfully catalytic Enacting Geographies session a lifetime ago. At the University of Southampton, David Conradson, Jürgen Essletzbichler, Alan Latham, and Donald McNeill were supportive and encouraging colleagues, both on and off the Astroturf.

Alan, especially, helped me to articulate my own research interests through a set of wider concerns and debates — many thanks for this and for the friendship.

Many people have made the labyrinthine institutional spaces of Oxford easier and more enjoyable to navigate, including Andrew Barry, Pam Berry, Gordon Clark, Chris Gosden, Tony Lemon, Linda McDowell, Richard Powell, Tim Schwanen, and Heather Viles. Particular thanks to Sarah Whatmore for advice and encouragement when it mattered. I shall be forever in the debt of Ali Rogers for introducing me to Wednesday LSI football nights — they have kept me moving at many points over the past few years. My time at Oxford has been enriched by the presence of wonderful graduate students, including Sebastian Abrahamsson, Janet Banfield, Becky Catarelli, Zoe Enstone, Joe Gerlach, Jeff Hung, and Thomas Jellis: their experiments with experience have helped me reflect upon the limits of my own. Equally, the persistent questioning of brilliant undergraduates at Hertford and Mansfield Colleges has helped me develop some of the ideas in this book.

Participation in a number of formative events, workshops, and gatherings informs the arguments of the chapters that follow. I am especially grateful for the opportunity to participate in events organized by Stephen Hodge, Petra Kuppers, Kanta Kochhar-Lindgren, Alan Read, Sarah Rubidge, and Jennie Savage. Sadly, Gill Clarke, who participated so fully in the event described in chapter 8, passed away as I was revising this manuscript. The ethos and sensibility of *Refrains for Moving Bodies* has been incalculably inflected by participation in richly inspiring events organized by the Sense-Lab in Montreal in 2006, 2007, and 2009. My heartfelt thanks to the many organizers and coparticipants for facilitating such generously open-ended experiments whose after-affects continue to reverberate and generate new connections. Thanks also to the editorial collective of *Inflexions* for the invitation to begin thinking about spaces of experiment. I am also grateful to all those people who, through their organization of and participation in various somatic and dance practices, contributed to the generation of atmospheres for experimenting with bodies and ideas. Thanks in particular to Dance Voice Bristol for helping me think through the relation between therapy and movement.

There are many other individuals, not already named, whose inspiring work, friendship, or generosity at various points have helped me make more of the thinking-spaces within which this book emerged: particular thanks to Peter Adey, Ben Anderson, Jane Bennett, Nick Bingham, David Bissell, William Connolly, Scott deLahunta, Mark Heffernan, Hayden Lorimer, Stephen McManus, Erin Manning, Brian Massumi, Mike Pearson, and Gary Timpson.

Courtney Berger is a wonderful editor with an uncanny ability to be perfectly attuned to the rhythms of thinking and writing that shape a project like this, and to know exactly how and when they should be modulated. I had the great fortune to have two marvellous readers for Duke University Press who responded to the first and second drafts of this book with exemplary attentiveness, generosity, and rigor. Thank you so much for your thinking time, and for your careful provocations. I am grateful to the brilliant team of people at Duke University Press for making the process of putting this book together such an easy one. Ailsa Allen in the School of Geography and Environment at Oxford did a fantastic job with the line diagrams, and Richard Beacham very kindly provided all the scans of Adolphe Appia's work.

Parts of this book draw upon and develop previously published material. Some of the ideas in chapter 1 were first exercised in "Drawing Out the Lines of the Event," *Cultural Geographies* 11, no. 2 (2004): 212–220. An earlier version of chapter 2 appeared as "Diagramming Practice and Performance," *Environment and Planning D: Society and Space* 23, no. 1 (2005): 119–147. An earlier version of chapter 3 appeared as "A Paper with an Interest in Rhythm," *Geoforum* 33, no. 4 (2002): 469–485. An earlier version of chapter 4 appeared as "An Event of Geographical Ethics in Spaces of Affect," *Transactions of the Institute of British Geographers* 28, no. 4 (2003): 488–507. Chapter 6 draws on ideas first explored in "Thinking in Transition: The Affirmative Refrain of Experience/Experiment," in *Taking-Place: Nonrepresentational Theories and Geography*, edited by Ben Anderson and Paul Harrison (Farnham, U.K.: Ashgate, 2010).

Special thanks to Fiachra for asking me what lies at the edge, to Cillian for knowing when to tell me to calm down, and to you both for your love of becoming whirling dervishes, good songs well sung, and Glen Campbell. Andrea, thanks for the verve you bring to our lives, and for your love and support over the last decade. Finally, thanks to my parents for that evening in the Abbey and much more besides.

Affective Spaces for
Moving Bodies

Refrains for Moving Bodies begins in the midst of a conceptual and empirical relation — between bodies and spaces — that at first glance can appear relatively uncontroversial. Uncontroversial because it seems all too obvious that bodies move through and within spaces. They move through corridors, across rooms, along streets. And they move thus with varying degrees of fluency and frustration. Uncontroversial also because it appears similarly obvious that certain spaces are designed explicitly to facilitate the movement of bodies for a range of aesthetic, cultural, or political purposes. Theaters, stadiums, churches, parade grounds, airports, and shopping malls are among the more obvious examples. What links each of these spaces, from the sacred to the profane, from the public to the more obviously commercial, is that they demonstrate how the movement, flow, and stillness of bodies is both enabled and constrained by various material architectures, habitual behaviors, and organizational technologies.[1]

The relation between moving bodies and spaces is more than physical, however. And this is because it is always more than a relation between two discrete things: it is a relation between things already in process. On one hand then, the claim that moving bodies are never singular or homogeneous is by now well established. Certainly, to suggest that the identities of moving bodies are in any way stable or fixed is no longer credible, thanks to the efforts of feminist and post-structuralist scholars across the social sciences and humanities. But the unsettling of bodies involves more than a critique of the performative articulation of their identities. It also involves thinking through and grappling with how to make sense of the affective materialities of bodies as they emerge from, and in turn fold into, worlds of difference in the making. It involves, as Erin Manning writes, thinking of bodies as "relational matrices" composed of multiple capacities for making sense of worlds that complicate any strict opposition between inside and outside.[2] It involves thinking of bodies as lively compositions crossing thresholds of intensive and extensive consistency whose limits are defined less by physical boundaries than by capacities to affect and be affected by other bodies.[3]

As this point suggests, the question of how to think moving bodies already presupposes the question of space. Yet space, similarly, is never undifferentiated. Certainly, space is not reducible to the status of a passive, three-dimensional container within which the intentional action of an embodied, moving subject unfolds. Space, in other words, is never a backdrop for something more dynamic. Nor, indeed, can or should it be juxtaposed to process or temporality in a way that privileges the latter. Instead, it is always more accurate to speak of space, or spaces, as multiple: spaces produced via a range of technologies and experienced through different sensory registers; spaces with variable reaches and intensities; and spaces that can often only be apprehended in and through the assemblages of movement and stillness of which they are composed.[4] Hence the question with which this book begins: if bodies and spaces are always already matters in process, how best to explore what social theorist Henri Lefebvre calls the *generative* relation between both in ways that do not presume the existence of one prior to the other? That is, how to explore and make sense of how bodies and spaces co-produce one another through practices, gestures, movements, and events?[5]

In *Refrains for Moving Bodies* I argue that making sense of this generative relation — that is, learning to think through and within the spaces produced for and by moving bodies — demands particular attention to the affective qualities of these spaces combined with a commitment to experimenting with different ways of becoming attuned to these qualities.[6] Affective qualities are those heterogeneous matters of the sensible world we often try to capture through terms such as emotion, mood, and feeling. As part of the "affective turn" across the social sciences, these qualities of everyday life have been explored in a range of interesting and important ways.[7] Bodies, in their manifold incarnations, are central to this work. Yet one of the key insights emerging from the affective turn is that affect is by no means confined to or contained by the physical limit of bodies. Affect is instead better conceived of as a distributed and diffuse field of intensities, circulating within but also moving beyond and around bodies.[8] At the same time, the movement of bodies generates disturbances and perturbations that transform the intensity and reach of this field. In the process, bodies participate in the generation of affective spaces: spaces whose qualities and consistencies are vague but sensed, albeit barely, as a distinctive affective tonality, mood, or atmosphere.

For much of the time affective spaces are being produced without much in the way of direct intervention: they emerge accidentally, sometimes surprisingly, as part of the circulation of what Kathleen Stewart calls "ordinary affects."[9] They are happened upon, sensed unexpectedly. They seize us as we are entering into them. Moreover, the qualities of affective spaces are transmitted and felt across bodies, which are then potentially affected by, or moved by, these spaces. In fact, when we start to think about this, it becomes extremely difficult to differentiate the affective qualities of bodies and spaces. Both are always in the process of actively enhancing and dampening the qualities of one another. To dance with others is to sense this. To sit in a theater is to sense this. To attend a football game, or indeed any other sporting activity that draws an audience, is to sense this. So also is to listen to radio commentary on sporting events. Equally, to watch moving images of moving bodies projected on a screen — on a laptop, in a cinema, on a phone — is to sense this. A myriad of practices, techniques, and technologies are employed deliberately to actively organize, work upon, and choreograph moving bodies with the aim of producing affective spaces and modulating their intensity. Indeed, one of the most remarkable features of contemporary Western societies is the sheer variety of means available for actively generating and modulating affective spaces for moving bodies in different ways.

While differing enormously, these spaces share a number of key characteristics that can be outlined briefly in the form of propositions for experimenting with thinking and feeling. First, these spaces are relational — they involve nonreducible relations between bodies, and between bodies and other kinds of things, including artifacts, ideas, and concepts, where neither these things nor bodies are ever stable themselves.[10] Second, affective spaces are processual: that is, they exist as worlds in ontogenetic transformation whose variations can be sensed through different techniques of attention, participation, and involvement — techniques that can and should be cultivated as part of the process of thinking. Third, affective spaces are nonrepresentational: that is, their force does not necessarily cross a threshold of cognitive representation in order to make a difference with the potential to be felt. That is, these spaces have a quality that cannot necessarily be grasped or evaluated through a representational model of thinking — or at least not initially, and not if these qualities are to be sustained in thought. Instead, these spaces generate vague but tangible shifts, twists, and turns in the multilayered sensibility from which thinking takes place. They are composed of fragile and sometimes fleeting combinations of percepts, affects, and concepts — ways of seeing, feeling, and thinking that can align in potentially eventful and novel ways. Pursuing possibilities for sensing and thinking through the relational, processual, and nonrepresentational qualities of these spaces, and drawing them out through different techniques and technologies for experimenting experience, is central to the project of *Refrains for Moving Bodies*.

Rhythms, Atmospheres, Refrains

Refrains for Moving Bodies deliberately emphasizes the claim that moving bodies participate in the generation of affective spaces. This emphasis on space and spatiality is quite deliberate because the project of diagramming the distinctively affective qualities of the spaces we inhabit is a key task for the contemporary social sciences and humanities. This, in turn, is a necessary element of generating opportunities for creative variations and inflections in the ethico-political tenor and tone of these spaces.[11] Equally, emphasizing spaces deliberately thus also provides a way of countering the tendency to think of space, and spatiality, as inimical to thinking pro-cessually.[12] Yet this emphasis is also a cautious one because what is really at stake here is the affective *spacetimes* in which bodies are generative participants — for this reason I use the term "spacetimes" throughout this book to designate the qualities of felt gatherings of affects, percepts, and concepts. Affective spacetimes do not just have extension: they also have duration and intensity. They have reach and resonance. Front and center of the project of *Refrains for Moving Bodies* is therefore a concerted attempt to grapple and experiment with a series of conceptual-empirical matters of concern that allow for thinking through the distinctive affective spacetimes in which moving bodies are generatively implicated. This book foregrounds three of these matters of concern as having particular value for thinking affective spacetimes: rhythm, atmosphere, and refrain. As the chapters work to demonstrate, each of these matters of concern provides ways of grasping the consistency or intensive "thisness" of affective spacetimes without necessarily reducing these spacetimes to the status of containers for moving bodies. Each performs a valuable and necessary process of gen-erative abstraction as part of a radical empiricism that folds thinking into the world at the same time as it draws out the affects of encounters within the world.

Of the three, rhythm has perhaps attracted most attention across a range of disciplines and practices. Such attention is nothing new. In a short essay called "The Original Structure of the Work of Art," Giorgio Agamben points to the long-standing importance of rhythm within Western thinking as a concept that offers a way of grasping the "authentic temporal dimension" of "man's being-in-the-world." The significance of rhythm in this respect, argues Agamben, is the fact that it "grants men both the ecstatic dwelling in a more original dimension and the fall into the flight of measurable time. It holds epochally the essence of man, that is, gives him the gift both of being and nothingness, both of the impulse in the free space of the work and of the impetus toward shadow and ruin."[13] Agamben's essay foregrounds the particular importance of rhythm to any understanding of the spatiotempo-rality of aesthetic experience. But the significance of rhythm in this respect goes beyond efforts to understand experience properly defined in terms of its association with self-consciously aesthetic practices. It also extends to efforts to connect an awareness of the temporalities of aesthetic experience to an interest in the more mundane and habitual spaces of the everyday.

Refrains for Moving Bodies therefore draws heavily upon a minor tradition of thinking in which rhythm figures as way of imbuing philosophical thinking with a sense of the importance of the everyday.[14] Elements of the work of Henri Lefebvre and John Dewey exemplify this tradition. For both Lefebvre and Dewey, rhythm provides a way of thinking the everyday as dynamic, processual, and relational. And it links conceptual concerns with those of a range of somatic and aesthetic practices. In their work, rhythm is a mobile concept that draws together the concerns of philosophically inflected thinking and the performative logics of a range of somatic, aesthetic, and performance practices. Informed in particular by encounters with Lefebvre and Dewey, the book holds fast to the simple proposition that to learn to be affected by affective spacetimes is to take up and be taken up in the rhythms of which these spacetimes are composed: that is, *Refrains for Moving Bodies* affirms rhythm as a conceptual-empirical vehicle for experimenting with experience. And yet a certain degree of tentativeness is necessary here. This tentativeness stems from an awareness of the way in which rhythm can easily be co-opted by theories and political practices that place particular value on its capacity to underpin a space of ethical and aesthetic harmony. In the process it becomes all too easy to pathologize certain styles of movement as arrhythmic or, as Agamben's comments above suggest, to universalize the relation between bodies and rhythm. Thus, while affirming the value of rhythm, it is important to be cautious about the tendency for it to become a concept of ethico-aesthetic capture. The rhythmic spacetimes that figure in what follows are therefore always affirmed at most as fragile orderings emerging from, and potentially returning to, chaos.

The second conceptual-empirical matter of concern that figures prominently in this book is atmosphere. The claim that certain spaces have a distinctive atmosphere is a familiar one to most people, as is an understanding that the presence of moving bodies makes a qualitative difference to the intensity and feel of such atmospheres. In that sense, atmosphere is a concept with an affective resonance that precedes any attempt to theorize it. Until relatively recently, concepts such as atmosphere were too vague for the terms of critical social science. With a renewed interest in questions of affectivity, however, atmospheres have received more attention because they offer ways of foregrounding the distinctively felt qualities of spaces.[15] In the context of an interest in affective spacetimes, the vagueness of atmosphere as a concept becomes a distinct advantage because it provides a way of grasping what Ben Anderson calls the "indeterminate affective 'excess' through which intensive space-times can be created."[16] As Gernot Böhme has argued, atmospheres offer a useful way of thinking about spacetimes precisely because they are the product of neither subject nor object: an atmosphere is a "floating in-between, something between things and the perceiving subject."[17]

The relation between efforts to employ moving bodies and their rhythmic movement and the production of affective atmospheres is central to this book. Two questions follow from this. The first is the most obvious: how are atmospheres actually produced through attending to and mobilizing the affective qualities of moving bodies? This question is simultaneously conceptual, practical, and technical. As Böhme suggests, performance spaces, and particularly the practices of set and stage design through which these spaces are produced, offer privileged opportunities for exploring this question.[18] Chapter 2 therefore explores efforts to produce performance spaces that generate affective atmospheres by virtue of the opportunities they afford for the rhythmic movement of bodies. However, at the same time, affective atmospheres are not defined solely by situations of proximity or copresence. A second important question is therefore how atmospheres can be understood as affective spacetimes sustained and transmitted across and between bodies at a distance. As detailed in chapter 5, techniques of event amplification such as running commentary upon sporting events provide an especially useful means of exploring how this process takes place.

Always facilitated by specific material configurations, the affective spacetimes explored in this book are not delimited by site specificity: they stretch out across and between bodies in situ, but also involve bodies and their ongoing spatiotemporal differentiation. Moreover, the affects of site-specific encounters have the potential to return again and again, simultaneously interrupting and supplementing thought at odd moments, taking place, repeatedly, through sometimes novel configurations of bodies, concepts, and objects. The conceptual-empirical matter of concern that best captures this quality of affective spacetimes, and the concept that forms part of the title of this book, is the refrain. Furnished by Gilles Deleuze and Félix Guattari, the refrain names the durational mattering of which affective spacetimes are composed.[19] Refrains have a territorializing function: that is, they draw out and draw together blocks of spacetime from the chaos of the world, generating a certain expressive consistency through the repetition of practices, techniques, and habits. These territories are not necessarily demarcated or delineated, however: they can be affective complexes, "hazy, atmospheric," but sensed nevertheless, as intensities of feeling in and through the movement of bodies.[20] While qualified by a certain spatiotemporal consistency, refrains are radically open: that is to say, while they may be repetitive, refrains are always potentially generative of difference, producing lines of thinking, feeling, and perceiving that may allow one to wander beyond the familiar.

As Deleuze and Guattari make clear, the refrain is radically impersonal, or at least more than human. It does not necessarily originate through the expression of some inner psychological impulse: hence the fact that any expressive territory, including, for instance, the markings produced by animals, can be considered as refrains.[21] To this extent the refrain is not a strictly phenomenological concept. Nevertheless the concept of the refrain also points to the affective consistency of what Guattari calls "existential territories": that is, it gestures to the fact that these territories are held together and held open by affective relations of various kinds.[22] Following Guattari in particular, affective spacetimes can be understood at least in part as existential territories composed of multiple refrains: kinesthetic, conceptual, "material," and gestural.

Rhythm, atmosphere, and refrain are not self-contained matters of concern: each has the potential to traverse and participate in the activation of the others. To focus on the rhythmic spacetimes of moving bodies is also to explore their potential to participate in the active engineering of affective atmospheres. Similarly, affective atmospheres can catalyze refrains of different intensities and duration that shape the quality of thinking in a range of contexts. It is precisely in the interplay between rhythms, atmospheres, and refrains that this book moves. That the refrain figures in the title is not because it is any more important or primary than rhythm or atmosphere. Nevertheless, the refrain — perhaps more so than rhythm or atmosphere — provides a way of grasping the transversal quality of affective spacetimes. That is, it offers a way of affirming these spacetimes as having a consistency by virtue of affects that can travel across and between bodies and the relations of which these bodies are composed. The critical point here is that the aim of what follows is not to apply any of these matters of concern in order to construct a conceptual framework through which to make sense of the world. Instead, the aim is to enact a radical empiricism as an experimentalism insofar as it experiments with concepts, and thus re-creates them, every time they participate in making something of the world more tangible and palpable than it had already been. In the process, both experience and the concept are transformed.[23]

Fieldworking: Experience and Experiment

The claim that rhythm, atmosphere, and refrain are simultaneously conceptual and empirical is central to the argument in this book. A key speculative proposition here is that conceptual matters of concern can sensitize thinking to the affective qualities of spacetimes in ways that generate opportunities both for renewing the promise of experimenting with experience and, in turn, for thinking with concepts. The question of experience is of course freighted with all kinds of difficulties and tensions. Certainly, it should not be taken to mean a stable, self-referential anchor from which to make sense of the world. Nor, however, can it be dismissed entirely in the wake of a post-structuralist critique of the security of self-identity. Instead, as thinkers such as William James and John Dewey remind us, experience is not so much a transcendent moment but a felt process of transition. In their terms, experience is experimented with — potentially — every time something in the world is encountered that offers the possibility for making this world anew, however modestly. Or, more precisely, if somewhat more awkwardly, *experience is experimented*: that is, as Isabelle Stengers reminds us, experience is not an object out there to be acted upon. Rather, it is a field of variation in which thinking is another variation.[24] When I use experimented in this book it is not, therefore, to reintroduce some experimental distance, but to draw a conjunctive and transitional relation between the process of thinking and the process of experience.

To learn to be affected by affective spacetimes is not, then, to strip away the experience of these spacetimes, but to make more of this experience through experimentation with techniques, concepts, and materials.[25] In doing so, the aim of experimentation is to multiply possibilities for life and living through modifications in thinking, where thinking is always more than a process of cognitive intellectualism. Figures such as Jane Bennett, William Connolly, Bruno Latour, Erin Manning, Brian Massumi, Nigel Thrift, and others also affirm this kind of experiment. For these figures, experimenting experience is a way of multiplying the forces, events, and processes that we admit as participants in this perplexing matter of worldly involvement.[26]

The experimental quality of affective spacetimes is not so much that they provide opportunities to prove or demonstrate a prefigured idea, but that they have the potential to generate a feeling of something happening that disturbs, agitates, or animates ideas already circulating in ways that might open up possibilities for thinking otherwise. Exploring these spacetimes therefore always involves more than the effort to demystify the processes through which they are generated, and more than the articulation of a distanced critique of how they become implicated in certain macropolitical constituencies. That is not to say that it involves suspending critique entirely. Instead, it requires the cultivation of an affirmative critique open to the possibility of becoming affected — or moved — by the spacetimes in which bodies participate while also remaining attentive to the limits and problems of this participation.[27] This critical openness is a variation on what is now a familiar Spinozist question: if we do not know what a body can do, we also do not know what spacetimes might be generated when bodies move, and how, in turn, bodies might be moved by these spacetimes. It is also a variation on Foucault's characterization of critique as an "ethos" concerned with an "analysis of the limits that are imposed on us and an experiment with the possibility of going beyond them."[28]

The cultivation of this ethos is a project both related to, and distinct from, the by-now familiar claim that Western thinking needs to become more embodied. It is related, in the sense that it shares the conviction that attention to the participation of bodies in movements of thought is of critical importance to the qualities of that thinking. And it is distinct, because it takes issue with the claim that a focus on embodiment provides a necessary corrective to an overly abstract or conceptual habit of thinking. Thus, instead of making thinking less abstract, the important question, pursued in chapter 7, is how abstraction might help us make more of the experimental relations between bodies, and the architectures of thinking, feeling, and moving in which these relations are composed and recomposed. As performances of abstraction, concepts are especially important here: they sensitize attention to become more attuned to different elements of experience. Concepts are not, of course, the only way to develop this sensitivity. Somatic and performance-based techniques that work upon the affective capacities of moving bodies offer important possibilities in this respect.[29] Equally, opportunities for learning to be affected thus can also be provided by encounters with a host of mundane things as part of everyday ecologies: objects, images, or sounds, for instance.[30]

Taken together, the process of experimenting experience in the different ways pursued in this book can be understood as a particular form of fieldwork. This emphasis on fieldwork is shaped by the disciplinary context from which this book has emerged: geography. Within geography, it is fair to say that fieldwork has often been framed as an activity in which the researcher goes out into the world and collects data before returning home to analyze or write up these data in a meaningful account. This division of labor has also tended to be underpinned by an implicit separation between mind and body, with the latter serving as the underacknowledged vehicle for the cultivation of the former. These distinctions have, however, been challenged in recent decades, with the field now understood as a distributed and differentiated space composed of practiced relations between bodies, texts, technologies, and materials. Rather than nuggets of information waiting to be discovered, data within this field are now understood as coproduced, affective materials.[31] Within geography — and indeed other disciplines such as anthropology — fieldwork has come to be seen as a process of generative participation within the diverse forces and agencies of which the world is composed.[32] This claim pertains to any context: it has a particular resonance for an interest in affective spacetimes, however, because much of what goes on in these spacetimes does not cross a threshold of representation in order to generate a felt difference or variation. To learn to be affected by these spacetimes is, then, to commit to a style of fieldworking in which experience becomes a field of variations in which to experiment with the question of how felt differences might register in thinking.

Of course, to affirm an experimental sense of experience might well be seen to merely foreground something that takes place all the time throughout the process of research. And yet it often still gets written out of accounts of research. How to write this experimental sense of experience back into accounts of research is therefore an important question. *Refrains for Moving Bodies* takes seriously the value of experimenting with the manner and style in which accounts of this fieldworking are produced, narrated, and addressed.[33] At certain key junctures, albeit in minor ways, it works to show how inventive interventions in fields of expression are just as important as whatever happens during what is often understood as the empirical moment in research.[34] This is more obvious in some chapters than others: chapter 3, for instance, is a deliberate effort to stretch the spacetime of expression as part of the practice of experimenting experience with rhythm. Even if they are less obviously experimental, other chapters work to show how the style through which one writes, draws, or choreographs expression is shaped by a sensibility inflected by variations in experience. In some cases this is nothing more than a shift in emphasis or the interruption of a chapter by the description of an empirical moment that opens up the chapter to forces that exceed its lines. In other cases it is a shift in mode of address that opens up the affective territories of writing in deliberately suggestive but nonprescriptive ways.

Exemplifying

Refrains for Moving Bodies presents a series of experiments with and within affective spacetimes generated for and through moving bodies. These experiments are presented here through the logics of exemplification. As Brian Massumi argues, because examples are unruly and excessive, exemplification is a way of remaining faithful to the singularity of the event-full qualities of relation-specific circumstances rather than presenting this singularity as a particular instance of a general rule or theory.[35] Exemplification offers a way of avoiding framing encounters by the already defined idiom of the case as what Lauren Berlant calls a "problem-event that has animated some kind of judgment."[36] More specifically, it provides a way of avoiding using these details as a case study of a process or phenomenon that has already been defined in advance. Instead, it works as a mode of presenting a sense of how participation within relation-specific affective spacetimes might be considered to make a difference to the sensibility through which thinking takes place: that is, how this participation works to complicate the initial terms of this encounter. Through exemplification the task becomes one of presenting a sense of the specifics of participation while also holding onto the possibility that participation has the potential to transform the sensibility that shaped it in the first place. The form of exemplification pursued and performed in these chapters differs, however. In some instances it consists of outlining a sustained encounter with the affective spacetimes of a particular practice (chapters 3, 4, and 5). In other cases it involves narrating the generation of an event of collaborative research-creation (chapters 1 and 8). And in other cases it consists of dwelling upon a particular moment, or generative interval, from which a germinal thought or feeling of tendency emerges (chapters 2, 6, and 7).

As an ethos, as a way and style of acting into the world, exemplification affirms a commitment to the activation of the details of the world such that they may circulate beyond the context of their taking place. That is, what is exemplified is not so much something that already exists prior to the situation of empirical encounter, but the qualities of the situation that make a difference to participants in ways that extend beyond the site of that encounter in a process, following Charles Sanders Peirce and Gregory Bateson, that might be called abduction.[37] As Andrew Barry has argued, situations matter, but how they matter is up for grabs because they are always already implicated in a shifting field of relations.[38] This means, in turn, that the question of how, in circulating, accounts of such situations may catalyze other minor shifts in ethical sensibilities remains an open one: it is not a question of proof, but more a question of potential. This potential is only actualizable insofar as these examples circulate and participate, through suggestive contagion more than causality, in efforts to experiment with experience elsewhere.

The chapters that follow consist of a series of essays that describe how affective spacetimes are generated through and for moving bodies and how, in turn, it might be possible to learn to be affected by these spacetimes in ways that contribute to the wider renewal across the social sciences and humanities of the promise of an ethos of experimenting experience. Each chapter works to explore the relation-specific combinatory mingling of concepts, percepts, and affects that afford opportunities for experimenting with relations across and between bodies in movement. Chapter 1 begins by addressing the relation between experience and experiment. Drawing upon the thinking of William James and John Dewey, it works up an experimental understanding of experience, one that can be pursued through the relations between techniques, concepts, and bodies. This understanding is put to the test in a specific event of research-creation — a week spent in the corridor and stairwell of the Chisenhale Dance Space in London. Insofar as what happens in that corridor can be understood as an experiment with experience, the outcomes of this experimentalism can be evaluated in terms of the emergence of speculative propositions that continue to resound as refrains in and for thinking.

One of the refrains emerging from the event in the Chisenhale is an ongoing interest in how the rhythmic movement of bodies generates affective spacetimes. This interest is also shared by various thinkers, perhaps most notably Henri Lefebvre and John Dewey. Both figures affirm the importance of cultivating an affectively imbued spatial sensibility through rhythmic movement. Both also leave this project unfinished. Chapter 2 takes up the invitations of these thinkers by revisiting the collaboration in the early twentieth century between Emile Jaques-Dalcroze and Adolphe Appia. This collaboration involved working on the rhythmic movement of bodies as part of an attempt to cultivate spatial sensibilities. The outcome of the collaboration was the production of performance spaces designed to generate affective atmospheres. Exploring some of the problems of these spaces vis-à-vis the writing of Dewey and Lefebvre provides a way of cautiously affirming the value of using the rhythmic movement of bodies to generate atmospheres in which to experiment experience. A discussion of rhythmic movement is developed further in chapter 3 through an encounter with the affective atmospherics generated by a contemporary movement practice called the 5 Rhythms. Drawing upon Gregory Bateson's interest in "patterns that connect," the chapter exemplifies how an emergent interest in rhythm, precipitated initially as a barely sensed feeling, but gaining intensity as a territorializing refrain, can be diagrammed creatively by drawing out the patterned relations of which this refrain consists.

The question of how to understand and affirm the experimental possibilities of therapeutic practices is the focus of chapter 4. On one level, practices such as the 5 Rhythms can be understood as therapeutic insofar as they reinforce the idea of an individual self that needs to be worked upon and managed. However, the question posed here is how therapeutic practices might be grasped in terms of relations operating transversally to the self. This question is pursued through exploring how one practice — dance movement therapy — generates affective-therapeutic spacetimes through ecologies of interventions, objects, and techniques of relation. Drawing particularly upon the insights of Félix Guattari and Isabelle Stengers, the chapter outlines how these spacetimes afford opportunities for generating and experimenting with affective refrains that open up modest virtual futures within what William James calls the "tissue of experience."[39]

The first four substantive chapters are all concerned with affective spacetimes in which bodies are relatively proximate or copresent. In chapter 5 the focus turns to the production of distributed affective spacetimes in which bodies move and are moved without the tactile presence of another physical body. Specifically, the concern here is with techniques through which these distributed yet affectively tangible spacetimes are performed. The technique considered here is, perhaps surprisingly, radio commentating on popular Irish sporting events. The argument developed throughout the chapter is that the function of radio commentating is not so much to represent what happens when bodies move. Rather, drawing upon Michel Serres, commentating is understood as a technique for producing distributed affective atmospheres through a process of semiconducting the materialist energies of moving bodies. Understood thus, commentating performs possibilities for being and becoming taken up in the relation-specific rhythms and refrains of which particular affective atmospheres are composed and felt.

The project of exploring opportunities for minor experiment in the affective spacetimes generated through popular cultural practice is pursued further in chapter 6 through an encounter with moving images of moving bodies. The point of departure for the chapter is the claim that representational understandings of moving images give only partial purchase on how the affects of moving bodies circulate via processes and practices of value generation within contemporary forms of biopolitical life. Chapter 6 therefore explores how moving images can also be grasped as affective refrains circulating across and within bodies and their own capacity to differ. A series of encounters with what Steven Shaviro calls the "postcinematic affects" of moving images become occasions for experimenting with this potential to differ.[40]

Elements of this discussion anticipate chapter 7, which revolves around the effort to work up an affirmative critique of abstraction for moving bodies. The aim here is to move against and complicate a pervasive and deep-rooted tendency to juxtapose the alienating force of abstraction and the vitality of living, moving bodies. To pursue this aim the chapter turns again to Lefebvre, dwelling upon the ambiguous status of abstraction in his work. Rather than reading Lefebvre as an advocate for a straightforward critique of abstraction, his work is taken to support the cautious affirmation of abstraction as a necessary element of thinking through and experimenting with affective spacetimes for moving bodies. This claim is developed further via an encounter with the choreographic experiments of figures such as Rudolf Laban and William Forsythe. In Forsythe's work in particular, the value of abstraction for experimenting within affective spacetimes for moving bodies is affirmed with particular intensity.

The final chapter marks a return of sorts to geography, where geography is less a discipline and more an ethos oriented toward experimenting with generating worlds of involvement through moving bodies. The focus here is on the effort by a group of researchers to coproduce affective spacetimes within and across which to diagram the relations between the geographic and the choreographic. The chapter narrates different practices of participation in this process and its enfolding in a specific event of research-creation — a daylong workshop that took place in May 2009 as part of a more distributed event. Even if these events are minor, their performance remains significant precisely because it provides opportunities for experimenting with the duration and intensity of affective spacetimes of experience. Critically, this concluding chapter foregrounds how these experiments provide important sources for thinking about the kinds of value implicated in generation of new refrains for moving bodies. Inflected by geography as a shared matter of concern, the emphasis in chapter 8 is on how refrains always operate in the midst of disciplines without ever being discipline-specific: they offer possibilities for drawing out the affective potential of milieus composed of bodies, concepts, and objects. And this serves to reaffirm the wider claim pursued in the book — namely, that however minor, informed experiments with moving bodies provide opportunities for reaffirming the promise of experience as a field of potential within which valued forms of life might be made and remade.

CHAPTER ONE

Transitions

For Experimenting (with) Experience

We move through and along corridors all the time. As spaces of transition, they allow us to pass between rooms, to travel to other places. As thresholds, they allow us to move between interior and exterior zones. As passages, they are defined both by their architectural structure and by movement through this structure.[1] Yet while we may move through corridors, we don't often spend sustained time in them. Sometimes, of course, we linger a little, held temporarily in place by a chance encounter, a conversation, or when our attention is drawn to a notice or an announcement. Rarely, however, do we take time to inhabit these passages, to dwell within them. Rarely do we heed, let alone act upon, George Perec's injunction for us to learn to live in these "species of spaces."[2] Rarely, unless they are spectacular or grand, do we pay much attention to the details, corners, nooks, and surfaces of these spaces. Because we take corridors to be overwhelmingly purposeful and directional, rarely do we consider the opportunities they afford for thinking.

In April 2001 I spent the guts of a week in a corridor at the Chisenhale Dance Space in London. I was there as a participant in an event of research-creation with Petra Kuppers, a pain-impaired performance artist and researcher, and Kanta Kochhar-Lindgren, a hearing-impaired dancer and researcher. I had been invited by Petra on the basis that I was a geographer interested in the relation between questions of space, affect, and bodily movement.[3] Under the heading of "Landscaping," our broad aim for the week was to explore the maps of movement that might emerge during the course of encounters between our ideas, interests, and bodies. Within the generous terms of this thematic constraint, we had no definite end point or terminus in mind: we were interested in the potential of cross-disciplinary practice and process, in the production of contexts within and from which new eventualities of thinking, moving, and relating might emerge.[4] We were interested in the question of how something novel, however modest, might happen, when the relations between space, affectivity, and moving bodies are foregrounded as part of the process of thinking. And we hoped the Chisenhale would prove a facilitating context for the performance of open-ended, processual research-creation across and between disciplines and traditions of thinking.[5]

That we end up spending much of the time in the corridor is not so much a choice: the building lacks an elevator, and access to the upper floor proves difficult, particularly for Petra. And so the corridor and lower part of the stairwell become our working space for a week. In itself this is hardly novel: Western performance practices have long since moved beyond the confines of the theater to explore and experiment with the site-specific possibilities of a multiplicity of everyday spaces.[6] If the corridor and stairwell are open ended, they are not quite empty: the week that comes to pass therein is already populated by suggestions, anxieties, ideas. For Petra, these include the possibility of site-specific exploration through performance of "alternative access and space's imprint on bodies."[7] For Kanta, these include the possibility of exploring the connections between hearing and deafness in distinctive kinds of performance space.[8] And for my own part, they include the possibility that collaboration with practice- and performance-based researchers might allow a geographer to think through the relations between bodies, affect, and spaces.

Anticipatory interests only take things so far, however, when faced with the prospect of a week of working in a corridor. Inevitably — almost immediately — a simple and obvious question emerges: what should one do for that week as part of the effort to work and think across disciplines? Furthermore, how does one learn to become affected by what happens during such a week? And how does one know when something of any consequence is happening? In preparation, and without a real sense of how they might make their presence felt in the Chisenhale, I buy and bring some comfort blankets. Maps: random, charity store, fifty-pence-each maps — India, Norway, Wisconsin, Chicago, Buckinghamshire, France, and elsewhere. Maps: familiar technologies of lived abstraction. Maps: they become participants in the process of working in the Chisenhale. They provide blocks of color in the bleak white-gray of the corridor and stairwell. Some end up on the wall, some in fragments. Some are pasted to the risers on the stairwell, becoming the color of discipline in unfamiliar territory. Others become graphic thinking-spaces: for instance, we generate ideas on the back of Norway.

One evening during the week I go bookshopping. Luxury books. A copy of Elizabeth Bishop's *Complete Poems*. The first poem in the book is called "The Map":

Mapped waters are more quiet than the land is,
lending the land their waves' own confrontation:
and Norway's hare runs south in agitation.[9]

I place the book as a series of lines of reference in an alcove in the corridor, adding to the geographies therein. Multiplying: the more available the better.

And so, in the process of thinking with maps, some familiar themes and concepts begin to populate the corridor and stairwell. A legend of sorts emerges:

Time
Space
Perception
Fantasy
Line

Cartographic legends can be understood, referentially, as the elaboration of the information contained on the map. And narrative legends can be understood as mythical fantasies with complex imaginative geographies. In the context of the Chisenhale, however, a legend becomes the shorthand for a form of creative collaboration providing inventive trajectories along which to begin to move in a white-walled week of thinking-space. Rather than a matter of fantasy, legends become lines of orientation for what Henri Bergson calls creative fabulation, a kind of inventive thinking into the potentiality of the event to come.[10]

As it turns out, many things happen during that week. Minor details: the difficulty of beginning to know what to do in a corridor; encroaching frustration, tedium, claustrophobia; needing some orientation; wanting a manner of beginning to move. An uncertain rhythm beginning to emerge. Work, break, work. End to end, wall to wall. Turbulence: the felt sense of minor eddies in the rhythms of an ordinary access space.

THIS CHAPTER DWELLS within the details and afterlife of this week as a way of considering the following question: how, even in the most mundane of architectural spaces for moving bodies, might opportunities for experimenting with experience be generated? On one level then, the chapter provides a rationale of sorts for the minor collaborative experiments that might be facilitated by one such space: a corridor. On another level, and more broadly, however, the week becomes an occasion to dwell upon the problem of how experience might be understood as experimental. William James and John Dewey offer answers to this question through their shared affirmation of a conception of experience as an ongoing relational process of transition rather than an after-the-event process of representational reflection. Critically, they also affirm experience as something experimental and provide some valuable points of orientation for thinking about how and where such experimentation might take place. In the process, however, they encourage us to avoid thinking of such spaces as corridors in narrow, three-dimensional terms. Following James and Dewey means thinking of how corridors offer relation-specific affective spacetimes for experimenting with experience through moving bodies.

Questioning Experience

To commit to spending a week in a corridor is to take seriously the proposition that something might happen when bodies move in that corridor. Moreover, it is to place a degree of faith in the possibility that whatever might happen during this week has the potential to produce modifications in experience that, in turn, might shape the sensibility through which thinking takes place. It is also therefore to become entangled — intentionally or not — with one of the most problematic of philosophical concepts. Experience is always already shadowed by all kinds of conceptual and empirical difficulties. It has been dismissed as a mere veil over the underlying truth of nature, and as the refuge for a brute philosophical materialism. Its unproblematic affirmation has been criticized on the basis that it assumes a shared set of values anchored in a universal and distinctively human subject. The championing of experience as a useful philosophical category is also often taken to assume the possibility of an authentic relation between self and world. Indeed, it is precisely the impossibility of this coincidence that a range of post-structural theories have sought to place at the center of philosophical and, indeed, ethico-political thinking. These theories have, of course, subjected experience to a particularly withering critique, the terms of which are by now relatively familiar. This critique works to expose and demystify efforts to intervene in experience on the basis that they inevitably posit some existential truth, or grounds, upon which this experience is based. It seeks to reveal how any appeal to experience as a category is also always beholden to a dream of presence. It explores how the meaning of experience is multiple, and how this multiplicity is enacted through a range of practices and technologies. It also, therefore, seeks to expose the political and ethical implications of privileging experience, and more specifically how such privileging works to sustain certain systems of value, and in ways that foreclose the futures of other values.

In the wake of this critique, any claim that experience serves as a straightforward touchstone for a thinking subject is difficult to justify. Consequently, as Giorgio Agamben observes, "the question of experience can be approached nowadays only with an acknowledgement that it is no longer accessible to us."[11] Yet while it can be approached only asymptotically, experience remains one of the central problematic object targets of contemporary Western capitalist societies and the biopolitical technologies that shape the affective life of these societies.[12] It continues to be modified through technologies and practices designed to produce distinctive and sometimes novel ways of thinking, feeling, and perceiving in a myriad of contexts. This is nothing new, of course: the work of Michel Foucault and others has demonstrated how the possibility of working upon experience through techniques has long been central to the fashioning of the self.[13] It is fair to say, however, that one of the distinguishing features of that structure of feeling named modernity has been the generalized rendering explicit of experience as a field of biopolitical intervention.[14] Experience has become both more available and more problematic. But as Agamben also observes, such has been the proliferation of techniques and technologies for working upon experience that it is no longer possible to think of it as something singular, homogeneous, or easily translatable from one context to another.

What then to make of experience in a context where its philosophical currency has been devalued through the terms of critique while also becoming the focus of an ever-expanding range of interventions that mobilize it in order to generate different kinds of value? Certainly, it would be possible to continue to develop and refine a critique of the category of experience. And to some extent this remains an urgent and necessary task. However, the question of experience — and all the problems and possibilities in which this question is implicated — is not exhausted by critique, or at least not if critique is understood as a project of demystification. Instead, as a number of prominent thinkers, including William Connolly, Isabelle Stengers, and Nigel Thrift, have argued, one of the key questions facing us today is how to develop an affirmative critique of experience: a critique that seeks to reclaim the category of experience as an occasion for thinking, without, at the same time, reinstalling it as an essential phenomenological category, or an existential ground for thinking. This critique affirms experience by opening it up to all those elements that are in excess of a phenomenology of presence: that is, it seeks to make explicit the non-, or more-than-human, participants in the processuality of experience as it comes to matter.

Affirming Experience

An important way of developing this critique is to foreground the traditional association between experience and experiment. As Raymond Williams notes, up to the sixteenth century, both terms were often interchangeable.[15] Subsequently, experience came to mean more than a process of empirical testing, and incorporated a sense of conscious awareness of a past state or event and the ability to use this awareness in the present. This divergence of experience and experiment parallels the split between subject and object. Experience became something possessed by the subject, a reservoir of worldly wisdom upon which to draw when making sense of the world. At the same time, experiment became defined and delimited to a greater and greater extent by well-rehearsed methodological protocols that worked to exclude, albeit under certain conditions, the influence of subjective experience.

An emphasis on experience as experiment persisted, however, in various minor strands of philosophy and social science. North American pragmatism is one of the most affirmative of these philosophical traditions, particularly the varieties developed by William James and John Dewey. Their respective work is affirmative in a number of shared respects: in the faith placed in the promise of a world of change and becoming; through a vision of an ethics of immersive involvement within this world as the basis of a renewed philosophical vision; and through the tone or style in which it is written. Yet what James and Dewey affirm, perhaps more than anything else, is the value of experience as a philosophical category: a concerted attempt at the renewal of this category for philosophy is one of the defining features of their respective writings. Pragmatism, in deed — in its doing — is nothing without experience.

A series of themes cuts across the respective visions of experience outlined in the writings of James and Dewey. For both figures, experience is of this world: it is not a secondary reflection of the world apprehended from a distance. Experience, in other words, is part of the sensible materiality of nature. Dewey is especially emphatic in this regard: "It is not experience which is experienced, but nature — stones, plants, animals, diseases, health, temperature, electricity, and so on. Things interacting in certain ways are experience; they are what is experienced. Linked in certain other ways with another natural object — the human organism — they are how things are experienced as well. Experience thus reaches down into nature; it has depth."[16] Similarly, for James experience is part of the ontogenetic materiality of nature: it is the "stuff of which everything is composed."[17] At the same time this primal stuff is by no means homogeneous but is infinitely differentiated: "There are as many stuffs as there are 'natures' in the things experienced."[18] If experience is in some sense coextensive with the sensible yet differentiated materiality of the world, then it becomes difficult to think of the process of experiencing as involving the activity of a mind representing (internally) to itself the details of an external environment.

To affirm a pragmatist conception of experience is, in other words, to take seriously the claim that experience can never be reduced to processes of representation. What is not present in experience for these theories is a representational picture of the world: indeed, these theories are relentlessly critical of any sense of experience as something that takes place through an act of cognitive representationalism. Experience is not our way of producing a synthetic facsimile of raw sense data. Nor is experience an after-the-event event: it is not (only) something we make sense of retrospectively through reflective contemplation. So pragmatism moves against a model of experience that would install a division between a perceiving subject and perceived object, precisely because in the process experience is reduced to the status of something upon which a thinking subject reflects through an act of separation and transcendence. As James puts it, "as 'subjective' we say that experience represents; as 'objective' that it is represented. What represents and what is represented is here numerically the same; but we must remember that no dualism of being represented and representing resides in the experience *per se*."[19] This means, in turn, that the subject and object of experience do not precede the event: they are created in and through it. Similarly, Dewey argues that the work of experience is not to produce a copy of an environment external to itself. If this were the case, the experience of an organism would actually be of a different environment than the one in which an organism lives and moves — a situation that would make its life infinitely more difficult. Dewey does not however deny the existence of cognitive experience: his claim is instead that "cognitive experience must arise from that of a non-cognitive sort."[20] Cognitive knowing, as one mode of experiencing, emerges from a background of nonrepresentational sense making.

The conception of experience emerging through the pragmatism of Dewey and James is anything but an internal, subjective state: it is "no slipping along in a path fixed by inner consciousness."[21] Experience is, instead, connective: it is the ongoing product of a multiplicity of "dynamic connections," involving all kinds of "specific affinities, repulsions, and relative indifferencies [sic]" between things in the world.[22] Where Dewey speaks of connections, James famously writes of relations.[23] For James, "pure experience" is fundamentally relational and the relations themselves are as real as anything else. Crucially, these relations are not just extensive or distributed — a relational conception of experience is absolutely not just a matter of drawing lines between different actors. The radical empiricism of James, and to a degree Dewey, hinges upon the claim that the relations of which experience are composed are also temporal. On one level this means that experience is never a static state of being — it is an active process of becoming in transition. But it also means that a pragmatist conception of experience has a particular orientation to futurity. For Dewey, this is expressed through the claims that anticipation is more primary than recollection, and that projection is more than the "summoning of the past."[24] A similar orientation toward futurity is found in James's vision of radical empiricism. He puts it thus: "We live, as it were, upon the front edge of an advancing wave-crest, and our sense of a determinate direction in falling forward is all we cover of the future of our path."[25] Experience, in other words, is never all there, but is always leaning into a "chromatic fringe" where the actual and virtual mix in a "more that continuously develops, and that continuously supersedes them as life proceeds."[26]

In this pragmatist vision, experience is therefore conceived as the relational stuff of the world, a processual "thisness" only ever grasped in the course of its transitional immediacy. This is not to say that experience cannot be known in the sense that we might recall an experience. It is just that this process is not a matter of reflection or representation — it involves the addition of more relations, more transitions. The actuality of experience is a process that cannot therefore be apprehended by the substitution of static representations because these cannot grasp the degree to which experience is a process of being in transition that is always becoming more than itself. Moreover, experience is a distributed, immanent field of sensible processuality within which creative variations give rise to modifications and movements of thinking. So, while Dewey and James sometimes write in a way that rehearses a subject-centered account of experience, they both open experience up to its nonhuman constituents: that is, they open it to those relations and processes that agitate and animate any self-coincident sense of experience as immediacy.

Experimenting (with) Experience

James and Dewey are not content to call for the affirmation of experience. As pragmatists, they also affirm the importance of finding ways of moving through the processuality of a world that, whether we like it or not, is always affirming its own becoming through the refrain of something that can be sensed in experience while always exceeding the actuality of this sensing. The crucial question for these thinkers is not therefore how to transcend experience through representation; rather, the crucial question is how to think the moving event of transition, or how to find "different ways of being in and of the movement of things."[27] And for both Dewey and James, answering this question is a matter of experiment. Thus at various points in their respective writings both speak of experience as something with which one can experiment — James, for instance, suggests that we can usefully experiment upon our ideas of experience before undertaking to change them through activity. Dewey's claims in this regard are based upon a kind of ethology of experience: for him the life of the organism is an ongoing process of testing and interacting within a shifting field of connections, and what he calls "undergoings" can be grasped as "experiments in varying the course of events."[28] This vision of experience as experiment is linked closely with the pragmatist orientation toward futurity. As Dewey puts it, experience in "its vital form is experimental, an effort to change the given. It is characterised by projection, by reaching forward into the unknown; connection with a future is its salient trait."[29] What Dewey and James do is to affirm an ethos of experience and experiment in ways that reveal the mutual imbrication of both terms as part of work of thinking relations in transition. To think relations in transition is to experiment, and to experiment is to provide possibilities for making more of experience. If pragmatism, in James's words, is radically empirical, it also takes experience to be always, at least potentially, radically experimental.

Affirming the potential for thinking to move in the midst of experience through a radically experimental empiricism is all well and good. But how might it take place? To read Dewey and James, it seems sometimes that such experimentation can take place anywhere: at any given point something might happen to force us to think, to create new lines of thought, to allow us to sense the genesis of variation in the moving midst of things. And in a real sense this is precisely what their respective philosophies suggest: the sense of the world as constrained yet open (within limits) in any given occasion, however mundane.[30] Dewey and James would seem therefore to move toward a position where the distinction between experience and experiment is no longer sustainable. A similar position has been articulated by Isabelle Stengers, albeit in the context of a discussion of the work of Alfred North Whitehead. Stengers uses "the verb 'to experiment'" in a sense akin "'to experience,' that is, without 'on' or 'with,' which would induce the idea of a separation between the experimenter and what she is experimenting on or with. It is thus a (French-inspired) neologism meant to signal a practice of active, open, demanding attention paid to the experience as we experience it. For instance, a cook would be said to experiment the taste of a new dish. In French, there is no clear distinction between the terms 'experience' and 'experiment' as there is in English."[31] This is a wonderfully generous approach to the world: it is radically empirical in the Jamesian sense of that term. And it is a form of words employed often in the present book.

Yet the prospect of the sheer potential affirmed here is more than a little overwhelming. Thankfully, James and Dewey point to a number of ways in which to make explicit the experimental qualities of experience. These elements do not necessarily add up to a formula. Rather, they provide a degree of generative constraint for experimenting experience.[32] Concepts are the first of these elements. To some extent this might seem counterintuitive, as both figures are suspicious of any effort to substitute static representations for the moving transition of experience. Yet their shared philosophical orientation insists on the necessity of affirming the pragmatic value of certain grammatical operators, especially prepositions in James's case, as ways of moving through or within experience without necessarily reinstalling a representational division between the subject and object of experience. If we think of concepts as performing a kind of work similar to prepositions — if we think of them as ways of moving in the midst of things — then James's critique of concepts as essentially static loses much of its force. Instead, by reading James against himself, it becomes easier to appreciate the claim that to experiment with concepts is to experiment with experience as a processes of transition. It is not a matter of capturing experience, but of exploring how different concepts afford possibilities for drawing out the relations and process of which experience is always being composed.

Equally interesting, however, is the enthusiasm shared by Dewey and James for practical techniques that make explicit the experimental quality of experience. As part of his wider effort to cultivate a radical empiricism, and with a view to ameliorating his frail physiological constitution, James advocated participation — and in some cases participated — in a range of techniques for experimenting experience. As Richard Shusterman observes, these included "ice and blistering (for counter-irritation), corsets, varieties of weightlifting, electric shock, absolute bed-rest, diverse water cures, vigorous walking, rapid mountain climbing, systematic chewing, magnetic healing, hypnosis and 'mind-cure' therapy, relaxation, spinal vibrations, vapour inhalations, homeopathic remedies, lessons in mental focusing to minimize muscular contractions, diverse programmes of medically prescribed gymnastics, cannabis, nitrous oxide, mescaline, strychnine, and varieties of hormonal injections."[33] Rather surprisingly, however, James has little to say directly about somatic practices that focus on the kinesthetic movement and organization of bodily experience. One exception is a lecture titled "The Energies of Men," during which he notes approvingly the value of participation in a range of techniques, including yoga. For James, these techniques point to the value of a "suggestive therapeutics" through which to engage in an "experiment in methodical self-suggestion."[34]

In contrast, Dewey's enthusiasm for somatic practices is more obvious, even if an explicitly philosophical engagement with the body is arguably absent from his writing. This enthusiasm is most apparent in his discussion of the Alexander Technique, in which he participated from his late fifties until his death at the age of ninety-two. While Dewey's championing of the practice needs to be set within his wider affirmation of the somatic basis of thinking and learning in society, it also reveals something of the experimental ethos informing his work. In a preface to a book by Alexander, Dewey notes: "I was, from the practical standpoint, an inept, awkward and slow pupil. There were no speedy and seemingly miraculous changes to evoke gratitude emotionally, while they misled me intellectually. I was forced to observe carefully at every step of the process, and to interest myself in the theory of the operations. . . . In bringing to bear whatever knowledge I already possessed — or thought I did — and whatever powers of discipline in mental application I had acquired in the pursuit of these studies, I had the most humiliating experience of my life, intellectually speaking."[35] Yet, as he continues, "in the study, I found the things which I had 'known' — in the sense of theoretical belief — in philosophy and psychology, changed into vital experiences which gave a new meaning to knowledge of them."[36]

Both James's and Dewey's life and work exemplify how an ethos of generosity and responsiveness to the potential affective energies that may emerge during participation in somatic practices can become part of the affirmation of an experimental sense of experience. That is not to say that such participation always generates positive affects — Dewey's remarks demonstrate this all too clearly. Both thinkers do, however, provide reminders that participation in somatic practices requires a commitment to tactically suspend certain habits of judgment while cultivating others, and to experiment with experience in ways that take thinking beyond a certain comfort zone, while also returning again and again to details that might, at first glance, appear unremarkable and unconnected. And they also provide reminders that the process of thinking through the affects of participation and their ongoing resonance is not a matter of going with the flow but of cultivating germinal experience through careful attentiveness to the variations of which it is generative. Both James and Dewey suggest therefore that participation in somatic practices should be understood not so much as an opportunity for reembodying thinking, but as what political theorist William Connolly calls techniques of thinking. As Connolly has argued, and as James's own life illustrates, any number of such techniques for experimenting experience exists.[37] The key thing is that such techniques offer opportunities for the cultivation of an ethical sensibility open and attentive to the "vicissitudes of experience."[38]

If techniques and concepts are the first two elements for experimenting experience that can be drawn from the respective writing of James and Dewey, the third is sensitivity to the organization and arrangement of the environments within which such experimentation takes place. James and Dewey developed their own ideas in an intellectual context in which the laboratory was becoming the focus of a range of efforts to treat human experience as an object of experimental procedures. Clearly, the laboratory is an archetypal or paradigmatic site of such experiment. The evolution of the laboratory can be seen in many ways, however, as an effort, albeit diverse and distributed, to fabricate and privilege a site from which any explicit sense of experience is evacuated. And the protocols and procedures of lab work achieve this evacuation in a publicly demonstrable way. In some respects the work of both James and Dewey is indebted to this vision of the lab. At the same time, their work can also be said to complicate this vision. For both, the laboratory was a site at which to experiment on and with experience. Thus, for Dewey, the laboratory could be understood as a pedagogical space for organizing and modifying experience in a manner that was determinedly experimental. His involvement in the University of Chicago Laboratory Schools attests to this. Equally interesting, however, are Dewey's ideas about the possibility of designing a pedagogical space for facilitating rhythmic modulation of student attention through movement within and between different zones.[39] According to Jason Kosnoski, this space was to be organized in such a way that movement between different rooms, or activity areas, could affectively modulate "the spatial and temporal qualities of the student's attention" toward different issues, generating sympathetic responses to difficult and sometimes challenging ideas.[40] If designed in the right way, the spatiotemporality of the learning experience would be akin to the constructive interference of a multiplicity of waves moving through a body of water. Thus, as Kosnoski notes: "As the students move up and down between the two floors of the school building they establish a rhythmic progression between their initial interests and the perspectives they gain through collectively investigating their original problem."[41] For Dewey, then, the task was to design buildings that would provide opportunities for experimenting with the rhythmic composition of bodies, spaces, and modes of attention.

James shared Dewey's concern for making more of spaces for experimenting experience by challenging the primacy of the laboratory. And he did so as someone whose own scholarly interests were intertwined with the emergence of the lab as a space for experimental psychology, particularly at Harvard. However, while he acknowledged the importance of the experiments undertaken in the lab, James certainly did not seek to confine philosophical experiment to such sites. Instead, he advocated a philosophical ethos that multiplied the spaces and sites at which to experiment experience. Indeed, as Francesca Bordogna has argued, for James philosophy was a "relational" space in both a metaphorical and literal sense: it required no privileged location but nevertheless benefited from fortuitous and often deliberately designed arrangements of materials.[42] For James and Dewey, then, the physical organization of spaces is an important aspect of their capacity to facilitate experiment with experience — their material architecture has the potential to play an important role in the enactment of pragmatism's radical empiricism. Yet these spaces are never reducible to the objects and materials from which they are constructed. They are also spaces in which concepts, affects, and percepts participate in unpredictable ways, adding to the relations of which such spaces consist.

Corridor Theory

There is a curious and little remarked-upon spatial imaginary informing this pragmatist sense of experience as experimental. Drawing upon the Italian pragmatist Giovanni Papini, James once described pragmatism as a "corridor in a hotel," out of which open "innumerable chambers." Thus, in "one you may find a man writing an atheistic volume; in the next someone on his knees praying for faith and strength; in a third a chemist investigating a body's properties. In a fourth a system of idealistic metaphysics is being excogitated; in a fifth the impossibility of metaphysics is being shown. But they all own the corridor, and all must pass through it if they want a practicable way of getting into or out of their respective rooms."[43] For James, pragmatism in its various guises did not share an overarching theory: rather, it consisted of an attitude, an orientation toward process and consequences rather than toward first principles, or universal categories. So pragmatism, as a kind of "corridor theory," was a space of transition: a philosophical orientation toward experience as the experimental process of becoming.[44]

If the relations between corridors and thinking can be articulated thus by James in metaphorical terms, what then of the possibilities for experimenting experience in actual corridors? In some ways this question is not new. In the early part of the twentieth century, for instance, school design in the United Kingdom and the United States began to utilize the corridor as a space within which to facilitate exercise and rhythmic movement. These "marching corridors" were envisaged as alternatives to more traditional school halls, and were supposed to allow for healthy indoor activity when the weather prevented students from moving outside. In the process, they linked concerns with ventilation and hygiene with the imperative to encourage proper habits of movement. Indeed, as the very name "marching corridor" suggests, they were not spaces for spontaneous, unregulated movement. They were spaces in which to produce well-disciplined, well-drilled bodies and subjects that would respond quickly to commands and that would feel part of a coherent, organic community.[45] In this context, the corridor became a space within which to channel but also to work upon the rhythmic movement of bodies.

These efforts to design corridors as spaces for producing and working upon experience have affinities for what happens elsewhere. Consider, for instance, the cloister. Sites of solemn contemplation, cloisters are hardly spaces full of radical, transformative potential. Indeed, "cloistered" is a byword for a dry, insular intellectualism divorced from the tangled mundane of everyday life and critiqued so extensively by figures such as James and Dewey. But the rhythm of cloister work is more interesting than such associations allow, particularly insofar as it exemplifies how the activity of thinking becomes articulated through the moving body.[46] Henri Lefebvre, for one, recognizes this. In *The Production of Space*, he refers to the medieval monastic cloister and "the solemn pace of the monks who walk there" in the context of his argument for the importance of rethinking and reanimating Western conceptions of spacetime by affirming the importance of bodies.[47] For Lefebvre the cloister is a thinking-space that moves between the corporeal and the absolute, connecting a "finite and determinate locality . . . to a theology of the infinite."[48] But the cloister is also interesting insofar as it reveals how the rhythmic relations between bodies and spaces are mediated through the generative power of gestures.[49] As he puts it: "Organized gestures, which is to say ritualized and codified gestures, are not simply performed in 'physical' space, in the spaces of bodies. Bodies themselves generate spaces, which are produced by and for their gestures. The linking of gestures corresponds to the articulation and linking of well-defined spatial segments, segments which repeat, but whose repetition gives rise to novelty."[50]

How might this help us think about what happens in a space such as the Chisenhale? Certainly, walking repeatedly up and down the narrow, white-walled corridor of the Chisenhale can start to feel vaguely monastic: like passing time in a cloister, or cell, albeit one without corners or openings onto the light relief of a central quadrangle. This encroaching sense of becoming cloistered might well work to close down rather than open up the potential for a corridor to facilitate thinking. Unlike a cloister, however, the corridor of the Chisenhale is a space of more obvious admixture. It is a space of and for mingled bodies.[51] As zones of transition, corridors generate perturbations by virtue of the mundane, transitory presence of passers-through. Furthermore, everyday movements in the corridor of the Chisenhale are not nearly so disciplined or regimented. And yet the rhythm of these movements is relatively predictable. Bodies go with the flow. Move along, nothing of interest here. To pass time in this space is not, however, to accede inevitably to its rhythms: it is also to modify them, and to generate new rhythms with the potential to be felt across and between bodies. It is to complicate the purposeful, linear, direct movement of bodies. In the process, the corridor can be transformed, however briefly, in ways that make it feel like a passageway for moving bodies — a passageway in which we work while "a distracted, urban audience" hurries "by us, on their way to the studios above, or out of the Chisenhale." A passageway in which, at times the "hurrying would arrest itself, stopping awkwardly in its tracks. A passerby would stop at the top of the stairs, seeing us blocking the path with our energies, diverting the flow of action."[52] A passageway in which bodies pass by, and pass through, mingling dances, or at the very least, mingling glances.

What is being worked upon here? What is being experimented? What is being experimented are the affective relations of which this space of movement is composed. Subsisting within any architectural context, including a corridor, are fields of affective potential. The affective potential of a corridor can be understood as a turbulent background field of relational intensity, irreducible to and certainly not containable by any single body or subject.[53] The affects of this field are radically autonomous — they are not contained by bodies. But that does not mean they are not felt. They can be felt as the registering of intensity in a sensing body before that intensity is recognized as a distinct emotion.[54] They can be sensed as disquietude before this sense becomes recognizable, or nameable, as fear. Conversely, they can be sensed as a joyful disturbance from which emerges a sense of anticipation moving toward a possible future. They can be sensed as the feeling of something happening before that process is named as such.

The concept of feeling is especially important here because it points to the possibility that minor variations within and between bodies may generate affective turbulence producing in turn a sense that some kind of difference is in the making. William James calls these variations "feelings of tendency": affective vectors that are "often so vague that we are unable to name them at all."[55] These feelings of tendencies are nonrepresentational — they do not exist as definite "images in the mind," or at least not as picture-like images.[56] Their existence is more akin to the "shadowy scheme of the 'form' of an opera, play, or book, which remains in our mind and on which we pass judgment when the actual thing is done."[57] These feelings are important because they make palpable the possibility that something is taking place even if it remains difficult to capture. As James suggests, this something is a halo or fringe of which we have a sense without it necessarily precipitating as a discrete object. It is a "feeling like any other, a feeling of what thoughts are next to arise, before they have arisen."[58] To experiment experience is to attend to these feelings of tendency, to take them seriously as part of the process of making more of thinking.

These feelings of tendency have the capacity to persist. The affective fallout of a week in a corridor is an ongoing process: its after-affects continue to resonate long after particular configurations of bodies, objects, and ideas come together. To work through the week is to respond to its affective tonality, and to the ongoing resonance of this tonality in thinking. And so, even if after the week in the Chisenhale things settle down and intensities dissipate, certain affects nevertheless persist: vague but tangible senses of resonating augmentation and orientation producing subtle shifts, twists, and turns in the multilayered sensibility from which thinking takes place. And the affective memory of the eventful corridor remains: not as the recollection through representation of an event, but as a point of inflection generating a field of virtual potential that never quite exhausts itself in the process of becoming more than it never (actually) was.

Sometimes, of course, the after-affects of the event do precipitate as blocks of affective spacetime that return. Thus, the return from a week in the corridor of the Chisenhale includes a moment of angular clambering pointing to the possibility of making more of abstraction (chapter 7); the spectral remains of an image complicating inventively the rhythmic movement of bodies (chapter 2); and a growing sense of the value of taking a line for a walk as a way of experimenting experience (chapter 4).

Relation-Specific Spacetimes for Experimenting Experience

Insofar as a corridor is a space for experimenting experience, it is both site and relation specific. There are elements of a week of working in that corridor that were obviously site specific, that is, that can only be understood in terms of the architectural constraint of that space. Thus, we played with the affordances of specific features of the corridor — its narrowness, the concreteness of steps, a nook and cranny here and there, the sheer face of white paint. There is something intuitively appealing about using site specificity as a way of understanding and lending legitimacy to the act of spending a week in a corridor. After all, site specificity seems to privilege locality, place, situatedness, positionality — all those things that work against an understanding of space as abstract and against thinking as an activity of distancing. Site specificity serves as a reminder of the importance of the fact that each view is a view from somewhere, and that sensing always takes place somewhere. To pass time in a corridor seems obviously site specific insofar as it involves a particular kind of performance work that "articulate[s] and define[s] itself through properties, qualities or meanings produced in specific relationships between an 'object' or 'event' and a position it occupies."[59] But site specificity only partly captures the qualities of a corridor as a space within which to experiment affective experience.

Perhaps a better way of understanding a week of activities in a corridor is in terms of what Brian Massumi calls relation-specific work.[60] This claim might seem little more than recognition of the fact that sites are composed of distinctive collections of objects, things, bodies, and ideas: this corridor, this stairwell, these three bodies. Relations are however always more than contextual collections of things or objects. They are also more than lines of connection between already existing actual actors and agents. To foreground relations does not simply involve joining the dots. As William James is always reminding us, it also means taking seriously the fact that relations are just as important as the terms to which they refer. Furthermore, as James also makes clear, relations are always just as temporal as they are spatial. There is always more to relations: a relentlessly necessary excess. And because of this, relations are always in transition, always in the process of moving on and arriving along what James calls the "chromatic fringes" that edge the actuality of experience with the potential of the virtual. Or, as James puts it, "the word 'and' trails after every sentence. Something always escapes."[61] And as it is with sentences, so it also is with corridors. To listen to James is to foreground relation specificity as much as site specificity as a logic for thinking through the fugitive processuality of spacetimes without reducing these spaces to attributes of a physical location. It is to recognize that relation specificity does to site specificity what situation does to site. Only much, much more. Put another way, relation specificity is always a processual arrangement of agencies and actors that never precipitates site as a "stable point of origin" or a "specific, 'knowable' point of destination."[62] To foreground relations in this way is to complicate any sense that events are specific to particular locations while also recognizing that they may be what artist Robert Irwin calls "site-conditioned": that is, they may emerge through close and responsive engagement with the details of particular surroundings.[63] The key thing is that site is sensed as a nexus of ongoing relations rather than something concrete existing in advance of these relations. This helps us avoid falling back upon a sense of site as a container within which bodies move; rather, relation-specific spacetimes for moving bodies consist of bodies and their surrounds emerging through the processual event of movement.

Crucially, relation-specific spacetimes never cease to have the potential to become something more than they actually are. The trick is to find ways of thinking this excess. This is fundamentally a matter of participation. However, the ongoing persistence of the affective wake of relation-specific spacetimes complicates the question of participation. The question is no longer only how to learn to participate in the process of which these spacetimes are composed, but how to remain open to the ongoing participation of the affective turbulence they generate in the process of thinking. Long after their actual enactment, events of participation return to participate, taking thinking off guard, even if only momentarily, moving one to think and write. To take seriously participation in experiments for moving bodies is therefore to become open to the value of revisitation as a process through which participation continues to resonate and move within experience. Furthermore, such responsiveness is not addressed solely toward relations between bodies. It is also responsiveness to the potential futures of these relations. Understood thus, the spacetimes of participation are always partly an involved orientation to potential futures: futures always actualizing from the untimely potential of the virtual.

Viewed retrospectively, then, certain things happened in the corridor of the Chisenhale: the recoding, rewriting, or remapping of an ordinary transitional space; a collaboration of sorts across disciplines always promising more. But no great revolution. Nothing turned on its head. No subversion, resistance, rupture. Not even any real dancing. And perhaps not even any real geography. More than anything else, what emerges from that week is the ongoing refrain of a simple proposition: "Bodies not only move in, but generate, spaces produced by and through their movements."[64] As Mike Pearson and Michael Shanks continue, "Movements — of dance, sport, war — are the intrusion of events into architectural spaces. And yet the reverse is always true. Each door implies the movement of someone crossing its frame; each corridor the progression that blocks it; each architectural space the intruding presence that will inhabit it."[65] Equally, we might add another proposition: architectural spaces such as corridors generate affective spacetimes through and for moving bodies. Thinking the generative relation between spacetimes and bodies together thus is one way of understanding what happens in a corridor and beyond.

In this context, a corridor affords the opportunity for a relation-specific experiment with affective experience as a process of transition between and with bodies, concepts, and techniques. Clearly, unlike James's corridor, the Chisenhale does not have actual rooms connecting with it — its physical open endedness is limited to a doorway and a stairwell. But it does serve as a transitional zone through which disciplinary interests pass. Save for the door onto the street, the corridor lacks actual doors: it does, however, have other openings. It opens onto a range of questions about how moving bodies might participate in the generation of spacetimes not as fixed points but as comings and goings, as transitions. And, like pragmatism, a week spent in a corridor might encourage experimentation with the transitions of which these spacetimes consist. Experimenting experience in this way involves the radically empirical activity of understanding the processual spatiality of moving bodies without ever precipitating either bodies or spaces as objects of thought. It involves the effort to respond to the ongoing possibility that encounters with moving bodies might provide opportunities for stretching experience, for modifying senses and sensibilities. And it does so in anticipation that such experimentation can contribute to the elaboration of an expanded terrain of ethical and political potential, articulated through affectively imbued dispositions and sensibilities, that might modify and work against the problematic tendencies of contemporary cultural and political life in corridors and who knows where else.

CHAPTER TWO

Rhythmic Bodies and
Affective Atmospheres

And so, at some point, let's say we are working in the corridor of the Chisenhale. Petra is reciting some lines in a slow rhythm and, at the same time, moving up and down the corridor in her wheelchair. She suggests taking up the rhythm of her movement. I begin trying, by walking up and down the stairs and corridor. Yet, beyond walking, nothing of any significance seems to happen. But Petra persists, encouraging. She continues reciting lines and moving up and down the corridor, inviting a response. It becomes easy to try too hard, to pay too much attention to walking — to want and wait too much for something to happen. How to know how to go on? How to proceed in a way that eases that awkward sense of discomfort arising from the fact that apparently nothing of any real importance is happening here? For the want of something else to do, I simply keep walking, advancing and retreating up and down the stairs to the rhythm of Petra's voice and movement (fig. 2.1). And I continue to think that nothing seems to happen for quite some time.

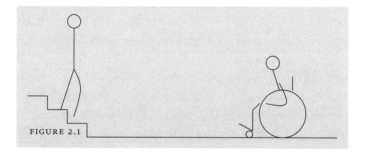

FIGURE 2.1

Suddenly, and with some relief, something happens (fig. 2.2).

FIGURE 2.2. *A rehearsal photograph of Orpheus and the Furies. Orpheus performed by Emmy Leisner.*

Through the repeated process of moving up and down to the rhythms of Petra's voice, an unsolicited but corporeally precipitated memory introduces a note of creative difference into the movement in the corridor, inflecting it with the memory of Orpheus's descent into the underworld, and, more specifically, a scene from a 1913 production of Gluck's *Orpheus and Eurydice* staged at a theater in Hellerau, a garden city near Dresden.

The performance at Hellerau, and the performance space in which it was produced, were the result of a collaboration between two figures — the composer and pedagogue Emile Jaques-Dalcroze (1865–1950) and the theater designer Adolphe Appia (1862–1928). Dalcroze is best known for devising "eurhythmics," a system for using rhythmic movement to enhance musical education.[1] In the years leading up to the First World War eurhythmics was one of the most fashionable somatic practices in Europe, its popularity briefly on a par with the tango.[2] Dalcroze undertook extensive demonstration tours throughout Europe, establishing institutes in cities such as Berlin, Kiev, London, Paris, Prague, St. Petersburg, Vienna, and Warsaw. After participating in a demonstration by Dalcroze, Appia became convinced that eurhythmics could provide a corporeal vehicle with which to carry forward his own ideas about the reform of conventional theater and performance space.

The collaboration between Dalcroze and Appia and its return as a minor disruption of that week of working in the Chisenhale serves to foreground two interrelated issues explored in this chapter. The first is the question of how rhythmic movement is employed to modulate affective experience through experiments with specific techniques. Delving into the practice and performance of eurhythmics provides a way of examining how efforts to answer this question have been central to concerns about the affective capacities of moving bodies in modern life. At the same time, examining eurhythmics in this way also provides an important opportunity to explore the relation between rhythmic movement and the practical effort to produce distinctive performance spaces. This opens up a second question: what kinds of experiments with experience are made possible by these spaces?

In pursuing answers to these questions, this chapter returns not only to the collaboration between Appia and Dalcroze but also to elements of the writing of both James Dewey and Henri Lefebvre. The point here is not so much to use the latter pair of thinkers as a necessary critical corrective to the practical experiments of the former: indeed, if anything, the example of eurhythmics actually serves to highlight some of the problematic elements of both Dewey's and Lefebvre's writing on rhythm. More important, however, is what emerges from these encounters: an argument for the value of a modest form of rhythmic experiment taking place through the production of affective atmospheres for and by moving bodies.

Thinking Rhythmically

Rhythm is one of the key concepts underpinning John Dewey's efforts to work up an experimental sense of experience. Like other philosophers, Dewey is drawn to rhythm because it offers a way of thinking differentiation in process. He emphasizes in particular the temporality of rhythm: it is first and foremost a variation in "intensity or speed."[3] In Dewey's vision, rhythm is not simply temporal, however: it involves instead a qualitative transformation in spatiotemporality. On this point he is quite clear: "There is no rhythm when variations are not placed."[4] Place here is not a static territory, but a dynamic process. "There is," Dewey observes, "a wealth of suggestion in the phrase '*takes place.*' The change not only comes but it belongs; it has its definite place in a larger whole. [Rhythm] is not a variation in a single feature but a modulation of the entire pervasive and unifying qualitative substratum."[5]

The placing of rhythm is the way in which rhythmic differentiation abroad in the world is sensed in experience as a disquietude or disturbance of spacetime. For Dewey, however, rhythm has particular value insofar as it points to how aesthetic experience emerges from the mundane spatiotemporalities of everyday life. He puts it thus: "The first characteristic of the environing world that makes possible the existence of artistic form is rhythm. There is rhythm in nature before poetry, painting, architecture and music exist."[6] Aesthetic experience would therefore not be possible in a world conceived in terms of either pure flux and flow or pure stasis. Rhythm, then, is differentiation in worldly experience: a variation in *tempo*, a difference in "where emphasis falls in the constant rhythm" of the relation between organism and environment.[7] If experience is grasped thus, the task of the artist — and indeed the philosopher — is less to represent rhythm and more akin to the amplification and expression of variations in experience. This aesthetic task is also an ethical one: it is about multiplying possibilities for living, both individually and collectively, by making more of the expressive qualities generated by rhythmic spacetimes.

Henri Lefebvre was not especially enthusiastic about pragmatism.[8] Nor was he particularly fond of using the category of experience in the way Dewey did, perhaps because it seemed to Lefebvre to appeal to an unmediated, nondialectical empiricism. Yet he shared with Dewey an enthusiasm for the promise of rhythm as a corporeal and conceptual nexus through which to grasp the spacetimes in which bodies participate.[9] Lefebvre's interest in this is expressed in his writings about rhythmanalysis, broadly conceived as an attempt to conceptualize and apprehend everyday spacetimes in processual and relational terms.[10] As such, rhythmanalysis involves both an ontological and an epistemological claim. The ontological claim is that the world — its objects, places, bodies, and events — is composed of a multiplicity of rhythms. Lefebvre articulates it thus: "There is neither separation nor an abyss between so-called material bodies, living bodies, social bodies, and representations, ideologies, traditions, projects and utopias. They are all composed of (reciprocally influential) rhythms in interaction."[11] Bodies are therefore spacetimes generated through the constructive entrainment and interference of a multiplicity of rhythms. Epistemologically, rhythmanalysis involves the cultivation of a peculiar style of attentiveness open to becoming affected by the rhythmic spacetimes of everyday life. This attentiveness is simultaneously practico-sensory and intellectual: the rhythmanalyst thinks with and through the body, while also making appropriate use of concepts. Her aim is to understand and mobilize the body as a set of rhythmic relations through which the spatiotemporal turbulence of everyday life registers as so many intensities of feeling.

For Lefebvre then, as for Dewey, rhythm is always spatial and temporal: it "invests places, but is not itself a place; it is not a thing, nor an aggregation of things, nor yet a simple flow. It embodies its own law, its own regularity, which it derives from space — from its own space — and from a relation between space and time."[12] And, like Dewey, for Lefebvre rhythm offers a way of implicitly affirming experience as a dynamic and distributed field of movement that is nevertheless also felt and sensed in moving bodies.

Moreover, both Dewey and Lefebvre share an interest in aesthetic practices and techniques that allow experiment with rhythms.[13] In *The Production of Space* Lefebvre hints that the nascent field of rhythmanalytic inquiry might be explored most profitably in the spheres of artistic and creative practice, including "poetry, music, dance and the theatre."[14] More specifically, Lefebvre claims that the "field of application par excellence [of rhythmanalysis], its preferred sphere of experiment, would be the sphere of music and dance, the sphere of 'rhythmic cells,' and their effects."[15] What might such experiments in the rhythmic cells of music and dance look like? In *Elements of Rhythmanalysis*, parts of which were cowritten with Catherine Régulier, Lefebvre points to some possibilities. He remains typically vague about the exact shape and style of such experiments, however: at most, he sketches a future research agenda for experiments in thinking through rhythmic spacetimes, offering an invitation for a project he claims has yet "to be undertaken."[16] It would be unfair to demand of Lefebvre that he outline a program of action or a recipe for rhythmanalytic experiment: indeed, part of the appeal of his writing is its suggestive, open-ended vagueness. It remains, at most, a speculative invitation to think rhythmically.

The Importance of Being Rhythmic

One way of taking up this invitation is by exploring how ethico-aesthetic experiments with rhythmic movement are enacted in practice. And in this respect there is a particular value in exploring experiments that share something of the philosophical and cultural context within which the ideas of both Dewey and Lefebvre emerged. This context can be understood in terms of what Hillel Schwartz calls a "kinesthetic": specifically, a late nineteenth- and early twentieth-century cultural-corporeal structure of feeling in which rhythm figured prominently as a transformative and expressive force.[17] Without any single point of origin, this structure of feeling was articulated through a range of spheres of activity, including art, psychology, philosophy, performance, and the design of technology.[18]

For those contributing to and caught up in the practices of which this structure of feeling consisted, rhythm worked as a key matter of concern through which the dynamism of modernity could be grasped, while also offering the promise of ameliorating some of its more negative effects on minds, bodies, and cultural sensibilities.[19] In philosophy, rhythm provided a conceptual vehicle with which to think through the generative processuality of spatiotemporality without relying upon the arresting and immobilizing terms of representation. In addition to the writings of Dewey and the early writings of Lefebvre, this sense of the value of rhythm could be found, for instance, in the process philosophy of Alfred North Whitehead and in Henri Bergson's writing on duration. For each, grasping the process of change — and the experience of that change — required some conception of differentiation and novelty in the flow of motion. And rhythm seemed to allow this maneuver. As Whitehead put it, "a rhythm involves a pattern and to that extent is always self-identical. But now rhythm cannot be a mere pattern; for the rhythmic quality depends equally upon differences involved in each exhibition of the pattern. The essence of the rhythm is the fusion of sameness and novelty, so that the whole never loses the essential unity of the pattern; while the parts exhibit the contrast arising from the novelty of their detail."[20] For Bergson, rhythm is also grasped as the differentiation of process. His thinking in this respect has much to do with ideas about time as a dynamic, creative force, the apprehension of which is badly served by popular representational habits of thinking that render it immobile through its analysis in spatial terms. Rather than a discrete object existing in space, lived time, or duration, is a creative, intensive process.[21] Furthermore, for Bergson duration can only be grasped through a method — intuition — that "seeks to recapture, to get back the movement and rhythm of the composition, to live again creative evolution."[22]

Bergson's thinking on these questions serves as an important point of orientation for Dewey's and Lefebvre's respective writings on rhythm. For both, Bergson is far too eager to affirm continuity. Sharpest, however, is Lefebvre's critique of "Bergsonism and the formless psychological continuum advocated by Bergsonian philosophy." Lefebvre's theory of moments, from which his rhythmanalytic project emerges, challenges Bergsonian continuity by "reinstat[ing] discontinuity, grasping it in the very fabric of the 'lived,' and on the loom of continuity."[23] For Dewey, Bergson's philosophy lacks a conception of effort with which to account for ethical participation in the flow of the world, and through which to avoid philosophical passivity in the face of the primacy of movement where the latter is never in a condition of risk. Dewey argues that an emphasis on the movement of experience is also a "call to effort, a challenge to investigation, a potential doom of disaster and death."[24] In other words, the continuity of experience does not provide an ethical guarantee, but a rationale for an ongoing process of testing out and risk taking by the organism at a range of scales and intensities. And yet Bergson is careful to insist that philosophical thinking — exemplified through intuition — demands such effort. Bergson himself makes this point clear in *The Creative Mind*: "I repudiate facility. I recommend a certain manner of thinking which courts difficulty; I value effort above everything. . . . But because I called attention to the mobility at the base of things, it has been claimed that I encouraged a certain relaxing of the mind. . . . One might just as well imagine that a microbiologist recommends microbic diseases to us when he shows us microbes everywhere."[25] Neither is Bergson claiming that human life is issued with an ethical guarantee. He does affirm the necessity of an ontological or ontogenetic principle that is always in excess of the actuality of experience. The life of this excess is never in question: but life as phenomenological finitude always is. Finally, the claim that Bergson's thinking is underpinned by a formless psychological continuum is also contestable. As Bergson puts it toward the end of *Matter and Memory*: "In reality there is no one rhythm of duration; it is possible to imagine many rhythms which, slower or faster, measure the degree of tension or relaxation of different kinds of consciousness."[26]

Within the context of the kinesthetic outlined above, such claims resonated with efforts to develop a rhythmic aesthetics across a range of artistic movements including fauvism, cubism, and futurism. The idea of rhythm as a nonrepresentational generator of differentiation in affective, kinesthetic, and perceptual experience was crucial to such work.[27] Rhythm was invoked to grasp the affective excess of spatiotemporal experience without necessarily reducing this experience to a static painterly perspectivalism. For cubists such as Albert Gleizes and Jean Metzinger, the point was to generate spaces for affective intersubjectivity in which the viewer, by means of his or her own creative intuition, could appreciate the rhythmic unity of the artwork.[28]

These philosophical and aesthetic ideas about rhythm were often linked with an emphasis on cultivating rhythmic thinking and feeling through movement. This, of course, was not necessarily new. A sense of the importance of rhythmic movement could be identified, for instance, in classical Greek culture, and in particular through an emphasis on "eurhythmy" as the graceful embodiment of rhythmic flow. And in part, it was these rhythmic ideals that various figures, perhaps most notably Isadora Duncan, claimed to have rediscovered through modern forms of bodily movement and expression. Relatedly, in a pedagogical context, the importance of the moving body was addressed through techniques and practices that worked on and attempted to modulate its rhythms: the aim of such instruction was the physical and moral invigoration of both individual and community. The key point here is that many practices were informed by an underlying belief in the enlivening and transformative effect of bodies moving rhythmically: that is, through a greater aesthetic appreciation of rhythm it might be possible to renew and reanimate the life of both the individual and society. Rhythm was in this sense a utopian vehicle through which to pursue more authentic forms of existence, particularly in the context of fears about the effects of industrialization and mechanization on the energies of the individual. Even if its beneficial effects and affects were only temporary, rhythmic movement could restore wholeness and organic unity in a life perceived as fractured and disordered.

The work of Emile Jaques-Dalcroze and the practice of eurhythmics can be situated squarely within this concern with rhythmic movement. For Dalcroze, rhythm was a vital force to be harnessed for the benefit of individual and society. It was "analogous to electricity and the great chemical and physical elements,— an energy, an agent — radio-active, radio-creative — conducing to self-knowledge and to a consciousness not only of our powers, but of those of others, of humanity itself."[29] Moreover, the appreciation of this force was to be cultivated as a form of "rhythmic consciousness." In 1907 Dalcroze outlined a series of principles capturing the relation between rhythmic movement and consciousness:

1 Rhythm is movement
2 Rhythm is essentially physical
3 Every movement involves space and time
4 Musical consciousness is the result of physical experience
5 The perfecting of physical resources results in clarity of perception
6 The perfecting of movements in time assures consciousness of musical rhythm
7 The perfecting of movements in space assures consciousness of plastic rhythm
8 The perfecting of movements in time and space can only be accomplished by exercises in rhythmic movement.[30]

Such principles were formulated during practical experiments with rhythmic movement. In 1892, and at the age of twenty-five, Dalcroze became professor of harmony at the Music Conservatory in Geneva. While teaching, he noticed a problem encountered by many of his students, who were often very good at writing and notating particular chords yet were much less able to discern them by ear. For Dalcroze the problem arose from the fact that existing methods of musical education did not provide students with "experience of chords at the beginning of their studies — when brain and body are developing along parallel lines, the one constantly communicating its impressions and sensations to the other."[31] He therefore introduced into his teaching "special exercises of a physiological nature" and soon noticed an improvement in the "inner hearing" of students who undertook these exercises.[32] Problems remained, however. Many of his students seemed to have a limited capacity to discern and reproduce "with any exactitude variations of time and rhythmic grouping."[33] For Dalcroze, the solution lay in the design of a system of musical education combining the development of the "auditive sense" with the cultivation of the sensory and motor processes of the body. As he put it, "musical sensations of a rhythmic nature call for the muscular and nervous response of the *whole organism*."[34] And such a response demanded a "system of musical education in which the body itself shall play the rôle of intermediary between sounds and thought, becoming in time the direct medium of our feelings — aural sensations being reinforced by all those called into being by the multiple agents of vibration and resonance lying dormant in our bodies."[35]

This system consisted of three distinct but interrelated components. The first element — rhythmic training — laid the basis for the second two, and was acknowledged to be the most innovative aspect of Dalcroze's work. In practical terms, teaching the individual child to "move and think accurately and rhythmically" began with exercises that directed attention to the basic rhythms of corporeality, including breathing.[36] Students would then progress to exercises designed to develop control over those corporeal rhythms that could be directed consciously. Walking was particularly important in this regard, as it was "the natural starting-point in the child's initiation into rhythm."[37] The capacity to control more complex rhythmic movements was then introduced through exercises that demanded the simultaneous movement of limbs to different rhythms:

> By marching the beats and accentuating the first beat of each bar with a stamp of the foot. Gestures with the arm accompany each step, and emphasise the first beat by means of a complete muscular contraction. On the weak beats, steps and gestures should be executed with a minimum of muscular effort. Then, on a sudden command, at the word "hopp," the pupil must contrive to prevent his arm from contracting or his foot from stamping. Or, again, the word "hopp" may be made to convey the beat, or to substitute a leg movement for an arm movement. It is extremely difficult to separate leg from arm movements, and it is only by dint of repeated exercises that, eventually, distinct automatisms are created.[38]

The development of these automatisms was allied with solfège, the second element of Dalcroze's system. The aim of solfège was the development of the "auditive sense," and it involved exercises combining bodily movements with listening, reading, and vocalizing music. So, for instance, in the course of singing a particular melody, a student might, on the command of the teacher, substitute bodily movements for the voice, and vice versa. Or she might "learn to sing a melody while executing a different rhythm by means of bodily movements."[39] The third element of Dalcroze's method, improvisation, combined "the principles of rhythm and solfège, with a view to their musical externalisation, by means of touch."[40] This involved exercises in which the student might "execute a fixed rhythm, concentrating on its melodisation and harmonisation. At the word 'hopp,' he must invent a rhythm of a different order."[41] It is here that Dalcroze's work becomes most obviously experimental, in the sense that it is a deliberate attempt to cultivate the capacity within students to respond creatively to the rhythms of music. More generally, however, the evolution of the system itself can be seen as an ongoing effort on the part of Dalcroze to experiment with moving bodies and their capacities to be affected.

Moving between Rhythmanalysis and Eurhythmics

Dalcroze's practical experiments resonate directly with elements of John Dewey's interest in somatic pedagogy. In 1925 a reader of Dewey's work, Margaret H'Doubler, published *The Dance and Its Place in Education*, in which she outlined the pedagogical value of expressive movement experience.[42] Rhythm was a crucial element of this experience, a claim H'Doubler supported with reference to the work of Dalcroze. Thus, as she put it, the "rhythms and harmonies" of music "satisfy one of the most fundamental needs of every normal human being, the need for satisfaction of the sense of rhythm that is grounded deep in his physical constitution."[43]

If the sympathies between Dewey's pedagogic ethics and the work of Dalcroze are obvious, then the relations between eurhythmics and the vision of rhythmic experiment outlined by Lefebvre are less so. For Lefebvre, eurhythmics may have been understood, less than favorably, as a paradigmatic exercise in rhythmic training, or *dressage*.[44] "Dressage" is the term Lefebvre uses to refer to the process through which humans, like animals, are entrained in rhythmic gestural economies. Evident most obviously in the military, dressage reproduces itself through repetition and is addressed to the body through the inculcation of well-rehearsed ways of walking, moving, and talking. It requires a corporeal discipline in which individuals begin to understand themselves, and their dynamic place in societies, through rhythmic entrainment. The suspicion that eurhythmics was a similarly disciplining practice chimes with early critical reactions to Dalcroze's work. For instance, in the years after the First World War, the poet Osip Mandelstam was a frequent visitor to the eurhythmic studios in Leningrad. He responded to eurhythmics in terms of its capacity for facilitating wider social and cultural transformation. "Rhythm" he argued, demanded "a synthesis, a synthesis of the spirit and the body, a synthesis of work and play. It was born of syncretism, that is, the fusion of non-differentiated elements."[45] Any successful system of rhythmic education needed to engage fully the bodies of its students. While eurhythmics had potential, Mandelstam was not convinced it provided a comprehensive answer. As he put it, "The system is best characterised not by estheticism, but by the spirit of geometry and strict rationalism: man, space, time, and motion are its four basic elements. However, it is not really surprising that rhythm, which had been banished from the community for an entire century, returned rather more anemic and abstract than it actually was in Hellas. The system does not belong only to Dalcroze. The discovery of the system is one of those brilliant finds like the discovery of gunpowder or steam power. Once a force is revealed it must develop of its own accord."[46]

Lefebvre may have had some sympathy with Mandelstam's comments, but it is also possible that he could well have understood the practice more generously. Kurt Meyer has suggested that Lefebvre would have considered the popularity of practices such as eurhythmics as a response to the encroachment of mechanical modes of temporal organization in everyday life. As such, eurhythmics and practices like it could have served to provide a cathartic relief from the repetitive rhythms of everyday life.[47] Lefebvre's own remarks about the transformative relation between "musical time and the rhythms of the *body*" would seem to support this.[48] Musical time, according to Lefebvre, has the capacity to reorganize and reassemble the rhythms of the body, making "a bouquet, a garland from a jumble."[49] Furthermore, after a period during which the relation between music and dance had been attenuated through systems of abstract orchestration and composition, modern music had reaffirmed their mutuality. As he writes, citing the example of jazz, music now "finds itself back in the body; rhythm dominates, supplants melody and harmony (without suppressing them)."[50] This reaffirmation was not only of aesthetic significance. It also had ethical value insofar as it provided a "compensation for the miseries of everyday life."[51]

Lefebvre could also have been generously disposed toward the sensibility eurhythmics encourages, particularly to the extent that it involves learning to be affected by rhythm. As Lefebvre reminds us, the rhythmanalyst is a figure that "calls on all his senses. . . . Without privileging any one of these sensations, raised by him in the perception of rhythms, to the detriment of any other. He thinks with his body, not in the abstract, but in lived temporality."[52] Both rhythmanalysis and eurhythmics encourage the cultivation of a form of thinking combining attentiveness and susceptibility. Eurhythmics is a technique for cultivating the corporeal capacity to respond and "realize" musical rhythms through the body without deliberate, representational contemplation of those rhythms. Similarly, for the rhythmanalyst the critical task is how to be taken up in and by the rhythms to which she attends. As Lefebvre puts it: "To grasp a rhythm it is necessary to have been *grasped* by it; one must let oneself go, give oneself over, abandon oneself to its duration."[53] Furthermore, by "grasping," Lefebvre means a mode of attentive hearing, a version of solfège, through which the "attentive ear begins to separate out, to distinguish the sources [of noises], to bring them back together by perceiving interactions."[54]

Both rhythmanalysis and eurhythmics can therefore be situated in relation to a loosely aligned set of psychological and aesthetic theories in which attention is conceived in terms of the operation and organization of a rhythmic economy transcending the division between mind and body. Such theories were particularly popular in the early decades of the twentieth century as part of the kinesthetic outlined above. For instance, in a 1904 essay about rhythm published in the *American Journal of Psychology*, Thaddeus Bolton described the rhythmic character of a range of physiological and psychological processes, including attention. Attention, for Bolton, "manifests itself in a wave-like form. It is a series of pulses."[55] Understood in this way, the development of rhythmic attention could be achieved through the deliberate cultivation of susceptibility to the affective and kinetic force of rhythms, whether in vocal, musical, or gestural form. Similarly, in the case of eurhythmics, the intention was to allow the body to hear and respond to the rhythms of music without the interference of intellectual contemplation. The body would play the role of "intermediary between sounds and thought.[56] The underlying aim was to allow the student to understand her body as an ensemble of rhythms, each of which could be isolated and controlled independently — given enough practice.

Initially such control would be deliberate and intentional on the part of the student. Over time the degree of effort required would diminish until the "time between the conception and realisation of the movement" was reduced to a minimum: in this way it would be possible to develop the capacity to facilitate a precognitive, corporeal transposition of "sound-rhythms into plastic rhythms."[57] This process happens so quickly that the "mind has no time to record all the elements of the musical rhythms; the body expresses them before the brain has even a clear idea of them."[58] For Dalcroze this process was a less a matter of "interpretation" than of "translation."[59] It was precisely this aspect of eurhythmics that critics of the practice found so problematic, however, because it suggested little more than a technique for the cultivation of mindless, unthinking, rhythmic automata. But such criticism is rather shortsighted. After all, cultivating "immediate" response is central to the development of many techniques that encourage skillful involvement. And, as various figures have argued, there is some evidence that much of what happens neurophysiologically takes place before this happening is registered in conscious thought.[60]

Qualifying Rhythmic Movement

Rhythmanalysis and eurhythmics share something else, however: a concern with the transformative potential of bodies moving rhythmically. Eurhythmics was obviously intended as a solution for some of the problems experienced by music students. But for Dalcroze it also had much wider application. It would solve the problem of "a general 'a-rhythm,' whose cure appeared to depend on a special training designed to regulate nervous reactions and effect a co-ordination of muscles and nerves; in short, to harmonise mind and body."[61] Following the First World War, Dalcroze argued that eurhythmics might reawaken the bodies and enhance the rhythmic "temperament" of distinct cultural groups. In an essay on this topic he provided a brief typology of the rhythmic characteristics of different European countries, identifying the kinds of treatment each might need. Dalcroze singled out one group of people for special attention in this regard, suggesting that "in every country, Jewish children should be especially urged to undergo a training in Eurhythmics, for, while their musical faculties and artistic intelligence are in general of a remarkably high order, their a-rhythm and lack of harmony in motor and nervous functions are liable to hamper their aesthetic development and their attainment of intellectual and physical balance."[62]

Such comments have obvious affinities with the racist rhetoric of eugenics, particularly through its articulation in German fascism.[63] They would not be significant if Dalcroze had been a minor figure in the emergence of German body culture in the first decades of the twentieth century. However, as Karl Toepfer observes, "Dalcroze looms over the relation between modernity and carnality in Germany before and after the [First World] war."[64] For Toepfer, Dalcroze's influence rests upon his establishment of "a pervasive didactic credibility for activities that, from a social perspective, even long after the war, might otherwise have seemed excessively aesthetic, mere narcissistic body worship."[65] Over the longer term then, the utopian potential of rhythmic movement could inform explicitly political choreographies. Arguments about the transformative and unifying power of rhythm could inform dreams of a body politic moving in unison and harmony, the most obvious expression of which was in the choreographic politics of German fascism.[66]

An awareness of eurhythmics' troubled histories should encourage close attention to how elements of the practice overlap with the conceptual concerns of thinkers such as Lefebvre and Dewey. In the case of the former, this is revealed most obviously through suggestions about the therapeutic potential of rhythmanalysis to modify and regulate rhythms that are simultaneously individual and collective, natural and social. In the process of affirming this therapeutic vision, Lefebvre mobilizes a conceptual vocabulary that resonates with some of the language used by Dalcroze to discuss eurhythmics. For the latter, terms like eurhythmy, polyrhythm, and a-rhythm were especially important in this respect, and provided a link between his ideas and the values of classical Greek culture. Lefebvre also makes use of some of this vocabulary. So, for Lefebvre, the rhythmanalytical project never loses sight of the body: "not the anatomical or functional body, but the body as polyrhythmic and eurhythmic (in the so-called normal state)."[67] And "intervention through rhythm . . . has a goal, an objective: to strengthen or re-establish eurhythmia."[68] This "eurhythmia" is a feature of "organism, organization, life (living bodies)."[69] And, in terms that would appeal to Dalcroze, Lefebvre juxtaposes eurhythmia with arrhythmia: "*Eurhythmia* (that of a living body, normal and *healthy*) presupposes the association of different rhythms. In arrhythmia, rhythms break apart, alter and bypass *synchronisation* (the usual terms for designating this phenomenon). A pathological situation — agreed! — depending on the case; interventions are made, or should be made, *through rhythms*, without brutality."[70]

Kurt Meyer suggests there are significant differences between eurhythmics and rhythmanalysis. Perhaps most importantly, while the former is concerned primarily with the unification of mind and body through rhythmic movement, rhythmanalysis is much more concerned with the "conflict zones" at which different spatiotemporalities encounter one another.[71] Lefebvre is indeed interested in how conflict zones within and between rhythms have the potential to generate creative differences in everyday spacetimes. But while it may well be the case that Lefebvre is more attentive to rhythmic conflict than Dalcroze, his vision of the practice as a transformative project is arguably underpinned just as much by a vision of rhythmic wholeness and unity that pathologizes arrhythmic movement.

A critical encounter with eurhythmics should also encourage qualification of Dewey's interest in rhythm. Certainly, it should make us cautious about his enthusiasm for the value of collective efforts to mobilize rhythmic movement. As he puts it: "To sing with another involves a contagious sympathy, in perhaps a higher degree than is the case with any other art. There is in the first place, as in the dance, a unit of rhythm. Rhythm is based on cooperation and in turn immensely strengthens the possibility of cooperation. When a company of people work on a dance or sing in rhythmic movement their efficiency and their pleasure are immensely increased."[72] This vision of collective rhythmic movement is underpinned by an ethico-aesthetic privileging vitality, harmony, and fulfillment. As Dewey asserts, "only when an organism shares in the ordered relations of its environment does it secure the stability essential to living. And when the participation comes after a phase of disruption and conflict, it bears within itself the germs of a consummation akin to the aesthetic."[73] Without this rhythm of order and disorder in which active interventions can be made, there is no possibility of an ethico-aesthetic moment. Experience therefore only becomes aesthetic when it realizes the potential harmony between thought and feeling, mind and body, inherent in the rhythms that give consistency to life. Such an emphasis points to the importance in Dewey's argument of the development of a form of intellectual, perceptual, and affective experience that tends toward unity and integration. As he puts it: "The rhythm peculiar to different relations between doing and undoing is the source of the distribution and apportionment of elements that conduces to directness and unity of perception. Lack of proper relationship and distribution produces a confusion that blocks singleness of perception."[74] This emphasis on the proper distribution of energies in an ongoing process of harmonization seems to support a vision of aesthetic experience as rhythmic ordering. But what of those ways of moving that do not accord with the well-balanced rhythms of the organism? And what of those experiences that do not precipitate a "movement toward an inclusive and fulfilling close"?[75] Put another way, insofar as experience is rhythmic, this rhythmicity might be as much to do with disorder as with order. And it might not necessarily assume a model of experiential, corporeal, and affective authenticity based upon progressive self-somatic improvement and realization.

In sum, then, efforts to restore continuity between the everyday and the aesthetic provide an important source of orientation for the attempt to cultivate thinking through somatic techniques of experience and experiment. But any rhythmic conception of experience should be attentive to how this experience might also have plateaus, fractures, and tears complicating a purposeful progression toward fulfillment. If rhythm is to serve as a key conceptual-empirical matter of concern with which to renew an ethico-aesthetics of the everyday through moving bodies, it needs to be employed in a way that does not pathologize "arrhythmic" experience — as the example of eurhythmics illustrates, such pathologizing can have dangerous resonances. Thus, as Stamatia Portanova argues, thinking rhythmically requires a sense of how "flows and cuts, energetic continuities and corporal singularities, constitute the rhythm of a human body which, rather than autonomous and isolated in its individuality, is always open and in relation with the outside, always incorporating external impulses and re-elaborating them in different ways."[76]

Rhythmic Spaces

The point here is not to argue against any affirmation of rhythmic movement as a source of transformation. Nor is it to claim that the relationship between eurhythmics and the affirmation of rhythm found in the work of figures such as Lefebvre and Dewey is by any means straightforward. Certainly, eurhythmics is not, by any stretch of the imagination, a direct exemplification of rhythmanalysis. But there are problematic resonances. These should not, however, discourage experimentation with rhythmic movement. And this might be pursued through thinking more about the collaboration between Dalcroze and Adolphe Appia. Appia thought eurhythmics had the potential to facilitate the radical overhaul of performance space. For Appia, theater design at the beginning of the twentieth century had a number of limitations. It was overly reliant upon static stage sets whose goal was representational — that is, they aimed toward the faithful reproduction of scenographic illusion. This arrangement tended, in turn, to diminish the expressive powers of the body: body and space were not understood as dynamic and mutually intertwined. Appia puts it thus: "The actor therefore is directly subservient to the inanimate setting. The place for the action is realised in one manner, the action itself in another; the two modes come into contact, but are utterly disparate."[77] Finally, for Appia the proscenium arch was too dominant in the architecture of theater design: the effect of this was to maintain an unnatural spatial division between audience and actor.

Renewing and reanimating theater space demanded an acknowledgment that musical and rhythmic sensibilities were also spatial sensibilities. It also required some sense of bodies as active participants in the generation of lively spaces. Appia's vision of the relation between bodies and space is remarkably similar to elements of the writing of Lefebvre. For both, bodies have the potential to generate spaces in the process of their movement. And for both, moving bodies have an animating quality inextricable from space and time. Appia writes: "It is not merely mechanically that we possess Space and are its centre; it is because we are living. Space is our life; our life creates Space; our body expresses it. . . . Our life creates space and time, one through the other. Our living body is the expression of Space during Time and of Time in Space. Empty and boundless Space — wherein we are placed at the start so that we may effect this essential transformation — no longer exists."[78]

How then to cultivate an appreciation of this creative relation between space and the body? Eurhythmics is, for Appia, crucial here: it is a practice that "generate[s] for itself a setting that emanates inevitably from the solid form of the human body and its movements."[79] As such, students of eurhythmics could begin to realize how, by moving, they had the capacity to produce spaces. As Appia puts it: "Trained in [eurhythmics] our body becomes a marvellous instrument of infinite possibilities. In contact with it, space comes to life and takes part in the living proportions of movement."[80] At eurhythmics institutes students would learn how to appreciate space as something actively created, something that was continuous with the movements of their bodies.

Training in eurhythmics was not sufficient, however. It was the task of the theater designer, as architect, to facilitate the full realization of this intimate relation between space, time, and the moving body. Indeed, without such intervention, the promise of eurhythmics would remain unfulfilled. This became clear to Appia in 1909, when he witnessed a production staged by Dalcroze in which the latter used "his own music, costumes, coloured light, etc." Appia was not terribly impressed: "I left the performance feeling depressed, and seizing paper and pencils I designed feverishly, each day, two or three *space designs* intended for rhythmic movement. When I had about twenty I submitted them to Dalcroze with a note explaining that his pupils were constantly moving on a flat surface. . . . My designs caused great enthusiasm. . . . This is how the style of space appropriate for the rhythmic movement of the body was first formulated. I shall call this *corporeal space*, which becomes *living space*, once the body animates it."[81]

On paper the designs appear two-dimensional; however, they were intended to provide a three-dimensional context within which bodies actively moved (fig. 2.3). They also provided the model for Appia's subsequent ideas about the design of rhythmic spaces. Such spaces were to be infinitely flexible, consisting of a variable architectural geometry composed of "simple and flat surfaces as well as obstacles, such as various stairs, platforms, ramps, walls, pillars, et al."[82] Clearly, these designs have an abstract quality, with clean, geometrical lines. The relation between these constructions and bodies was not passive, however. Rather, the former were "designed to render the body more conscious of its balance and flexibility, of the infinite possibilities in its expressive power."[83] For Appia, such designs would afford possibilities for the cultivation of distinctive spatial sensibilities.

Appia and Dalcroze had the chance to experiment practically with such designs at Hellerau, one of the first "Garden Cities" in Germany. Established in 1908 by Wolf Dohrn and Karl Schmidt, Hellerau was planned as a utopian community based upon the value of combining art and labor in a harmonious and self-enriching manner. Physical activity was also an important part of the ethos. In 1908 Dohrn attended a demonstration given by Dalcroze in Dresden and was immediately won over by it: he felt that it was exactly the sort of corporeal practice around which the aesthetic and cultural life of the community at Hellerau might be based. Subsequently he invited Dalcroze to establish an institute for rhythmic education at the site, an offer the latter accepted, not least because of the resonance between the utopian gestures of eurhythmics and the social reformist agenda of the community at Hellerau.[84] At the center of the institute was to be a new kind of performance space, one that would allow both Appia and Dalcroze to realize their shared interests in the expressive and transformative potential of rhythmic movement. The plans and eventual construction of the performance space, produced by architect Heinrich Tessenow,

FIGURE 2.3. *Appia's 1909 design for a "rhythmic space," titled "Escalier en face."* *Munich, German Theatre Museum (inv. IV. 749).*

reflected the particular influence of Appia's ideas about the need to rethink the relation between moving bodies and spaces. Constructed with no proscenium arch, no orchestra pit, and no fixed stage, the auditorium was designed to facilitate mobile, flexible, and rhythmic relations between bodies and spaces. It was also a deliberate effort to explode the boundary between performers and audience, a spatial arrangement that Appia felt was arbitrary but "implanted in us: the book *and* the reader; the picture, the statue *and* the public."[85] Appia was especially critical of this arrangement insofar as it engendered passivity in audiences sitting in comfortable seats in semi-darkness. Instead, drawing upon Brahman philosophy, Appia claimed that audiences should "participate actively" in the work of art, "sensing" themselves in the process. As with the actor, the spectator "must start with his own body out of which the living art must radiate, expanding into space and bringing it to life. It is this body that dictates the arrangement of settings and lighting; it is this same body that creates the work of art."[86] For Appia, then, such a space would become a work of total art in which every element, including the audience, might actively participate.

Appia insisted that the goal of these rhythmic performance spaces was not primarily to produce representational scenes. They were attempts to engineer an affective atmospherics through specific configurations of bodies, music, movement, objects, and light. The task of the theater designer, he writes, is "not to represent a place as it would be seen by someone transported to it," but to produce an atmosphere that expresses the mood contained in the dramatic or musical text.[87] Consider, for instance, the relation between an actor and a forest. For Appia, the role of the director is not to realistically represent a forest, but, as the rhythmic design in figure 2.4 illustrates, to produce the effect of a forest as a "particular atmosphere encompassing the actors, an atmosphere which can only be achieved in relation to the living and moving beings."[88] Careful manipulation of this atmosphere would allow the spectator to sense subtle shifts in the tone and affective intensity in the relations of which it is composed.

Light was an essential element of this atmospherics. As a complement to sound, light was for Appia the "aesthetic regulator of brightness — capable of modifying its intensity."[89] Indeed, understanding the rhythmic relation between light and sound demanded the cultivation of "a new sense . . . called musico-luminous sense." Unsurprisingly, eurhythmics provided the corporeal vehicle through which to undertake this cultivation, and eurhythmics institutes provided venues at which to experiment with this sense as part of a new domain of aesthetic-technical study.[90] For Appia, "merely 'to render visible' is not light in this sense at all, and on the contrary, . . . in order to be form giving or plastic, light must exist in an atmosphere, a luminous atmosphere."[91] The creation of such atmospheres involved specific technical requirements: footlights and spotlights were insufficient. Instead, a complex system of electrical illumination sophisticated enough to produce rapid and subtle variations in atmospheres was required.[92] At Hellerau, this luminous atmospherics was provided by a system, designed by Alexander Salzmann, in which hundreds of light bulbs were placed behind translucent screens.

The most obvious expressions of this vision of an atmospheric performance space were the productions of the scenes from *Orpheus and Eurydice*. According to some of those who witnessed them, the most affecting scene was the descent into the underworld (fig. 2.5), during which Orpheus "entered at the highest point of the scenic structure, in a glare of light, and slowly descended the staircase into ever greater darkness, confronted

FIGURE 2.4. *Appia's 1909 design for a "rhythmic space," titled "La clairière matinale."*
Bern, Swiss Theatre Museum (inv. 07g).

and opposed by the Furies. Dressed in black, they were in constant motion; carefully coordinated with the ebb and flow of music. Arranged along the steps and platforms; their naked arms and legs seemed like snakes, and formed a moving mountain of monstrous forms. The whole scene was bathed in an otherworldly blue light."[93]

Those in the audience responded enthusiastically to the production. For one observer, "it was beyond imagination. The space lived — it was a conspiring force, a co-creator of life."[94] Another witness, the American writer Upton Sinclair, described a version of the performance in his novel *World's End*: it was "music made visible" and after it had ended, "a storm of applause shook the auditorium. Men and women stood shouting their delight at the revelation of a new form of art."[95]

In an important sense then, Appia's practical design can be seen to anticipate much more recent concerns with atmospheres as aesthetic and affective spaces. The German philosopher Gernot Böhme, for instance, has argued for the importance of the concept of atmosphere as a way of thinking about the significance of staging to contemporary aesthetics.[96] More specifically, the design of stage sets, he argues, can teach us much about the

FIGURE 2.5.
*Appia's 1912 Hellerau
setting for Gluck's*
Orpheus and Eurydice,
Act II: *The Descent into
the Underworld.*

generation of atmospheres as affective spaces in which bodies participate.[97] Similarly, the concept of atmosphere allows Appia to conceive of spaces not so much as three-dimensional containers for activity, but as shifting configurations of bodies, materials, and ideas taking place with different degrees of affective intensity and duration. At the same time, Appia's work also encourages us to think of atmospheres in terms of how they facilitate the radically empirical activity of understanding the processual spatiality of moving bodies without necessarily precipitating either bodies or spaces as discrete, separate objects.

The life of these atmospheric experiments was short: with the outbreak of the First World War, Appia's collaboration with Dalcroze came to a premature end. These collaborations continued to have an influence on Appia's thinking and writing, however, particularly his vision of what he called "Living Art": a nonrepresentational ethico-aesthetic in which the individual cultivated an appreciation of the collective body by "awakening" his own corporeal potential through practices such as eurhythmics. In this living art the distinction between actor and audience disappears as part of a generalized "social" collaboration between all participants. Such ideas reveal the heroic optimism in Appia's writing. They also explain why his writings can be seen to anticipate elements of the corporeal and choreographic politics of the Third Reich.[98] Yet it is important not to overdetermine retrospectively the potential futures of Appia's writing. As a designer or architect, Appia saw his task as both pedagogical and anticipatory: his was a vision of a performance space that would "lend itself to continuous transformation in order to encompass in space the evolution of works whose very nature is to remain resilient and tentative."[99] These spaces would need to be designed with sufficient flexibility and openness to facilitate experimentation: "I imagine a rectangular, empty and unadorned hall equipped with complete lighting installations. On either side are large annexes for storing sections of three-dimensional units. These would be built with lines and proportions appropriate to the human body and broken up into segments that could be joined together to form every possible arrangement of levels, whether horizontal, vertical, or sloping. . . . This would be called the 'study site.'"[100]

Such study sites would not necessarily be limited to the halls described by Appia. They would also extend to a range of other locations. He himself claimed to have noticed "remarkable anticipatory signs" of a greater flexibility in the creative use of spaces as part of the breaking down of distinctions between different modes of performance.[101] In this sense, Appia's study sites are not necessarily site specific in the sense discussed in chapter 1. Rather, Appia is outlining a vision of relation-specific spaces of experimentation through which experiment remains, however, site conditioned.

Perhaps then, as Richard Beacham has argued, one of the most important aspects of Appia's work is the extent to which it anticipates, without determining or realizing, an experimental performance space reducible neither to body nor physical location.[102] These suggestive yet nonprescriptive empty spaces can be imagined as contexts in which different styles of thinking and working might be explored, and in which the "art of staging will never cease being empirical."[103] In outlining a vision for these performance spaces, Appia is also of course anticipating a practice of utopianism. This is not the kind of utopianism that seeks to transcend the everyday. Rather, the performance spaces with which he is concerned are those within and through which utopianism takes places as an immanent and imminent practice: this utopianism is an ongoing conviction that there is more to come from the affective and rhythmic relations between bodies, space, light, and music.[104] And such utopianism might be enacted through contemporary experiments, however modest, with the rhythmic relations between moving bodies and spaces and in ways that do not necessarily rehearse the ethos of inclusive harmony that underpins Dalcroze's vision.

It is tempting, when thinking critically about a practice such as eurhythmics, to evaluate it retrospectively, and especially so in light of its affinity with the corporeal politics of European body cultures between the First and Second World Wars. Such retrospective judgment is all too moralizing in its impulse, however. This is not to deny the problems with eurhythmics. Perhaps the critical problem with eurhythmics is the fact that it is based on the virtue and necessity of shortening the interval between hearing music and the expression of movement such that the duration of the interval becomes a problem to be overcome. In the process, eurhythmics works toward the contraction of thinking-space to a nontemporal point of immediacy. It fails, therefore, to affirm the multiple spatiotemporalities within which moving bodies are implicated and of which they are generative.

Acknowledging this situational multiplicity is crucial to any attempt to experiment with and within spacetimes of rhythmic movement. It bears upon how rhythmic spacetimes might exist as ongoing durations, or in the persistence of affective refrains that might precipitate as atmospheres in which it is possible to experiment with the question of what bodies can do. As André Lepecki has argued, foregrounding the multiple spacetimes of dance and movement practices has the potential to "activate sensations, perceptions, and memories, as so many stirring affects bound not to what has once happened and then disappeared into a 'lost time' — but to an intimacy to whatever insists to keep happening."[105] For the most part, Lepecki's comments refer to contemporary choreographic practices and experiments. But they can also inform encounters with a range of techniques for moving bodies, encouraging attention to how they can generate multiple spacetimes.

By way of concluding, we might therefore revisit that moment in the Chisenhale when the memory of *Orpheus and Eurydice* returns. We might stretch it out in order to think again about what happened. To think about how, in advance of the research residency at the Chisenhale, and knowing only that the space in which the week would take place is a narrow corridor and stairwell, sketches are scribbled in a notebook, among which is the drawing in figure 2.6.

Such drawing is obviously an act of preparation. And such sketches provide diagrammatic orientations for future movements in a space as yet relatively unknown. Like Appia's plans, they anticipate the architectural

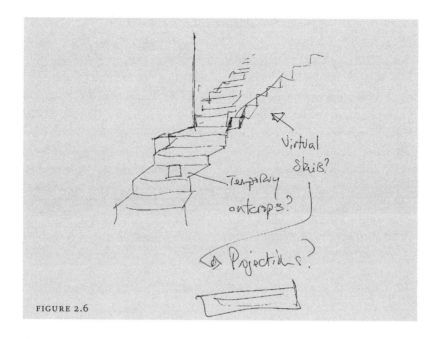

FIGURE 2.6

geometry of this corridor as a series of lines of movement through and against which the movement of the body might be creatively juxtaposed. They do not, however, provide a representational plan framing or choreographing in advance what might happen in the Chisenhale. Instead, they act as affective lures for potential futures, opening, however modestly, a zone of potential from which new lines of movement might emerge.

Some of this potential is actualized in that corridor. More specifically, in combination with Petra's words, movement generates an affective atmosphere of expectancy, sensed as a feeling of tendency toward the possibility that something might be happening within, between, and across bodies. From this atmosphere certain feelings of tendency have the potential to precipitate as memory. And in that corridor and stairwell the event of memory emerges implicitly but affectively in the constructive interference between the repetitive rhythm of footsteps up and down the stairs and along the corridor, and the refrain of Petra's ongoing invocation. In retrospect, then, the becoming present of memory might be sensed as the kind of aesthetic experience about which Dewey is enthusiastic without the idea of ordered consummation that underpins this experience.[106] The becoming present of memory might be a modified version of a Lefebvrian "moment";

a brief, affectively charged modulation in lived spacetime without Lefebvre's recourse to dialectics: "a lacuna, a hole in time, to be filled in by an invention, a creation."[107] Or, put another way, what happens is that an interval of variable length is generated in a field of movement and thinking, an interval from whence memory emerges. And, in the process, it may be that it is precisely by affording the opportunity for generating these intervals that affective spacetimes become experimental: that is, they become experimental when rhythmic movements in a corridor generate atmospheres within which precipitate memories of an event that is always in the process of differentiating itself and the affective lives of those bodies in which it continues to participate.

CHAPTER THREE

Diagramming Refrains

A Chapter with an Interest in Rhythm

Limbering Up

These lines began in the middle of series of bare and empty rooms: a community hall, a church, a chapel, a school gym. For the sake of convenience let's settle on one with wooden floors, with benches along the sides, where first one, then gradually two . . . three . . . four . . . five . . . six . . . seven . . . eight . . . nine . . . ten or so people present, some stretching and walking and lying on the floor, others changing or removing shoes. Join and sit, rooted: looking around while trying not to look, taking an age to remove your own shoes. Shuffle nervously, looking for some hints or pointers as to how things will begin, how things will get going, and how you will join in. Help arrives from the other side of the hall, from a man standing at a sound desk, who changes tracks and James Brown! I remember. GET UP, GET ON UP, GET UP, GET ON UP . . . for a moment at least, back to 1992 at the Point Theatre in Dublin . . . a memory of a gig to mark the occasion of a birthday, GET UP, GET ON UP but not yet, the next song then GET UP, GET ON UP go on, do it as more people arrive and get into the same routine STAY ON THE SCENE and begin doing something at least like S t r e t c hing, S t r e t c hing, LIKE A SEX MACHINE and God I can't touch my toes LIKE A LOVING MACHINE: how long is it since I did this? Not since some basic youth football training regime or another: touch your toes, and stand with feet apart . . . shifting pressure from one knee to another, while grabbing your foot and pulling your leg up as far as it would go HUHHHHH! GET UP, GET ON UP and now, another look, more people, at least twenty-five, with James Brown fading out, and the guy at the side asking *can we all come together in a circle please?*

Have we any new people tonight? Three or four hands. *We have. Well, for those of you who have not been here before, what usually happens is that we go through a wave of the rhythms, through flowing, staccato, chaos, lyrical, and still-ness. At this point there is nothing more you need to know, except perhaps that, at least here, there is no failure, and that you should trust the fact that your body, you, know what to do.* After these instructions, and some encouragement, an invitation to find a place in the room. Find a corner, with nothing, or no one behind — keep your distance — and a good view of the hall. Music, gently working its way into the space. An invitation to close your eyes, and with your eyes closed, to

Begin to take yourself inside yourself, and begin to focus your attention on your feet, feeling where they touch the ground, slowly shaking out all the tension in your feet, gently, and after some time, now shifting your atten-tion to your knees as they also begin to move, following the music, moving in gentle circles, before your attention moves up to your hips, that's it, letting them do it, letting them take the rest of you with them, and from your hips let the movement come up into your spine, slowly, letting your spine move at its own pace, taking care, breathing into its gentle curve, letting the rhythm of your movement find its way from your spine up into your head, and when your head wants to, allow it to pass the movement down through your neck, flowing down into your arms, and now your arms begin exploring their movement, as you allow them to go wherever they want to go, exploring the shapes they can make, the spaces they can make, and now begin taking this movement into your hands as they too begin to enter into the dance, before all of you at once, begin moving, perhaps finding a pattern, a line, following it for a while, before allowing another to emerge. . . .

By limbering up thus, however awkward and forced, thinking finds itself becoming a movement of sensation and affect. And from somewhere there emerges a growing sense that perhaps "one writes initially through a wave of music, a groundswell that comes from the background noise, from the whole body, maybe, and maybe from the depths of the world or through the front door, or from our latest loves, carrying its complicated rhythm, its simple beat, its melodic line, a sweet wafting. A broken fall. One cannot grip one's pen but this thing, which does not yet have a word, takes off."[1] This something is vague, indeterminate: barely palpable as a feeling of tendency about the potential for something to happen. Something that is never the product of an individual intentional subject, but which takes shape through a series of contingent encounters, relations, directions, forces. Something that might be named after the event as an interest in rhythm, sensed initially as an affective imperative, a kind of "impulsion which, as soon as found, carries one forward of itself. This impulsion, once received, sets the mind off on a road where it finds both the information it had gathered and other details as well."[2] An interest in rhythm whose affects overfill the experience of moving in one hall or another to become generative of various questions that persist in thinking: How do rhythmic affects, registering as so many intensities of feeling, participate in the movement of thought? How, and in what ways, might the generativity of this participation be sustained through careful use of concepts? And what might it meant to compose a style of expression that allows these affects to continue to resonate through and within experience?

Such questions are pursued here in different ways: through an ongoing return to the affective territories of which the 5 Rhythms consists as a way of learning to be affected; through a series of encounters with the concepts that circulate in the work of Gregory Bateston, Gilles Deleuze, and Félix Guattari; and through the generation of a diagram of the patternings that draw out the relations between the rhythmic affects of participation and the possibility of thinking with conceptual feeling. In the process, an emergent interest in rhythm might be disclosed for what it virtually is: something more than personal, a refrain composed of differentiating patterns of affects, percepts, and concepts that exceed any effort to explain, to figure out, the when, where, and why of what happens when body, sound, and light mingle with different degrees of intensity; a refrain that nevertheless holds together affective, conceptual, and textual milieus as a kind of signature, or style, drawn out as a series of lines of creative variation.

Learning to Be Affected

The basics: the 5 Rhythms is a somatic movement practice developed by the late American dancer and artist Gabrielle Roth. The practice is organized around five distinct but mutually implicated rhythms (flowing, staccato, chaos, lyrical, and stillness), each of which Roth claims affords different opportunities for moving physically, affectively, and spiritually.[3] Roth does not claim to have created these rhythms herself, only to have discovered them gradually through her own experience of experimenting with movement and dancing — both alone and with others.[4] Roth's writing gives a sense of the distinctive qualities of each of these rhythms. *Flowing* is described as "the state of being fluid, of hanging loose and being flexible." Flowing connects individuals with the underlying rhythmic continuity between bodies and world, akin to how breath does. It is given shape by Roth as an ongoing recursive curving. Flowing is rhythm without break or rupture, continuous change as opposed to sharp break or interruption. Furthermore, flowing is a feminine, maternal, and promiscuous rhythm, even if Roth uses basketball player Michael Jordan as an example of someone whose movement embodies a sense of natural, organic flow. For Roth, Jordan's "internal rhythm connects with the energies of the ball, his team, his opponents, and the court, until they all merge into one organic entity and it becomes as natural for the ball to swoosh through the net as it is for breath to flow in and out of our bodies."[5]

In contrast, the second rhythm, *staccato*, is more angular, an expression of lines and edges akin to "geometry in motion."[6] Rather than continuity, staccato is characterized by discontinuity, breaks, separateness. It is the rhythm of "childhood," characterized by rapid changes of attention and by shifts in activity and emphasis. It is masculine because it involves the drawing and marking of boundaries, of limits: the expression of a kind of processual decisiveness. Roth illustrates this angular economy of rapid-fire movement through the description of a bartender, albeit one who also seems to play basketball:

He doesn't move from one position to the next, he starts and spins on an invisible edge that only he can see. He dodges the other bartender as if he were dribbling a basketball. He doesn't stoop to get the ice from under the counter, he does a series of sit-squats. He whips the glasses out of the rack, throws the ice into the martini shaker, spews it into the glasses, sets it down, picks up the money, pivots right, flicks the register, slams the money in, pivots left as his right hand leaps from his side to slide back his hair and his dark eyes dart across the crowd.[7]

In turn, the rhythms of flowing and staccato "collide and create the rhythm of *chaos*."[8] As Roth notes, the roots of the term "chaos" can mean empty space or abyss. Roth, however, prefers to see chaos in terms of plenitude: this is a space "loaded with potential, free of all the strictures and structures of the ordinary world."[9] The rhythm of chaos is full of wild currents and generative energies that come from nowhere. And understanding these energies involves a process of letting go: chaos is therefore the most cathartic and overtly expressive of the 5 Rhythms. The fourth rhythm outlined by Roth is *lyrical*. After the deep abandon of chaos, lyrical is lighter, but no less grounded. It is characterized by a sense of possibility and "openness in movement."[10] Lyrical is the most "intricate" and "elusive" of the rhythms, with an airy quality akin to playful flight. Roth illustrates this through the description of a dancer "moving weightlessly and effortlessly as a bird," whose movements are "whimsical, nimble, airborne — intoxicating to watch."[11] Lyrical involves a kind of maturity conducive to improvisation. Following lyrical, the last of the rhythmic maps described by Roth is *stillness*. It is an attentive quietude that follows the more obviously kinetic rhythms preceding it. She describes its arrival thus: "Finally stillness enters your dance, calling you into spaces between the beats, between your bones, between your moves. Your body shifts through many shapes, sometimes holding them, feeling their vibration, sometimes letting them go. Your attention is drawn to your inner dance, where everything is alive, awake, aware. You have disappeared into the dance, and the dance has disappeared into you."[12]

For Roth, each of these rhythms provides a map for exploring the basic "geography of emotions."[13] Roth describes herself as a "cartographer obsessed with surveying the geography of inner space."[14] This emotional geography can be mapped in terms of identifiable rhythmic patterns of movement existing as "an infrastructure underlying all our experience, a living language."[15] Hence her claim that "energy moves in waves. Waves move in patterns. Patterns move in rhythms. A human being is just that, energy, waves, patterns, rhythms. Nothing more."[16] This affirmation of an ontology of rhythms and waves is coupled with a strong emphasis on the individual as the agent of self-development. Roth encourages and affirms shared rhythmic movement as a cathartic process that aims ultimately at the achievement of a state of individual ecstasy through an affectively charged alignment of mind, body, and spirit. Such claims draw upon a blend of Eastern philosophy, contemporary shamanism, and psychological theories of self-development that support a vision of moving rhythmically as a process of "moving meditation." This is described by Roth as a "healing" process: it "makes us aware that there's a lot of stuff between us and the ecstatic experience. By stuff, I mean all forms of inertia — physical, emotional, mental. Each of us must carve a path through our own inner wilderness. Movement as medicine gives us a way to dynamically transform that inertia into energy and, ultimately, ecstasy."[17] Roth positions the practice as part of a wider cultural process of self-renewal through movement, part of a "dancing revival" that "reflects a culture-wide yearning not only for a reunion of body and spirit, but of men and women and lovers of all persuasions."[18]

This emphasis on the therapeutic potential of movement reflects the influence on Roth's work of the human potential movement, elements of which she encountered during the late 1960s in California, and particularly at the Esalen Institute.[19] Founded in 1962, Esalen was at the forefront of the emergence of the human potential movement, and is one of the key sites at which New Age practices were popularized on the West Coast of the United States. These influences mean that the 5 Rhythms seems like the archetypal New Age practice, mixing as it does the affirmation of an underlying more-than-personal force — rhythm — with the claim that the potential of this force can be realized only through an individual journey of self-discovery. In addition, its explicit trademarking seems to signal an attempt to stake a claim in a highly commodified and competitive market for somatically based spiritual practices. At the very least, the 5 Rhythms needs to be positioned squarely in relation to the ethical and aesthetic imperatives of New Age somatic practices and their associated "expressive identities" and "networked spiritualities."[20] Read through the critical lens of sociological accounts of late modernity, the 5 Rhythms might well be understood therefore as one of many commercialized technologies of the embodied self that seek to capitalize on a range of contemporary existential insecurities and anxieties. It trade(mark)s on the possibility of cultivating an authentic rhythmic relation with self and world through the repetition of movement patterns.

Claims about authenticity might provoke a degree of suspicion — as might Roth's gendering of different rhythms as essentially masculine or feminine. Such suspicions should not inevitably foreclose other ways of responding to a practice such as this. Other possibilities may emerge in the course of an encounter with 5 Rhythms: the possibility, for instance, that encounters with its rhythmic affects might afford opportunities for experimenting experience in ways that supplement rather than short-circuit thinking. And so, while an initial encounter with the 5 Rhythms may generate the sense of affective disquietude that sometimes registers as the feeling of tightening called a cringe, this disquiet should not preclude the possibility of promising shifts in the sensibility in which thinking takes place. But sustaining this responsiveness demands a moderation of certain habits of critical thinking, and particularly those that prioritize demystification and disenchantment as stock responses to practices and events that seem to run counter to the intellectualism of scholarly thinking. It requires a commitment to learn to be affected by practices in the hope that they can help move or modify thinking. It involves openness to how dance and movement practices might facilitate an experiential experimentalism by their provision of a degree of generative constraint for moving bodies.[21] As José Gil suggests, dance "operates as a kind of pure experimentation with the body's capacity to assemble, thus creating a laboratory where all possible assemblages are tested."[22] Gil's comments are directed at dance practices that are experimental in an obviously aesthetic and artistic sense. Dance's experimentalism extends beyond more avant-garde practices, however. Even in the most unlikely of circumstances, dance affords opportunities for a kind of minor affective-somatic experimentalism — for the exploration of different configurations of bodies and movement through the generative constraint of technique. As Judith Hamera observes, "dance technique is a relational infrastructure" with which to make explicit and experiment with the "micro-connections between bodies."[23] To experiment with these relations is to return, *now* and *again*, *here* and *there*, to *that hall* (and others) in and from where, in different ways,

"One ventures from home on the thread of a tune, along sonorous, gestural, motor lines,"[24] lines now warmed up, becoming familiar with movements that seem to come from nowhere, taking hints from others: "Imagine you are all circles and curves, arms around, spine undulating, hands soft, hips rolling gently, knees loose. Allow your body to weave an endless stream of circles — powerful, relaxed, earthy. Surrender to your feet, each part of you partnering with your feet — elbows and feet, shoulders and feet, hands and feet — having dialogues in space."[25] Begin looking for the security of a phrase, a gesture, a line along which to move, before becoming more adventurous, as that phrase, that gesture, that line becomes something other by moving through you, and now a track change, and music comes with curves that circle around, picking up and folding into the speeds and directions of another, until before long a roomful of bodies becomes a multitude of curves, each of which is enhancing, inhaling, rising, expanding, and opening, into the curves of another . . .

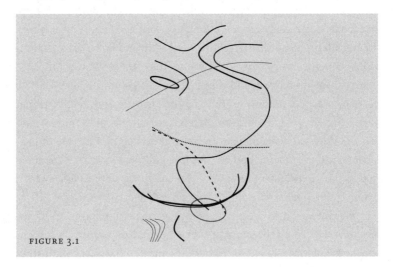

FIGURE 3.1

Patterns That Connect

One way to modify the critical habits of thinking that frame encounters with a practice like the 5 Rhythms is to consider how elements of the practice resonate with the respective ideas of philosophers and social theorists for whom rhythmic movement is a technique of thinking: figures, already encountered, including Dewey and Lefebvre. Roth shares a number of claims and commitments with these figures. They share an ontological claim that this world and the things in it — including humans — are composed of the interaction between rhythms. They share an economy of attention oriented toward the rhythmic details of everyday life: Roth frequently describes street scenes as a cacophony of rhythms in ways that resonate with the writing of Lefebvre, for instance. And they also share a belief that rhythmic movement is transformative and potentially therapeutic: transformative in the sense that it provides a way of working upon and modulating experience, and therapeutic in the sense that it affords the opportunity for attending to and ameliorating rhythmic disruptions. Clearly, these thinkers might have some problems with Roth's vision of the five rhythmic maps of a world of movement: Lefebvre, in particular, might well recoil from some aspects of the 5 Rhythms, not least the extent to which it encourages an ethics and politics of individual self-transformation. Dewey might also share this disquiet. Nevertheless, in their own ways Dewey and Lefebvre display an ethos of presumptive generosity toward somatic (and other) practices because they provide opportunities for experimenting rhythmic experience in ways that inventively supplement thinking. They affirm rhythmic practices as potential sources for experimenting with thinking.

Dewey and Lefebvre can provide philosophical encouragement for an emerging interest in rhythm sensed initially through the affects of an encounter with a movement practice called the 5 Rhythms. There is another figure, however, through whose life and work a more direct connection with the affects of this encounter can be traced. Writing of her time at the Esalen Institute, Roth remarks:

Gregory Bateson, the noted anthropologist, was there. He had become Esalen's community sage. He was dying of cancer, and he was doing it openly, bravely, gracefully. He participated in several of my ritual theater labs, and we even co-led a workshop we called "The Shaman and the Anthropologist," his last appearance as a teacher. Gregory was one of the most inspired and inspiring individuals I ever knew. Many powerful teachers had appreciated my work and recommended it to their students, but Gregory actually did it. He surrendered himself to it totally. Seventy-seven years old, his lungs shot, his feet so swollen he could barely walk, he never missed a beat, much less a session. My workshops are intensely physical, and yet this frail giant explored all the phases of the movement and immersed himself in the massage and ritual theater work. He was able to play with his prodigious intellect and vast knowledge and simply be in what he was doing. His mind was both full and empty. . . . Gregory and I — the thinker and the dancer, a most unlikely duo — met on a common ground, coming from different directions. We had both spent our lives investigating what Gregory called "the patterns which connect." I call them maps, maps to choreograph our energy and lead us to ecstasy, wholeness.[26]

Who knows why a figure such as Bateson might have been drawn to rhythmic dancing, what he may have taken from this encounter, and how it may have shaped the experience of his dying days? Bateson did however have a sense that his own work was part of an ecology of ideas extending beyond his life. So rather than speculate upon what it could have meant in the context of Bateson's passing away, his participation in the 5 Rhythms provides a point of entry into a series of wider themes and issues found in Bateson's writing and thinking that help sustain in thought the intensity of rhythmic affects.

Most obviously important here is the fact that Bateson's work exemplifies an interest in rhythm, one that emerged in part through his fieldwork encounters in Bali. These drew his attention to the role that dance played as a form of "kinesthetic socialization," one that prepared the individual for a state of altered consciousness or trance.[27] In this context, cultivating certain ways of moving encouraged receptivity to techniques of affective modulation common to a given group. Put another way, dance, and the simple, repetitive rhythmic movements of which it consists, could be understood as a technique through which bodies developed the capacity to be affected by other bodies. And yet, while dance was obviously rhythmic, for Bateson rhythm was not a quality possessed uniquely by dance: nor indeed was it the preserve of a distinctly human form of movement. Writing in *Mind and Nature*, Bateson argued instead that animate life might be understood as an ongoing experimenting, or testing, of the patterns of rhythmic relations and interferences between organism and environment — a claim remarkably similar to some of the ideas developed by John Dewey in *Art as Experience*. Furthermore, for Bateson, like Dewey, rhythm is a quality of aesthetic experience that predates the existence of prose. It is part of the originary aesthetic patterning of the world. It is a characteristic of "archaic behaviors and perceptions that rhythm is continually modulated; that is, the poetry or music contains materials that could be processed by superposing *comparison* by any receiving organism with a few seconds of memory."[28] Bateson described this in terms of the phenomenon of moiré: a combination of rhythmic patternings whose interference generates another patterning. This effect here is not to reduce rhythm to a derivative of spatial extension: rhythmic pattern is a process of spatiotemporal differentiation. The pattern, in this sense, is a dynamic block of spacetime. And the repetitive quality of rhythmic patterning reveals the difference that makes a difference in aesthetic territories.[29] According to John Shotter, Bateson's sense of "pattern through time" demands attention to "something like, say, 'musical shapes,' to the invisible 'time contours' of events — to 'shapes,' we must add, that never come to an end (for life only comes to an end in death!); they thus always generate further anticipations of yet more to come."[30]

Furthermore, paying this kind of attention involves what Bateson, following Charles Sanders Peirce, terms "abduction." In *Mind and Nature*, Bateson calls abduction the "lateral extension of abstract components of description."[31] Abduction involves abstraction, but abstraction as a way of grasping, on the basis of an intuitive hunch, the possibilities of future comparison that might emerge from any given encounter or experience. This generative anticipation is developed by tracing similarities across a range of disparate activities and by producing more descriptions of these activities. As Bateson suggests, "every abduction may be seen as a double or multiple description of some object or event or sequence."[32] That is not to say that abduction involves the generation of a rigidly fixed model imposed as a frame upon the world. Rather, as Shotter, drawing upon Bateson, argues, abduction is a process that proceeds from the sense that something is happening — something that only really emerges as a kind of proposition in thought through ongoing comparison and affective assay across a range of somatic encounters.[33] Insofar as it makes visible what he calls "the patterns that connect," abduction provides one way of foregrounding a broader concern of Bateson's, developed more explicitly in the later years of his life, with the role that aesthetics plays in drawing attention to the ecological character of mind. For Bateson, thinking is distributed within relational ecologies of mind that do not prioritize one level of thinking over another. But certain practices, particularly aesthetic practices such as dance, are important precisely because they provide what Bateson calls "bridges" between different kinds of thinking. As Bateson puts it: "Artistic skill is the combining of many levels of mind — unconscious, conscious, and external — to make a statement of their combination. It is not a matter of expressing a single level. Similarly, Isadora Duncan, when she said, 'If I could say it, I would not have to dance it,' was talking nonsense, because her dance was about combinations of saying and moving."[34] So abduction might lead to the anticipation of generative patterns across a range of practices and styles of thinking.

Learning to participate in the 5 Rhythms can become an occasion for developing a kinesthetic socialization through abduction as process of sensing patterns that connect. For Roth this is a matter of seeing those patterns in movements of all kinds. For the attentive participant in the 5 Rhythms, the task is a more modest matter of taking up and becoming taken up in the distinct rhythmic territories of the practice in order to produce possibilities for generative abstraction. In the territory of flowing, for instance, it might involve experimenting with a particular gestural curve, exploring its pathways, its limits, its speeds, until the curve becomes the movement itself, becomes a flourish with durational intensity of who knows how long, until from somewhere else another possibility arises, and the affective pathway of another curve takes over. Each rhythm has its own such possibilities, and at some point, these begin moving between rhythms, as one begins experimenting with staccato-chaos, or flowing-chaos. Hybrid, bridging rhythms emerge, passing from one body to another through the movement of a hand, an arm, a leg, a hip. Returning time and time again, session after session, night after night, the gestural repetitions of each rhythmic territory emerge without effort, without the act of thinking too much, becoming familiar shapes of trajectories. But this familiarization takes time. And sometimes it doesn't work, and then everything falls flat on its face in a bundle of self-consciousness tied loosely together with the question — what am I doing here?[35] And sometimes it works wonderfully.

It is one thing to become open to the unsettling affects of such participation and the opportunities it affords for experimenting experience. This raises further questions, however: How to present a sense of the affectively imbued thinking emerging in the process? How to draw out the affects of this thinking without necessarily remaining faithful to the "world of the symbol and that penny-in-the-slot resolution called meaning"?[36] How to compose a sense of the movement of this thinking in ways that draw together the affects of moving bodies and the movements of thought of which these bodies are generative? Such questions are simultaneously ethical and aesthetic: they pose the problem of learning to be affected by moving bodies in terms of a matter of expression. The trick here, through a form of abduction, is to find ways of describing the patterns connecting the affects of rhythmic encounters. And in some ways Bateson's own work exemplifies this: much of his writing is an attempt to enact a kind of aesthetic patterning, a kind of dance on the page defined by an "economy, a parsimony of description" to be gained by taking advantage of the "repetitive and rhythmic nature of what is to be described."[37] Bateson suggests that the process of choreographing writing — perhaps as much as dancing — enacts a commitment to thinking as the making and unmaking of rhythmic patterns. Following Bateson, writing with the animating potential of an interest in rhythm becomes a matter of drawing out a degree of creative consistency between the affective intensities of the 5 Rhythms and a conceptually informed exploration of rhythmic movement. Writing, and a deliberately performative writing, is a technique for rendering rhythmic patterning visible. Such a claim is hardly novel. And as performance theorist Peggy Phelan writes, it risks "reciting redundancy, flirting with a new marketing ploy, re-naming something that has existed for a very long time with little or no fanfare." Yet, Phelan continues, "I risk these things because I want to promise that there is a way to move even within the stone vaults to which too many of us have been vanished. I want to promise it rather than prove it. I may be wrong and we'll be frozen forever on cold rocks. But I may not be wrong (which is different from being right) and to dream of dancing while whiling away the hours in the waiting room is better than some other alternatives I can think of."[38]

Clearly, there are limits to the opportunities afforded by the 5 Rhythms in this regard. Not least of these is how it follows almost slavishly the narrative-like movement of the flowing-staccato-chaos-lyrical-stillness wave. In reality, however, the experience is rarely so linear. It is possible, for instance, to introduce chaos into flowing, staccato into flowing, lyrical into stillness, and so on. There is always another new line along which one can move in a way that allows a venturing from home, along

Sonorous, gestural, motor lines, lines that move on through another track change, another vocal intervention, this one offering an invitation to begin moving into staccato, the second rhythm, moving to the rhythm of a pulsing beat that demands clarity, definition, gestural geometry: "Focus on your exhale, the sound of it. Connect yourself to the thrust of your body as you push out the air. Let your movements be sharp, each one distinct and separate from the next. Think of angles, jagged edges, karate, shadow

boxing. Be forceful and linear. Create boundaries. Define yourself."[39]
Show others with your movements that this is your territory, your living
space, beginning to explore how it is to have others enter that space,
crossing lines, exploring how you want to respond, reject, embrace,
exclude, open those lines, as movements begin to delineate, demarcate
with an angle of elbow, marking space, making space . . .

FIGURE 3.2

The Refrain of Conceptual Feeling

If we think of thinking in the way Bateson does, the rhythms of both dancing and writing become part of the differential patterning of an "ecology
of mind." But there are other elements of this ecology that make a difference to how thinking takes place: concepts. Concepts can be seen as the
enemy of movement, static reference points that serve as substitutions for
real understandings of what William James calls "transitions in our moving life."[40] A suspicion of concepts also runs through the writing of Henri
Bergson. For Bergson, one of the problems with philosophy as he saw it
was its apparent ability to mistake a static representation — or concept — of
movement for the lived duration of that movement in itself. Such concepts
divide up the world, parceling it out for the purposes of analysis in the

service of an immobile thinking. So, while duration "can be presented to us directly in an intuition," it cannot, Bergson argues, be "enclosed in a conceptual representation."[41] And yet, taking seriously these claims does not lead automatically to jettisoning concepts in favor of a mindless return to some kind of preconceptual immediacy. Instead, for Bergson, the point is to go beyond "inflexible and ready-made concepts" to create "flexible, mobile, almost fluid representations, always ready to mould themselves on the fleeting forms of intuition."[42] Concepts, then, serve to amplify and intensify the duration of intuition: something sensed, an "impulse felt" that always wants to "slip away"; not a "thing, but an urge to movement."[43]

Concepts participate in ecologies of thinking not so much by acting as fixed reference points but by foregrounding and also generating variations in the patterning of that ecology: they modify its rhythms. Concepts are not used or applied: they make a difference within thinking, becoming what Erin Manning calls "events in motion."[44] And they make a difference insofar as they catalyze relations with and between bodies, facilitating a "novel distribution" of these relations.[45] Bateson's own work provides a famous example: plateau. Emerging from his research in Bali, plateau is used in the context of a description of the experience of continual intensity through which the inevitability of climax is muted and deferred. This experience is characteristic of "music, drama, and other art forms." In the case of music, this "typically has a progression, derived from the logic of its formal structure, and modifications of intensity determined by the duration and progress of working out of these formal relations. It does not have the rising intensity and climax structure characteristic of Western music."[46] The concept of plateau is not treated at any great length in Bateson's writing. Nevertheless, it makes a great deal of difference to the ongoing creation of ideas extending far beyond his life or writing: difference revealed in part through the plateau's participation as an ethico-aesthetic principle in the writing of Gilles Deleuze and Félix Guattari. Famously, Deleuze and Guattari use this concept to give their writing a nonreducible, nonlinear, intensive consistency.[47] These plateaus have no single point of orientation and do not aim toward a particular point of meaningful closure. Their intensive consistencies are traversed instead by a multiplicity of relations and movements. As such, they are territories of resonant potential, blocks of spacetime that constructively interfere with one another in myriad ways. To read A Thousand Plateaus is to encounter a moiré pattern of singular complexity composed of relations that run across and between plateaus.

One of these plateaus resonates with particular intensity: "1838: On the Refrain." Here Deleuze and Guattari define the refrain as "*any aggregate of matters of expression that draws a territory and develops into territorial motifs and landscapes.*"[48] The refrain, as an ethico-aesthetic concept par excellence, offers a way of conceiving of territories as processual compositions, matters of both ethos and style. There are different refrains, however. Some refrains assemble territories, generating a home: these refrains mark out space, drawing lines. There are functionalized refrains that play a particular role in the process of territorializing: for instance, the refrain of certain occupations or songs that give a loose consistency to blocks of spacetime. There are refrains that pass between territorial assemblages, redistributing relations between bodies as they do. And there are refrains that open onto an infinite outside through a molecular deterritorialization.

The refrain is not a singular entity, nor is it a self-contained concept: as Deleuze and Guattari remind us, concepts are never self-contained — they have histories and hinterlands composed of dynamic relations with other concepts. Moreover, concepts are composed of components "that may, in turn, be grasped as concepts."[49] The refrain already vibrates with the intensities of other components, each of which can also be considered as a concept in its own right:

1 Chaos: a condition of generative potentiality, a "non-localisable, nondimensional . . . tangled bunch of aberrant lines,"[50] which nevertheless is "not without its own directional components." These components are the "ecstasies" of chaos.[51]

2 Milieu: a "vibratory . . . block of space-time constituted by . . . periodic repetition" of certain directional components of chaos.[52] A body can be understood in terms of the relations between different milieus — internal, intermediary, exterior, and so on.

3 Rhythm: the "milieus' answer to chaos."[53] Rhythm is a "transcoded passage between milieus," a communication or co-ordination between spacetimes that is never metric or dogmatic.[54]

4 Territory: territories emerge from the rhythmic passage between and within milieus, when this passage becomes dimensional rather than directional, when it becomes expressive rather than functional. Territorializing refrains take place through the emergence of matters of expression or qualities that "express" the relation of "the territory they draw to the interior milieu of impulses

and exterior milieu of circumstances."[55] These matters of expression can be understood as a signature or style grasped through the relations between territorial motifs and territorial counterpoints.

Chaos, milieu, rhythms, territories: these concepts do not add up to the refrain. Nor, as Deleuze and Guattari emphasize, is the movement between these concepts an evolutionary one that climaxes with the refrain. Rather, the refrain is the differential patterning emerging through the relations between these components. Rather than an after-the-event artistic product, it is a moving matter of passages, bridges, and tunnels between chaos, milieu, rhythm, and territory. The refrain is the sensed consistency of these components, the distinctive way in which heterogeneous elements hold together as a matter of expression.

Consistency, it must be said, does not imply an infinitely predictable series of events through time. To be consistent is not to do the same thing again and again. Consistency is more akin to spatiotemporal thickness — the density and intensity of a block of spacetime expressed as a signature. Nor does consistency mean closure. As Deleuze and Guattari put it, "what holds an assemblage together is not the play of framing forms or linear causalities but, actually or potentially, its most deterritorialised component, a cutting edge of deterritorialisation. An example is the refrain."[56] The refrain is not, therefore, a pattern of "deathly repetition": it also opens up onto lines of flight through which the sensate finite is dynamized by the potentialities of the infinite, or what Deleuze and Guattari call the Cosmos. This is a space of infinite molecular movement whose forces can be captured by the consistency of the refrain at the same time as they always move beyond the threshold of individual perception. This movement is *like a passage from the finite to the infinite*, but also from territory to deterritorialisation. It is indeed the moment of the infinite."[57] To some degree, this sounds remarkably resonant of the kind of spiritual kinesthetics of the 5 Rhythms, summarized by Roth in the following terms:

> More and more the worldviews of advanced physics, chemistry, and astronomy parallel those of the traditions such as Buddhism and, in effect, the esoteric core of the great traditions. We find that the deeper we probe the matter of creation the more we bump up against the mystery of nonmatter, uncreated energy, infinity. In a word, spirit. As the Hasidic masters taught, the spark of the infinite that energizes each of us derives from the same ultimate source.

We needn't interpret this source theistically, but it is easy to think of it as a universal energy in which everything participates to some degree. Hence, freeing the spirit means fanning the spark of infinity into a consuming fire, channeling the ultimate into the now, embodying the infinite in our finite lives.[58]

While Deleuze and Guattari are not pursuing a kind of spiritual theism, invoking the notion of the Cosmos is suggestive of an effort to harness a kind of mobile mysticism, which, in turn, runs the risk of denigrating corporeal form in a moment of cathartic deterritorialization. However, the point of invoking the Cosmos is not to escape or overcome the flesh, or what usually passes for the body. Instead, it involves a generous commitment to admit the creative potentialities of incorporeal bodies and forces in the habits of corporeality.

The refrain does not therefore provide a concept to be *applied* to an encounter with a practice such as the 5 Rhythms. Rather, it furnishes a conceptual machine or a "set of cutting edges that insert themselves into [an] assemblage undergoing deterritorialisation" offering possibilities for "drawing variations and mutations."[59] So let's say the assemblage undergoing deterritorialization in this case is an emerging interest in rhythm: the refrain provides a conceptual machine giving this interest in rhythm a consistency that opens onto an outside. In the process, an interest in rhythm might become a refrain: a refrain that is not so much the expression of an individual subject or body as the territorializing expressiveness of the connections between the rhythms of different milieus — kinesthetic, conceptual, textual. The refrain gives these milieus a degree of "*consistency*: the 'holding together' of heterogeneous elements."[60] This consistency is not produced through a model of linear, externally imposed hierarchical order. Nor does it produce homogeneity where previously there was heterogeneity. It is an emergent "act that produces consolidated aggregates, or succession as well as of coexistence, by means of three factors . . . : intercalated elements, intervals," and a "superposition of disparate rhythms, an articulation from within of an interrhythmicity."[61] The important act is that which gives an emergent consistency to a way of moving, one which engages the logics of sensation at the same time as it opens onto the incorporeal, the virtual, or the infinite. This is a matter of realizing how relations between motor, sensory, neurochemical, and other milieus are given a fragile consistency as rhythmic spacetimes that provide opportunity for[62]

Venturing from home on the thread of a tune, along sonorous, gestural, motor lines, lines that move on through another vocal intervention offering an invitation to begin moving on into the next rhythm, Chaos, as a track changes, sounding on into a heavier, pounding, bass thumping beat that finds feet, and, still dancing, could we begin forming a circle, a wide circle, a dancing circle, while keeping the feet of that bass rhythm, while as if from nowhere, the pathways of lighter rhythms begin to arrive, taking arms and moving through the still thumping bass while heading in directions with speeds and lines that take off from no point in particular, and whenever you want, take your dance into that circle, one, two, or three at a time, moving into the middle, moving in between for a moment . . .

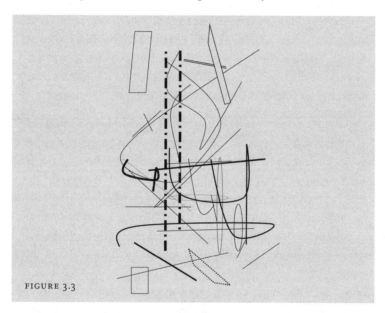

FIGURE 3.3

Diagramming Refrains

Because the refrain holds together an expressive territory, the question of moving is also a question of ethico-aesthetics and style, where style is not added after the important work has been done, or after the groundwork has been laid. Furthermore, if the refrain is a patterning of spacetime always open to an outside, it can therefore be grasped ethologically as much as ethnologically. As an expressive territory, it goes beyond the creative activity of human beings: it is open to earthly and animal becomings. Given the properly sonorous qualities of the refrain, birdsong is the most obvious example. Yet the animality of the refrain is not only sonorous: it also extends to patterns and styles of movement. As Deleuze and Guattari point out,

> Every morning the *Scenopoetes dentirostris*, a bird of the Australian rain forests, cuts leaves, makes them fall to the ground, and turns them over so that the paler, internal side contrasts with the earth. In this way it constructs a stage for itself like a ready-made; and directly above, on a creeper or a branch, while fluffing out the feathers beneath its beak to reveal their yellow roots, it sings a complex song made up from its own notes, and at intervals, those of other birds that it imitates: it is a complete artist. This is no synesthesia in the flesh but blocs of sensations in the territory — colours, postures, and sounds that sketch out a total work of art. These sonorous blocs are refrains; but there are also refrains of posture and colour, and postures and colours are always being introduced into refrains: bowing low, straightening up, dancing in a circle and lines of colours.[63]

Animal refrains are just as expressive as those emerging from and between milieus that have a more human flavor. What happens in either context is that the refrain catalyzes expressive territories moving in a zone of indiscernible sensation between human and animal: the refrain marks a process of becoming animal through a process of becoming artist. So there is a relation between gestural, sonorous, and artistic refrains transversal to human and more-than-human forms of life. Moving through the material of one therefore offers the possibility of amplifying the forces and rhythms of the other.

In these terms ethico-aesthetic interventions become less matters of mimetic representation and more like tactics for apprehending the affective force of the logics of sensation. This, of course, is what many human artists try to do: draw out the more-than-human affects and rhythms of duration. This effort is present, for instance, in the painting of early twentieth-century cubist and rhythmist painters whose work was influenced loosely by the thinking of Bergson. Attempting to apprehend the rhythms of duration by means of breaking down the unified extensity of the image on the canvas, in the work of these artists, "objects portrayed frequently dissolve into abstract planes, causing our attention to fluctuate between the representational content and the non-representational volume. It is the rhythmic interrelation of such volumes which instigates our intuitive apprehension of the painter's organisational matrix."[64] The effort to amplify the rhythms of sensation is present also in Wassily Kandinsky's endeavor to "paint music." In order to do this, Kandinsky mobilizes a kind of elemental geometry, about which he writes in *Point and Line to Plane*. The first of these is the incorporeal, invisible singularity, materialized in the graphic intervention of the point. The second is the line, "a force which develops not with the point, but outside of it. This force hurls itself upon the point which is digging its way into the surface, tears it out and pushes it about the surface in one direction or another. The concentric tension of the point is thereby immediately destroyed and, as a result, it perishes and a new being arises out of it which leads a new independent life in accordance with its own laws. This is the Line."[65] In turn, points and lines enter into relations of composition on a third element, plane.

For Kandinsky, this compositional geometry reveals the harmony between the inner spirituality of the artist and the force of the infinite. Here what matters less is Kandinsky's attempt to delimit the fundamental geometry of spiritual harmony on the canvas than his attempt to compose territorial refrains that "consist in dynamic trajectories and errant lines, 'paths that go for a walk' in the surroundings."[66] What matters also is the fact that his compositional effort derives in part from a familiarity with dance.[67] For Kandinsky "in the dance, the whole body — and in the new dance, every finger — draws lines with very clear expression. The 'modern' dancer moves about the stage on exact lines, which he introduces in the composition of his dance as a significant element. The entire body of the dancer, right down to his fingertips, is at every moment an uninterrupted composition of lines. The use of lines is, indeed a new achievement but, of course, is no invention of the 'modern' dance: apart from the classic ballet, every people at every stage of their 'evolution' work with line in the dance."[68]

Kandinsky is not the only source of orientation for drawing out the affects of moving bodies. Deleuze and Guattari argue that other artists harness, perhaps more affectively, the expressive force of the refrain. Paul Klee is one of these. Klee, like Kandinsky, takes lines for a walk, but remains less in thrall to the dependence of the line on the point as a center of origin and departure. And also like Kandinsky, Klee is interested in making visible the rhythm of sensation but in a way that departs from the spiritual geometry of Kandinsky's work. In the wandering lines and loops of Klee's work there is also a greater sensitivity to the discontinuities of duration. Consequently, many of Klee's paintings "are perhaps best thought of as rhythmic scripts that blend the cultural and the natural together through simple repetition, regular alternations, various syncopations built up out of overlaps and irregularities, delicate filigrees, sudden, even brutal, shifts and pointed, even barbed poundings. Such scripts continue to grow and evolve, being therefore both latent and propulsive."[69]

As Deleuze argues, Francis Bacon develops further this relation between sensation, rhythm, and painting. Bacon's art renders the rhythm of sensation through the space of the figural: his art can be set within the context of the effort to break with the figurative. With its focus on representation and signification, figuration fails to harness the particular violence of sensation. It also works on a canvas already populated by a myriad of representational, illustrative, and narrative clichés. In contrast the figural — exemplified in the work of Bacon — harnesses the material forces of sensation in order to produce a nonfigurative space of the figure whose elements are deformed and decomposed. The figural designates a "semiotic regime where the ontological distinction between linguistic and plastic representations breaks down."[70] It is also an "energetic space of forces" in which the recognizable — if also often prereflective — coordinates of corporeality and visibility are complicated and deformed.[71] The figural is also a profoundly rhythmic space. Indeed, it is in his discussion of Bacon's paintings that Deleuze affirms most emphatically the transversal power of rhythm. As he puts it:

> The painter would thus *make visible* a kind of original unity of the senses, and would make a multisensible figure appear visually. But this operation is possible only if the sensation of a particular domain (here, the visual sensation) is in direct contact with a vital power that exceeds every domain and traverses them all. This power is rhythm, which is more profound than vision, hearing, etc. Rhythm appears as music when it invests the auditory level. This is a "logic of the senses," as Cézanne said, which is neither rational nor cerebral. What is ultimate is thus the relation between sensation and rhythm, which places in each sensation the levels and domains through which it passes. This rhythm runs through a painting just as it runs through a piece of music. It is a diastole-systole: the world that seizes me by closing in around me, the self that opens to the world and opens the world itself.[72]

Deleuze's discussion of Bacon pertains properly to the realm of painting and the full panoply of materials within which it works — including color. Yet it also reveals the role of intermediate interventions that engage matters of rhythm and refrain beyond painting. The diagram is of particular importance here. In Bacon's work the diagram acts as a modulator of forces that provides the painter with the possibility of moving beyond the strictures of the figurative. As Deleuze puts it, "the diagram is indeed a chaos, a catastrophe, but it is also a germ of order or rhythm. It is a violent chaos in relation to the figurative givens, but it is a germ of rhythm in relation to the new order of the painting. As Bacon says, it 'unlocks areas of sensation.'"[73]

Discussed by Deleuze with specific reference to painting, the diagram can also work to draw out the rhythmic affects of moving bodies. Admittedly, as Deleuze observes, Bacon is not so much interested in the moving body as in the effect of movement "on an immobile body."[74] But the diagram can also draw out the sensations of moving bodies through a figural space. This points to the possiblity of an emergent inventive diagrammatic practice taking seriously how the force of sensation implicated in sonorous and gestural refrains distorts and deforms the very matter and fact of this emergence: a diagrammatic practice that takes lines for a walk in ways that move toward — without reaching — the figural.[75]

The point here is not to propose a way of recording an interest in rhythm as it resonates across moving bodies and movements of thought, but to experiment with possibilities of diagramming refrains across different matters of expression. None of these refrains can be prioritized over any other. Nor are the shapes of each to be apprehended in terms of snapshots, outlines, essential moments. Instead, they become the pattern of a movement along the transversal lines of a process, not of a product: a process that has consistency, not necessarily continuity.

Drawn together, the differential lines of the refrain give consistency to a material pragmatics that works upon and through the movement between different regimes of signs. This diagrammatic component "consists in taking regimes or forms of expression and extracting from them particle-signs that are no longer formalized but constitute unformed traits capable of combining with one another. This is the height of abstraction, but also the moment at which abstraction becomes real."[76] The lines of these diagrams have no beginning or end: they are a cutting edge open simultaneously to the limits of several matters of expression, holding these together in non-subjectifying relations of consistency, while at the same time offering potential trajectories for moving otherwise. In this way the diagram becomes "a map of relations between forces, a map of destiny, or intensity, which proceeds by primary non-localizable relations and at every moment passes through every point."[77] And diagrammatic practice becomes a way of drawing out variations that allow one to

> *Venture from home on the thread of a tune, moving along sonorous, gestural, motor lines, lines that move on from chaos, through another track change, another vocal intervention, this one offering an invitation, now, beginning to move out of chaos into lyrical, into lighter notes, lifting sounds. Find yourself a group of three, a moment of apprehension, of glancing around another glance, taking one toward two, into mixed movements, one leading another, an arm tracing an arc into a phrase and following begins for a time until beginning then follows, moving beyond giving and taking, and at some point two becoming three, moving faster, touching, feinting, darting away, in a play of ducking and weaving and chasing through lines that always seem to be opening onto others . . .*

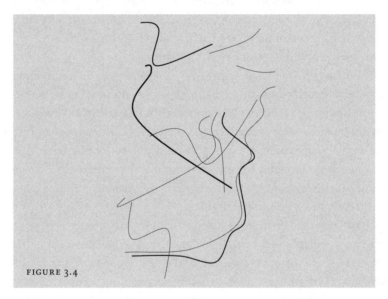

FIGURE 3.4

Refraining from Concluding

An encounter with a specific practice precipitates an emergent affective assemblage named initially as an interest in rhythm. A conceptual machine, the refrain, plugs into this assemblage and opens it up as a matter of formative territorial expression. The expressive qualities of these territories are then drawn through the lines of the diagram, which becomes, in turn, what Brian Massumi has called a "technique of existence."[78] These lines are ethico-aesthetic abstractions functioning nonrepresentationally, and in at least two ways. First, they do not seek to depict something — an object — that already exists. Second, they mark the possibility of drawing out those affects and percepts of the world that are excessive of figuration.[79] In this sense, the lines of the diagram do not so much join fixed points on a territorial or inscriptive surface, but can be understood as traces of the process of wayfaring. As Paul Carter observes, thinking the line through its rhythmic variations opens up the possibility that designs might become abstractions that "make room for things to happen. They should be scores that mediate between the abstract and the actual, encouraging improvisation."[80] Carter suggests that this is not just a technical challenge, but a social, ethical, and aesthetic one. To engage in drawing lines is, therefore, to contribute to a nonrepresentational geography oriented toward the drawing out of worlds that do not escape abstraction: this geography works instead in the hidden "linings" of the lines of abstraction in order to render them imaginable and inhabitable differently.

In the process of drawing out these lines, diagrammatic practice becomes a matter of interweaving ethics and aesthetics so that they are no longer content to remain "residing in the relation between a subject and an object, but rather in the movement serving as the limit of that relation, in the period associated with the subject and object," a movement in which perception is in "the midst of things."[81] Diagrammatic practice disassociates movement from the self-evident presence of an "I" that perceives and points to the emergent lines of a world of performative relations, events, and encounters, a world in which, in the words of Louis MacNeice:

We are always doing and making
Not to display our muscles but to elicit
A rhythm, a value, implicit in something beyond us.[82]

Beyond us not in the sense of the divine, but in the sense of the force of sensation that moves in a zone of indiscernibility between animal and human, along passages and bridges emerging between the affective territories of the 5 Rhythms and the conceptual territories of the refrain. Beyond us insofar as an interest in rhythm is a composite of vibrations, resonances, and reverberations from encounters that are never simply personal, never incorporated in organic form, in a subject, in an act, but that are always caught up in the speeds, intensities, and affects of corporeal, intercorporeal, and incorporeal forces. To think this beyond is not simply a matter of being seduced by the attraction of speeds of sensation, of becoming afraid to stop, and perhaps to breathe. Perhaps it is a matter of admitting (without demanding) how the refrain is the possibility of a creative resingularization, if only fleeting, of the "subtle pleasure of inventing, within the plurality, one's own conduct, one's own language, one's own individual work and private existence, one's body itself,"[83] where one is never an individual, but the individuating movement of an interest in rhythm that, even now, is

> *Venturing from home on the thread of a tune, moving along sonorous, gestural, motor lines, through one more track change, one more vocal intervention, inviting one to begin moving into the last rhythm, stillness, with slower sounds, and gestures that begin to wind down while allowing other movements to come into play. The flow of sweat, the rhythm of a re-emergent pulse. Take stock, but not just yet. Thinking is still caught up in the afteraffects of movement, the kinesthetics of desire, resonating, reverberating, more gently perhaps, though no less intensely. Thinking is still moving, moving still, still making a difference that is itself always in the making. And then, at last one senses that now, "the final moment is arriving. The return to measured time. The music stops. A brief encounter, life starts again. But it is no longer altogether the same."[84]*

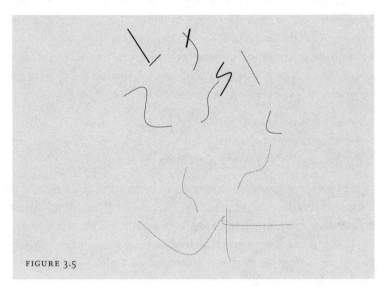

FIGURE 3.5

CHAPTER FOUR

Ecologies of Therapeutic Practice

This chapter presents an account of an event of participatory experiment in a somatic therapeutic practice called dance movement therapy (DMT). Though the style and regulation of its enactment differs from context to context, DMT is "founded on the principle that there is a relationship between motion and emotion and that by exploring a more varied vocabulary of movement people experience the possibility of becoming more securely balanced yet increasingly spontaneous and adaptable."[1] As this loose definition suggests, DMT privileges the claim that experimenting with movement is a way of working on experience in an ameliorative and therapeutic sense. In that respect DMT is not alone, but is merely one of an array of somatic practices in Western life based on the claim that working on and with moving bodies is potentially therapeutic. Broadly defined, such somatic therapeutic practices are organized activities that privilege moving bodies as the locus of transformative potential in subjectivities. They aim to generate a transformative intervention in subjectivities by reworking somatic, affective, and cognitive processes. In many cases these practices implicitly and sometimes explicitly challenge the mind-body dualism often taken to underpin much of Western intellectual and political thinking. In that sense they can be and often are mobilized as part of the philosophical project of making more of the participation of moving bodies in the process of thinking. And yet somatic therapeutic practices are also caught up in the performative positivity of biopolitical apparatuses — that is, they contribute to the proliferation of fields of actionable experience through techniques that value and perform certain forms of life over others on the basis of their security against everyday contingencies and disruptions. The existence and proliferation of practices such as DMT might therefore be taken to exemplify the wider problematization of moving bodies in contemporary Western societies within therapeutic techniques and assemblages that aim to govern affective life through securing this life against the vicissitudes of experience.[2]

However, an encounter with such practices is badly framed if limited to the terms of a critique of their implication in biopolitical regimes of self-making, not least because this critique immediately sets up such practices as problem cases whose ethical and political limits have been decided in advance. Just as important might be the opportunities such practices can offer for exploring the question of how, precisely, and under what conditions, the very possibility of experimenting experience through moving bodies becomes actualized. The question animating this chapter can therefore be framed thus: how might participation in somatic therapeutic practices disclose some of the ways moving bodies are generative of a sense of experience as an experimental field? The point of thinking about this question is not to excavate from a practice such as DMT an experimental sensibility in spite of the therapeutic ethos of the practice. Rather, it is to ask how participatory experiments within the affective spacetimes of DMT might generate opportunities for drawing out the value of a more-than-critical therapeutic style of thinking. In what follows I elaborate on how DMT works through a composition of techniques, objects, and ways of relating that, sustained by particular protocols and constraints, can produce opportunities for a minor experimentalism that is therapeutic because it allows for the invention of different ways of going on in the world. The therapeutic imperative of DMT takes place through the careful cultivation and enactment of an ethical and aesthetic orientation that values new ways of thinking, feeling, and going on as they emerge in the felt process of moving. What is at stake in an account of participation in DMT is not therefore the retrospective evaluation of its outcomes, nor a precise description of every aspect of its enactment, but the question of what demands, or obligations, DMT, as what Isabelle Stengers calls an "ecology of practices," places upon those who participate in it. Following Stengers, the proposition explored in this chapter is that a therapeutic form of thinking might be one committed to participating in an experimental situation while "giving to the situation the power to make us think, knowing that this power is always a virtual one."[3] What emerges, therefore, is a modest argument for the value of experimenting experience in DMT considered as an ecology of practices that might become the source of refrains which are therapeutic inasmuch as, following Félix Guattari, they re-singularize subjectivities.[4]

Dance, Movement, Therapy

The claim that dance has a healing or reparative function is by no means recent, nor indeed is it specifically Western — dance and movement perform these functions across a range of cultures and traditions.[5] More recent, however, are claims about the therapeutic potential of dance and movement and the formalization of various practices that aim to realize this potential. Thus, what is now called DMT only emerged after the Second World War as a constellation of explicitly therapeutic movement practices regulated by professional bodies and requiring a degree of professional training. In the United States, the emergence of DMT was influenced by the experiments of dancers working collaboratively with and sometimes within psychiatric institutions, most notably Irmgard Bartenieff and Marian Chace, both of whom had formative experiences with patients in medical contexts.[6] Dance movement therapy in the United Kingdom emerged rather later, in the 1970s, and was heavily influenced by elements of the work of movement artist Rudolf Laban.[7]

Even if formalized relatively recently, the emergence of DMT needs to be situated in relation to a number of important developments within a distinctively modern and Western structure of kinesthetic feeling, elements of which were discussed in chapter 1.[8] Crucial here was the affirmation by artists, choreographers, and performers of dance and movement as activities with an expressive capacity whose realization did not depend upon the narrow strictures of formal choreographic training or discipline. As Kristina Stanton-Jones suggests, the emergence of DMT would have been "unthinkable" without the development of "artistic and choreographic ideas that centered on direct emotional expression and abandoned formalism."[9] The possibility of tapping into, becoming aware of, and actively drawing out this inner expressiveness made a transformative and therapeutic relation with movement — both of one's own and of others — possible and practical. Self-awareness as the prelude to self-transformation could therefore be linked with affirmation of the apparently limitless capacities of the moving body as a source of authentic affective experience.

A second development was, of course, an increasing interest in affectivity as a dynamic force itself and, equally, in the manner in which this force was expressed through the efforts and movements of individual bodies. The influence of figures such as Charles Darwin and William James looms large here, particularly insofar as they highlighted, albeit in different ways, the bodily basis of emotional expression. For Darwin, patterns of emotional expression evolved in the same way as other characteristics: as a result, it was possible to identify relations between emotions and their expression across cultures. In developing this claim Darwin drew upon the experiments of Guillaume Duchenne, who stimulated facial muscles in the effort to discover their relation with specific emotions.[10] Influenced to some extent by Darwin, William James also explored the question of how emotions were expressed through bodily movement. Crucially, James extended elements of Darwin's thinking by arguing that bodily movement or posture was not necessarily the straightforward expression of an inner impulse of the mind: the "bodily accompaniments" of emotions were more "far-reaching and complicated than we ordinarily suppose."[11] Rather, emotional experience, and what is taken to be its expression through bodily movement or posture, was the effect of emotional behavior. As James put it, "bodily changes follow directly the PERCEPTION of the exciting fact, and . . . our feeling of the same changes as they occur IS the emotion."[12] This argument was and continues to be contested: the crucial point is that it emphasized the importance of exploring the relation between bodily movement and emotional experience.[13] Furthermore, while much subsequent scientific research has tended to focus on specific sites or types of emotional behavior, James suggests that emotions are global disturbances in the affectivity of bodies. As he puts it, "the immense number of parts modified in each emotion is what makes it so difficult for us to reproduce in cold blood the total and integral expression of any one of them. We may catch the trick with the voluntary muscles, but fail with the skin, glands, heart, and other viscera."[14] While not traceable directly to James, a similar idea of the body as a dynamic-affective expressive entity in totality rather than a system of interconnected organs is central to the ethos and practice of DMT: in this context, to modify movement is to modify the global affective economies of bodies and vice versa. The emphasis here is on experience as a series of incremental explorations of possibilities for thinking, moving, and feeling. As Carol Bruno writes, "to the extent that individuals move as they feel, they develop an adjustable, movable, dynamic way of perceiving, responding, and adapting to an ever-changing environment."[15]

In turn, and third, such work provided a scientific and philosophical parallel to efforts to systematically analyze the relation between movement and the expression of emotion. Similar analytic imperatives were of course already present in the work of Darwin, but other figures also shaped the emergence of movement as the object of systematic analysis.[16] For instance, during the early and middle decades of the nineteenth century, François Delsarte undertook a systematic analysis of the expressive qualities of the body, based upon a correspondence between physical, mental, and spiritual processes.[17] Delsarte's work anticipated Laban's through a shared concern with analyzing movement systematically as the expression of an internal impulse.[18] Underpinned by the claim that a direct relationship between emotion and movement exists, Laban devised a system through which the effort of an individual could be analyzed and notated. This system linked the kinesthetic and emotional qualities of movement, providing an interpretive framework through which to explore how movement is expressed affectively in any given context: in this respect it focused less on the form than on the shape of the feeling of movement — its dynamic-affective qualities as they are expressed through factors such as space, time, weight, and flow. For the dance movement therapist, then, this loose framework provides a set of kinesthetic resources not just for thinking about movement, but for thinking with and moving with others.[19]

Such interest in the systematic study of the emotionally expressive moving body could be given a distinctively therapeutic twist when allied with a concern with the psyche as the dynamic and experiential locus of individual transformation. At about the same time as forms of dance in the late nineteenth and early twentieth centuries began to valorize the "truthful" intensity of wordless expression, these movements were increasingly "'pathologized" by medical and psychoanalytic practices as "symptomatic" of problematic, inner, unconscious forces.[20] As Peggy Phelan has argued, the relationship between psychic topographies and corporeal choreographies provided the basis for an explicitly therapeutic employment of dance and movement. As she puts it, at the heart of psychoanalysis is an "ideology of movement, of the curative potential of moving, joining the psychic with the physical and the physical with the psychic is the task of analysis. The body's movements are the roaming rooms in which psychic 'truths' are lodged."[21] That is not to say, however, that DMT is merely psychoanalysis with a corporeal inflection. Dance movement therapists draw upon psychoanalysis in different ways, upon sometimes divergent traditions, and to varying degrees of influence.[22] Kristina Stanton-Jones clarifies this point:

> The verbal psychoanalyst is interested in unconscious determinants of neurotic symptoms, its role in the formation of sexuality and personality, and in manifestations of the unconscious in the transference relationship with the analyst. In contrast, DMT concerns itself with the creative aspects of the unconscious; that is, with the symbolic expression of the emotions through movement and imagery which arise from the patient's unconscious. DMT gains access to the unconscious through allowing the patient to free associate, using both verbal and non-verbal channels. DMT capitalises on the propensity of the unconscious to make new and unexpected connections between ideas, movement and imagery.[23]

In many ways, DMT serves as an important reminder that a central part of the psychoanalytic tradition is a concern with the unconscious as a productive force in which affectivity is a potentially generative participant: in this sense, DMT provides a necessary qualification of the alignment between psychoanalysis and versions of post-structuralism that foreground texts or representations, albeit with the aim of radically destabilizing them. It highlights instead how the development of psychoanalysis is part of the emergence of the imperative to attend to nonverbal activities as an element of a concern for the affective economies of psychic life. In this respect, DMT can be seen to operationalize the psychoanalytically inspired insights developed in the work of Daniel Stern, in which fine-grained observation is used to generate an understanding of the affective relations between individuals.[24]

Crucially, in DMT the productive propensity of the unconscious is not necessarily expressed through an economy of verbal or linguistic significa-tion. Indeed, as Kristina Stanton-Jones suggests, one of the most important things about DMT is the way in which it works to "use movement experi-mentation to explore new ways of being and feeling, and to gain access to feelings that cannot be verbalized."[25] In doing so DMT avoids the tendency to short-circuit the creative potential of the prepersonal force of the uncon-scious by incorporating it into an oedipal order of signification or reducing it to the therapeutic enactment of what Michael Henry calls a "logic of representation."[26] Equally, DMT does not usually use transference nearly as much as more conventional psychoanalytic therapies. Again, as Stanton-Jones comments, unlike verbal psychoanalysts,

> Dance Movement Therapists make different claims about what their
> therapy can do for a patient. . . . Whereas the psychoanalyst's role is
> to help patients gain insight into their personality and relationships
> by allowing the patient to transfer feelings that they had towards
> their parents onto the analyst, the Dance Movement Therapist does
> not use this transference phenomenon to anywhere near the same
> degree. In contrast, DMT's primary aims are: first, to help patients
> use movement to reconnect the psychological and physical aspects
> of emotional experience; secondly to use movement interaction in
> group processes to raise the level of interpersonal functioning; and
> thirdly, to employ creative movement as an access to unconscious
> feelings within the individual and the group.[27]

To participate in DMT is to negotiate a set of practices influenced by and entangled within a range of intellectual, therapeutic, and choreographic traditions. These traditions provide a set of ways of thinking about the relation between moving bodies and therapy, and shape the style within which DMT is enacted. Yet it is by no means inevitable that the enactment of DMT in particular contexts is overcoded or overdetermined by traditions such as psychoanalysis — indeed, some of the commentators noted earlier suggest precisely the opposite. And, if this is the case, then by deliberately backgrounding these traditions, as the remainder of this chapter does, it might become possible to pay more attention to DMT through the ecolo-gies of practices for experimenting with experience that define it. This is not to ignore the influence of these traditions — it is, however, to refuse to allow them to determine in advance the affects of participation in relation-specific ecologies of practice.

Learning to Attend

To participate in DMT sessions is to foreground the question of how attention takes place as and through movement. This is a matter of shared concern for therapists, for clients, and for anyone interested in understanding how this practice works. My own participation in DMT formed part of research into how a range of technologies and practices are employed to modulate and transform affective spacetimes. This participation eventually lasted for about eighteen months, much of which consisted of attendance at weekly drop-in sessions lasting about an hour and a half, and usually involving an opening assessment of energy levels and a directed warm-up, followed by a combination of client-initiated (where possible) and therapist-facilitated activities. Sessions would end with a warm down, often followed by informal chat and tea. I also participated in two week-long summer schools at the same center, each of which was attended by about twenty people. Designed as introductions to DMT for those considering embarking upon professional-level qualifications, these courses provided a contextual framework within which to place my ongoing experience of the drop-in sessions.

This is a familiar, unremarkable origin story of research. Equally important here, however, is the fact that I came to persist with participation in DMT not because it was immediately obvious how the relation between affectivity and movement was organized and experienced through the practice: indeed, my first impression was that little of any consequence was happening at such sessions. Certainly, when compared to the deliberate intensity of a practice like the 5 Rhythms, the activities at DMT sessions were far less energetic. Moreover, at least initially, it was by no means obvious, methodologically or conceptually, how to make sense of what goes on during DMT sessions. This has much to do with the challenge of talking about movement as it is happening. For instance, during DMT sessions it can prove difficult to identify an appropriate point at which to say "Stop for a moment and tell me what is happening here" or "What does it mean for you to be moving like that?" In part this is because such questions are inappropriate given the group nature of sessions. It is also because posing these questions in an appropriate way requires a certain learned skill and practiced judgment. But it is also because therapists rarely ask these questions during sessions.

Why then should one begin trying to understand a somatic therapeutic practice through interventions and methodological techniques that work against its ethos of enactment? The response to this question is not necessarily to talk to clients or participants after sessions have concluded. That is not to say that talking about practices has no value — of course it has. But it is limited with respect to thinking about what is happening during a DMT session because it tends to get people to provide some interpretive, after-the-event sense to something that, as it is playing out, does not always seem to require such sense to happen. Despite the fact that movement is crucial to what happens during sessions, something of the sense of this movement as a happening in process disappears during efforts to capture it through meaningful reflection.

For want of something better to do, I stopped trying to capture what happens during DMT sessions via the logics of postevent conversations. This may well be an admission of a failure (of sorts); nevertheless it also provides an opportunity that might be understood as therapeutic because it opens up new ways of going on. In my own case, participation in DMT allowed a forgetting or suspension of the imperative that had prompted participation in the practice in the first place: the imperative in question involved the effort to understand what was happening in the playing out of an event by apparently going beyond or behind either a surface understanding of or immersion in that event. The suspension of this imperative encouraged a shift away from the effort to do justice to the experience of other participants in DMT through providing representations of, or "giving voice" to, their experiences. Indeed, if anything, it became clearer that an effort to do justice to the thinking or inner experience of the participants is precisely what makes it difficult to become faithful to the affective relations and movements in which the enactment of DMT consists.

How then to begin attending to movement through participation in DMT? Consider the following scenario.[28] It might begin like this. Everyone in the room is asked to get into pairs. You are invited to lead your partner around the room. The person being guided must keep his or her eyes closed, and the exercise is nonverbal. With your right hand, you take your partner's left hand and hold it a little out in front of you, experimenting with different ways of holding. You find a position: loose, yet hopefully influential, and very slowly begin to guide this hand around the room, taking care that your partner does not bump into anyone or anything else, and allowing changes in direction and in the pressure of your hand to be as smooth as possible. Continuing, the contact between your hands becomes a moving surface of orientation, and guiding becomes more than one person directing another. What moves and guides is that space of relational touching: a space of orientation always in-between.

Invited to reverse roles, you find yourself closing your eyes and your partner is now taking your hand and finding a comfortable way to hold it, before beginning to move, now sensing the shape of relating, walking side by side with hands slightly out in front, moving, feeling the touch, the micropressure, now sensing changing directions, directions that guide as flickering anticipations of what might be happening around the room, directions that move through a stream of sunlight varying in warmth and with intensities that have no definite shape, and all the time the proximity of shufflings and quiet, apologetic expressions following unanticipated encounters. And then an instruction for you to swap partners and, after partner swapping, the course of things begins following the same pattern: the taking of a hand, a guiding throughout the room, a taking care. You begin encountering objects in the room: they add variety, offering material invitations. Your movement is drawn toward an encounter with the shape, touch, and texture of material and, with great care, you find yourself being invited to explore the surfaces of a chair. Moving on, you encounter material on the floor, coming in contact with a surface that, in no time at all, takes shape as a beanbag, a beanbag that affords a range of possibilities, all of which lose out to the invitation of the hand inviting you on. Coming to rest, you briefly lose contact with the hand that guides before another takes over, a hand without a face, a hand without a name, a hand with a different style, firmer: a style that squeezes when it wants you to stop. And all the time you find yourself paying close attention to movement, but also attending through movement: the movement of a subtle shift in posture, the movement of the intensity of light, or the movement of hands that "do not move with their own goals in view; [but hands that] are moved, troubled by the touch of the other with which they make contact."[29]

Differentiating Affectivity

To participate in DMT is to attend to and through movement. It is also to begin to realize the value of differentiating affectivity as part of the process of attending. It is to begin to realize that conceptualizing affectivity does not inhibit opportunities for experimenting experience. Nor does it close down fields of potentiality: if anything it opens them up. The distinction between affect, emotion, and feeling is potentially helpful here. To recap: emerging from Deleuze's rereading of Spinoza, and particularly the elaboration of this reading in the remarkable writing of Brian Massumi, affect can be understood as a kind of turbulent background field of relational intensity, irreducible to and not containable by any single body or subject. Affect is never just personal, even if it can be registered, or sensed, in bodies.[30] Then, and second, feeling can be understood as the registering of intensity in a sensing body before that intensity is recognized as a distinct emotion. Feeling is the sense of disquietude experienced by a body before this sense becomes recognizable, or nameable, as fear, joy, hope, and so on. As William James reminds us, feeling is the visceral stirring of the body as an affective complex undergoing some sensed modification.[31] Emotion, in turn, is the qualification of the felt intensity of affect within the processual materiality of the social. Emotion is affect felt and expressed, through language — but also through a look, a glance, a gesture. These terms are not, of course, mutually inclusive. And to distinguish these terms does not automatically mean privileging any one over the others, nor does it imply that any one term refers to a more authentic affective register than the others. These terms do perform different kinds of pragmatic-conceptual work in relation-specific contexts, however. For instance, where affect is conceived as a field of potential, emotion is understood in relation to a set of discursively constituted categories in terms of which the felt intensity of experience is articulated. Invoking emotion is therefore to position affective experience in relation to an already meaningful field of experience. And in this respect it has a certain value. But insofar as it is about positioning in a field of meaning, it provides less purchase on forces that exist prior to such meaning.

Differentiating affectivity thus is not quite the same as codifying or capturing it: rather, it can help cultivate sensitivity to different flows of affective intensity within and between bodies, and can direct attention to processes and events that may not otherwise be considered important. In the context of a DMT session, this differentiation has demonstrable pragmatic value. Consider the following example: weekly drop-in sessions usually begin with the therapist asking each of the participants to say something about the energy they have. Prompted by the example of the therapist, most of the responses are in the form of "I have high energy" or "My energy is medium today."

Sometimes there are finer gradations that draw a laugh, such as "high medium" and such. It is perfectly acceptable to say more, but not required. Rarely is anyone invited to talk about how they are feeling. Encouraging this way of talking is not to deny the importance of emotional expression. It does however allow the facilitating therapist to get a sense of the level of intensive energy of people in the group, without falling back on the temptation to qualify this intensity in terms of discrete emotions. By speaking in terms of energy, these interventions operate — at least implicitly — on a model of affect as "the capacity that a body has to form specific relations."[32] Their purpose is not so much to get a sense of how a particular individual feels, or to solicit emotional expression, but to elicit an initial sense of what a body can do, what capacities it might have for relations with other bodies, all as part of an ethics that seeks to ensure the availability of as many relations as possible, an ethics of "healthy relations," one that "precisely concern[s] the body, [and which] can be formulated as follows: those relations which ensure an open future, which is to say, those which promote the formation of new compounds."[33] Focusing too obviously on emotional disclosure at this state would foreclose affective potential by reducing the vagueness of affectivity through the demand of specificity.

Part of what is therapeutic about a participatory encounter with DMT is therefore a shift away from a concern solely with how movement is made meaningfully emotional after the fact of its taking place, and toward an attentive immersion in the affective relations and movements catalyzed during the enactment of the therapeutic space of which DMT consists.[34] This is also a shift away from treating emotions as the outward expressive representation of some inner subjective entity, away from the "persistent illusion" that emotion "is an abstract and detachable 'it' upon which research can be directed."[35] When thinking about affectivity, it is easy to "elide the challenge" of how it shapes forms of life by analyzing "texts, symbols, material objects, and ways of life as representations of emotions."[36] Such an approach proves particularly unprofitable in the context of an encounter with a practice like DMT. So perhaps participation in DMT only begins to become therapeutic when it catalyzes a move away from the imperative to understand and identify how discrete states of affective experience are represented, and toward attending to and valorizing the processuality of affective variations grasped in passing as a smile, a movement, a gesture, the playful use of an apparently useless object, the movement of the body when talking about movement, or the touch of a hand given over to the response of another.

The broader point here is that different ways of understanding affectivity have different ethical implications. That is, an ethics of emotion is not necessarily the same as an ethics of affect. Again, these ethics are not mutually exclusive: the crucial thing is to become aware of the different opportunities these terms afford for thinking about ethics as a process of experience and experiment. An encounter with a therapeutic practice such as DMT can therefore sensitize participants to the pragmatic and ethico-political value of developing a differentiated conceptualization of affectivity as part of the cultivation of an affectively imbued ethical sensibility.

Therapeutic Objects

If a differentiated conception of affectivity provides orientation for participation in DMT, so also does attention to the way in which DMT involves more than solely human participants. To learn to attend to the affective spacetime of DMT is to foreground the ways in which objects participate in the generation of affective relations. Another way to think of these objects is as therapeutic props. Dance movement therapists often use a whole range of props, including material (of all lengths, textures, and colors), sticks, hula hoops, balls, beanbags, streamers, clothes, hats, cloaks, Lycra bands, Grobags, parachutes. These props might be understood, following William Forsythe, as "choreographic objects" that provide opportunities for "transition from one state to another in any space imaginable."[37] As Erin Manning has written, choreographic objects allow for the rearranging of everyday relational spaces in ways that open up possibilities for moving differently: "You may decide to paint the room, taking out the furniture, only to realize that the orientation you've always taken in the space is not the most interesting one. It's not the objects that have kept you from attending to spacetimes of creation in this particular environment. It's that you forgot that objects have a life, that they create space. And that how the space moves you is synonymous with the eventness of its objects."[38]

The participation of choreographic objects in a more obviously therapeutic context can also be understood in these terms. These objects furnish opportunities for moving in different ways. In a therapeutic context, the role of these objects is also catalytic. They catalyze transversal affective relations that open up fields of potential in the actuality of sensible movement. And their force in this regard comes from the fact that most of them are so indeterminate. Consider the following example: at one point during a DMT summer school, a number of different types of sticks are brought into the room. These include bamboo poles with a plastic bulb at the end; thin, flexible plastic rods of different colors; and short wooden sticks about a foot long. Almost immediately someone picks up one of the wooden sticks and says, "Feel the force, Luke."

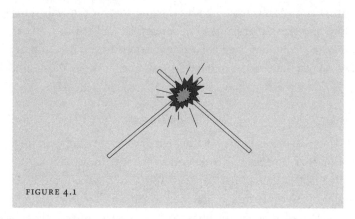

FIGURE 4.1

To the side, while this is happening, a therapist puts the theme from *Star Wars* on a stereo in the room. Everyone begins to move around the room, some with light sabers in hand, as other shapes, other movements come into play; spaceships, aliens, the dark side . . .

What happens here is not that the stick works as a representation of *Star Wars*. The stick represents nothing, phallic or otherwise. Rather than a matter of representation, the event of this encounter is transversally catalytic: it catalyzes an affective complex — or refrain — in the actuality of moving bodies. Specifically, what is catalyzed here is the *Stars Wars* affect, an abstract yet moving complex of gestural, figural, and musical refrains that, by dint of repetition, has crossed a threshold of cultural consistency. As Félix Guattari reminds us, this is a refrain in the same way that refrains are associated with celebrated composers or public figures.[39]

Catalyzed by the participation of objects, such refrains can easily become part of the dynamic and inventive affective field of DMT. This often takes place without any deliberate or deliberative summoning on the part of human participants. A therapeutic prop becomes a catalyst for a refrain that seizes a body, opening up universes of possibility. This, of course, sounds ever so grand: in actuality it is much more modest. Consider the following example: at one point during a DMT summer school, various long, flowing, colorful cloaks are introduced to the room, sifted through, and donned. Now there is a room full of superheroes. And one Father Ted.[40] Earlier in the week, one of the summer school participants remarked that I sound like Father Ted. The remark has become a running joke, and now in the midst of all the superheroes, donning a cloak becomes the event of my becoming a priest, becoming Father Ted Crilley. What happens is this. Every so often, I catch the eye of the person who initiated the joke and raise my arms as if to offer myself to God, and she laughs. Then I move in the midst of things until at some other point I repeat the gesture, and she laughs. It becomes a little refrain, animating the space, however briefly. This is not an effort to try to be Father Ted. Nor is it the moment at which the positional politics of cultural identity are revealed. Rather, it is the playing out of an abstract set of actions and movements that, in momentarily organizing movements, provides opportunities for creatively manipulating spacetimes.

Therapeutic Interventions

Through the use of therapeutic props and invitations, the dance movement therapist becomes implicated in pathways of pragmatic intervention. The process involves a series of ongoing risks, taken by both therapist and client. Insofar as they aim to catalyze movement, sometimes these interventions work, sometimes not. Sometimes they arrest things, or stop things in their tracks, as the vagueness of affect becomes territorialized in a refrain that closes in on itself. Consider the following example: an invitation from the therapist — "everyone throw a Paddy."

What?

A room full of mad, mad movements and silly, silly noises. It must have seemed obvious to everyone else how to respond, but not to me. Or at least not immediately. The whole thing throws me. Mad, mad movements and silly, silly noises and one very still, still very confused Paddy who does not know what it means, kinesthetically, to throw a Paddy. Very unbecoming. As it dawns on me, I'm not so much offended as fascinated. The other participants did not hear a culturally articulated affective-kinesthetic stereotype. Before they thought of anything like that, they were moved by an utterance to move, and in a very unfamiliar way, or at least to me. I stood there, motionless, arrested, with a stiff upper lip, throwing back a "Brit." But no one seemed to catch it. Sometimes interventions do not work: that is, they fail to catalyze movement because their affects become captured in webs of semiotic meaning.

The invitation to "throw a Paddy" is definitely a form of instruction. However, this should not undermine the claim that the underlying approach of dance movement therapists is nondirective. It remains an approach that works toward creating the conditions for opening up new modes of thinking and feeling, but it is also one that on occasion fails. A nondirective ethos does not mean an absence of intervention. The therapist intervenes all the time, in a process of minor experimentation. She tries moving in a particular way and finds after a while that it does not move things on. And then she tries something else, all the time noticing, waiting, intervening. These interventions are akin to offerings, a gifting of potential relations that may or may not be taken up by another. As Kristina Stanton-Jones suggests, DMT performs a therapeutic ethos in which the aim

> is not to move more freely, or more perfectly, which may be the aim of therapeutic dance activities, but to use movement experimentation to explore new ways of being and feeling, and to gain access to feelings that cannot be verbalised. In therapeutic dance activities, the dance teacher uses specific dance movements to direct the patient to feel in a particular way. The teacher may ask students to jump, or use their arms in a floating way to feel lively, or feel joyful, in contrast to the dance movement therapist who is non-directive, and neither prescribes the emotions the client is to express, nor instructs the clients on how to move.[41]

This distinction is crucial. Therapeutic interventions are absolutely necessary, but they do not need to take the form of an injunction to move in a specific way. Instead, therapeutic interventions can be understood as an ongoing set of efforts to keep relations open to variation through minor experiments with experience that could always fail.

Techniques of Relation

Much of what happens during DMT sessions involves attending to and modulating affective relations across and between bodies. This is facilitated by techniques through which the therapist attends to the capacity of her own body to amplify or dampen the intensity of these relations. Mirroring is one such technique. An example: an instruction of sorts — all participants get into pairs and sit facing one another on the floor. Each pair takes a piece of white gauzy material and arranges it over themselves (fig. 4.2).

The facilitating therapist instructs each pair to experiment at client-therapist role-play. Each pair decides who shall adopt each of the roles. The aim of the exercise is for the person playing the role of the therapist to engage the attention of the client. The brief for the person in the client role is simply to be very uncommunicative. The exercise is not a question of imagining that one is a therapist or client, but of trying to move in a particular way by attending to the movements of another in the relational immediacy of a specific situation.

Consider the following scenario. With a partner, let's say you assume the role of the client. Initially, you don't know how to do this. Because you do not want to act, pretend, or mimic, you therefore feel uncomfortable. So you simply take hold of the material with both hands and move it in your clenched fists. It makes a raspy noise. You might decide that this is a little refrain, a way of being comfortable in the situation in which you do not yet know how to go on. So you do this and wait for the therapist to begin doing something. She begins by facing you. Slowly she begins moving her hands in gentle curves, something you don't find particularly engaging. But at some point she stops making the gentle curves with her hands and begins scrunching the fabric in a way similar to your movement. You notice, curious, wondering where she will take it. At some point, she begins punctuating the movements with quick openings and closings of her hands. Again you notice this, but it does not engage you. It seems that she is trying to get you to stop your little refrain. But you might be happy with it, because it makes you comfortable in a situation you find uncomfortable, artificial, contrived, and so at this point you do not want to stop. But you wonder what the therapist will do. She takes up your scrunching action again, but does not open and close her hands. Instead, always mirroring your refrain, she moves her arms in different directions. You begin to follow it. Not as a client, not as student, but as a following. But you don't want to move too much. So you mirror her movements, but reduce their extent and intensity so that they are only barely noticeable. You want the therapist to notice this, to know that you are not going to do everything on her terms. This continues for a while until the facilitating therapist draws the exercise to a close.

To engage in such mirroring is different from mimicry: it is to take up and be taken up in the rhythms of relational movement.[42] To mirror in this sense is not to pretend or copy, nor is it to repeat what another is doing: it is a relational orientation toward the affective-kinesthetic space generated by the movement of another body. In the process, one's own affective-kinesthetic space is modified and modulated. In terms borrowed from Daniel Stern, mirroring may be understood as a way of acknowledging the "quality of feeling of a shared affective state, not necessarily [an] imitating [of] the exact behavioural expression of the [other's] inner state."[43]

Conversely, DMT also sometimes requires responding to movement without necessarily mirroring that movement through the physical displacement of the body. Some dance movement therapists employ a technique called witnessing, developed from a set of ideas called authentic movement.[44] During a DMT summer school the technique is illustrated as follows. A therapist gets up and moves in the middle of the circle for about a minute. She sits down and invites people in the group to describe the movement. There are different responses. Some describe short sections of the movement. Others describe the direction, speed, and so on. Others suggest that at points the movement was graceful, relaxed, and so forth. The therapist then gives some feedback, pointing out the different ways in which people talked about the movement. She highlights those ways of talking that make assumptions about what people might have been feeling while they moved or why they moved the way they did.

Let's say you then try the same exercise, breaking into pairs, one mover and one witness. You are the first to witness. With her eyes closed, your partner begins moving while you sit and pay attention to her movements. When this has finished, the therapist asks those who have moved if they would like to invite their partners to witness their movement. Your description takes the following form:

From a sitting position you stood up. Then you took a number of
steps forward. You lowered yourself to assume a kneeling and crawling position. You turned around and began crawling in a different
direction. You made contact with someone. I had a sense of surprise.
After crawling some more you raised yourself to a standing position.
You raised your right arm and as you did you made contact with the
hand of another. You remained in hand contact and made large circular movements. I had a sense of comfort and enjoyment. After
a short while you lost contact and began to walk around the space.

On first inspection it might appear that the neutrality of this description
refuses to acknowledge the full relationally implicated presence of another,
reducing the response to the movement of another to a form of detached
description. But this problem only holds if talking is held to be a representation of something working behind the movements of the world. It doesn't
hold if talking is taken as a way of going on in the world, a pragmatic and
affective intervention, a way of moving bodies. Thus, if witnessing in this
context is to be "authentic," it must involve a particular "way of talking
about" movement. The witness describes movement in an objective, non-
emotive language in order to avoid mobilizing ways of speaking about the
movements of another that make an evaluative judgment about internal
emotional experience or expression. Witnessing does not preclude speaking of emotions, but in speaking about movement the witness "owns" any
emotions that may be experienced during the movement. Hence, "I had a
sense of sadness while you moved," rather than "You moved as if you were
sad." In this approach, the witness obeys a grammar of affective relations
that divides the world up into "the space of my feeling" and the inaccessible
affect of another. Such an approach does not deny the relationality of affect.
On the contrary, it is an effort to remain faithful to the catalytic potential of
affect through a different style of relating. Indeed, it is precisely in the effort
to speak in an unemotive, nonevaluative way that the mode of speaking
implicated in witnessing acknowledges the importance of the performative
force of speaking as the capacity for affecting bodies and for maintaining
relations between bodies and allowing new relations to form.

This bears as much upon gesture as it does upon speech, as both are
implicated in fields of affective intensity and their modulation. Authentic
witnessing therefore involves a particular corporeal disposition that works

to avoid giving back to another whatever it is you assumed he felt by gesturing or moving in a particular way. Thus, when witnessing, the witness is encouraged not to give feedback through gestures. Indeed, some therapists sit on their hands when witnessing. As Shira Musicant suggests, the witness "attends to the temporal and spatial logistics [of the mover], keeping eyes open and attention on the mover. At the same time, the witness pays attention to and quietly contains his or her own judgments, feelings, sensations, and impulses to move."[45] In the context of DMT, the ethical importance of this way of moving/witnessing is the degree to which, by cultivating a commitment not to rush to specify the vague positivity of affect with interpretive sense, it facilitates the emergence of a spacetime of affective potential in which the mover can move as authentically as possible — that is, in a way, as far as possible, undetermined by the presence of the witness. Furthermore, by not commenting verbally or gesturally upon the inner experience of a mover, authentic witnessing is an effort to bear witness to the limits of witnessing. It seeks, however modestly, to be faithful to the belief that the possibility of testimony rests upon the impossibility of recovering experience.[46] This sense of witnessing is not simply part of the specific technique of authentic witnessing, but is an "intrinsic part of any therapeutic process, indeed, part of what makes therapy therapeutic."[47]

Thinking and Therapy

It is one thing to present a series of techniques and relation-specific moments in this episodic manner. But in what sense might such minor participatory experiments be understood as therapeutic? One way into this question is via the relation between thinking philosophically and the promise of therapeutic transformation. Here we might point, for instance, to Wittgenstein's understanding of philosophical investigation as a therapeutic process that allows us to go on in the world by demonstrating that there are other ways of thinking about or picturing the world than those to which we are accustomed.[48] Equally, we can think of philosophical writing that affirms the therapeutic quality of participation in somatic practices. For John Dewey, a practice like the Alexander Technique could help revive awareness of the somatic basis of public life and culture, through focusing attention on that which was most invisible to us — our own "habits and ways of doing things."[49] This was not a superficial cure or temporary remedy, but would be part of a thoroughgoing reworking of the sensibility of future generations.[50] As he put it in a preface to a book of Alexander's essays, through experience of this technique, "men and women in the future will be able to stand on their own feet, equipped with satisfactory psycho-physical equilibrium, to meet [with] readiness, confidence, and happiness instead of with fear, confusion, and discontent, the buffetings and contingencies of their surroundings."[51] Figuring somatic movement as therapeutic in the way Dewey does rehearses a much longer philosophical tradition in which care of the thinking self is understood to be enhanced by care of and for the body.[52] The pragmatist philosopher Richard Shusterman has called this "somaesthetics," an ethics defined by attention to somatic experience as a necessary element of critical engagement with wider formations of the embodied self and subject.[53]

Admittedly, this somatic self-fashioning can be grasped as a therapeutic individualism, one that draws upon a neo-romantic sensibility. Certainly, despite their very different intentions, there remains something of the spirit and reveries of Rousseau's solitary walker in Dewey's affirmation of the therapeutic quality of participation in somatic practices.[54] It would be a mistake, however, to caricature what Dewey advocates as amounting necessarily to an experimental aesthetic individualism. If anything, such experiments with habits, movements, and rhythms are always articulated as part of a process of exploring the environment of relations from which thinking is emergent. The same can be said of the rhythmanalysis developed in the work of Lefebvre and Bachelard, respectively.[55] As Bachelard puts it in *The Dialectic of Duration*: "A sick soul — especially one that suffers the pain of time and of despair — has to be cured by living and thinking rhythmically, by rhythmic attentiveness and repose." And the effect of rhythmanalytic therapy would be to generate benign and positive emotions: thus, "we would emerge from these rhythmanalysis sessions feeling more serene. Our repose would be more cheerful, more spiritual and poetic, as we lived this well-ordered temporal diversity."[56] Similarly, for Lefebvre, rhythmanalysis went beyond psychoanalysis insofar as the former could identify, analyze, and ameliorate arrhythmic movements and relations as part of a contribution to the wider project of valorizing the lived experience of the everyday. Rather than affirming a therapeutic individualism, rhythmanalysis — as a therapeutic project — intervenes into the rhythmic relations of which self, body, and world are composed: to think rhythmically is therefore to become aware of how lived experience is always emerging from the generative flux of rhythmic spacetimes. And to experiment experience therapeutically allows thinking to become open to a world that is already participating within experience. It provides a way for individuals to become more attentive to the individuations of which they are composed. In this way, rhythmanalysis encourages thinking of therapeutic intervention as always taking place within distributed, relational, rhythmic spacetimes.

Even if there are elements of a therapeutic ethos in his work, Lefebvre, in particular, might have reflected a little more on the logics of therapeutic interventions as part of thinking about spacetime. His writing could go much further in drawing out what is at stake in the articulation of a therapeutic mode of thinking that participates in and seeks to modulate the rhythms and refrains of moving bodies. The writing and thinking of Félix Guattari offer more in this respect, at the same time as they amplify Lefebvre's concern with rhythm. The significance of Guattari's work in this respect is at least fourfold. First, central to Guattari's thinking are claims about the prepersonal quality of the affective relations between bodies. Guattari draws upon Bergson and Spinoza to develop a working definition of affect as a kind of prepersonal, transitivist phenomenon. As a "prepersonal category, installed 'before' the circumscription of identities," affect always operates prior to the individual subject.[57] At the same time, affect is not static, but is a crucial element of the creative processuality of subjectivity: it is, as he suggests, a "process of existential appropriation through the continual creation of heterogeneous durations of being."[58] This is an especially important point: Guattari is critical of the subject as a self-enclosed entity while also affirming subjectivity as a generative process of existential creation. He is not so much antihuman as he is affirmative of the nonhuman participants in subjectivities.[59] Affect is nonhuman in the sense that it can become implicated in sensible transformations of experience across and between bodies. Crucially, affect is for Guattari more than relational in a personal or interpersonal sense. It has a transversal quality — it operates as a catalytically eventful relay between a multiplicity of movements and events. Both the more-than-personal and transversal qualities of affect are critical to Guattari's sense of what might count as a therapeutic intervention: therapeutic interventions open up the actuality of experience, transversally, to the relational excess of affect across and between bodies.

Second, Guattari reminds us that therapeutic approaches that have emerged from psychoanalytically inflected traditions of thinking are not necessarily overdetermined by these traditions. He encourages a cautious responsiveness toward some of these traditions without necessarily accepting all they stand for. As his writing with and without Deleuze suggests, Guattari is intensely critical of psychoanalysis, but only insofar as psychoanalysis tends to reduce subjectivities to the terms of symbolic analysis or oedipal dramas lodged in the psyche. Rather than dismissing psychoanalytically influenced work entirely, Guattari suggests that it needs "to get off the couch." This work has everything to gain from expanding the repertoire of means and methods for generating existential experimentalism: it can play with "words, but just as well with modeling clay . . . or with videos, movies, the theatre, institutional structures, familial interactions, etc."[60]

In turn, and third, Guattari's practical experience of therapeutic practices and institutions informs his affirmation of the value of relation-specific therapeutic spaces and the ecologies of practices of which they are composed as sources for resingularizing subjectivities. If organized appropriately, such institutions, for Guattari, always pose the question of how to live, through a myriad of modest experiments that generate event-centered singularities in processual subjectivities. Guattari's thinking here is shaped by his own active and sustained involvement in the institutional life of La Borde, a clinic near Paris, the underlying ethos of which was the establishment of a space in which transformations in processual subjectivities could be facilitated by revalorizing the affective relations emergent in very ordinary contexts. For instance, Guattari describes the kitchen at La Borde as a territory that

> combines highly heterogeneous social, subjective and functional
> dimensions. This Territory can close in on itself, become the site of
> stereotyped attitudes and behaviour, where everyone mechanically
> carries out their little refrain. But it can also come to life, trigger
> an existential agglomeration, a drive machine — and not simply of
> an oral kind, which will have an influence on the people who par-
> ticipate in its activities or just passing through. The kitchen then
> becomes a little opera scene: in it people talk, dance and play with
> all kinds of instruments, with water and fire, dough and dustbins,
> relations of prestige and submission.[61]

For Guattari, relation-specific therapeutic interventions at La Borde worked to the extent that they opened up new horizons of potential through novel (albeit modest) opportunities for thinking, feeling, and acting. The trick was to generate institutional spaces in which to cultivate responsiveness to these opportunities and to experiment via an expanded repertoire of interventions.[62] Furthermore, and equally importantly, these institutional spaces also had a therapeutic function insofar as they generated a distributed background field of nondetermining yet affectively felt encouragement of this openness. In this way, therapeutic institutions had the potential to facilitate a certain inventive transversality of thinking, feeling, and acting by producing atmospheres conducive to experiment.

A fourth important aspect of Guattari's thinking about therapeutic practices and institutions is an emphasis on the relation between the ethical and the aesthetic. Therapeutic practices are ethical in the sense that they are concerned with the Spinozist question of what bodies can do, and what they might be able to do if the generative conditions are opportune. They produce opportunities for expanding the range of ways in which bodies can be affected by other bodies, and, in the process, open up new possible forms of life whose value is not specified in advance. This is a different model of ethics from the code-centered model governing certain aspects of what happens during therapeutic practices. Admittedly, a code-centered model of ethics is useful in many ways, not least in a therapeutic context such as DMT, where it provides guides for professional contact and formalizes careful responsiveness. And yet it also has important limits. As political theorist Jane Bennett puts it, "many models of ethics are based on the undemonstrated presumption that if one does not endorse a command ethics one can have no ethics at all, that only a code-centered model can ensure a care for others."[63] In the process, ethics can all too easily be reduced to an auditable checklist that seems to speak for itself. Ethics, in other words, becomes detached from the question of experiment as a process that puts experience at risk. Ethics becomes indifferent to a field of differentiated affective processes and practices through which novel refrains may emerge, an emergence to which theory is a modest yet enlivening and pragmatic supplement. Again, this does not necessarily mean dismissing or ignoring the rules or techniques that shape conduct in a given situation: instead, to take Guattari's therapeutics seriously is to recognize that rules form part of a relation-specific ecology of practices affording opportunities for cultivating an affectively imbued ethical sensibility — or ethos — through which to experiment experience. This ethical sensibility is also an aesthetic one for Guattari because it takes affect and sensation as necessary elements of the remaking of subjectivites and the ecologies in which they participate.

Therapeutic practices are aesthetic, for Guattari, insofar as the process of resingularizing subjectivities through therapeutic interventions is a creative one that encourages the expression of affects across different domains of life without necessarily locating the source of such expression in any individual. Aesthetic practices are privileged techniques in this context because they provide opportunities for stretching out fields of expression across subjectivities and for generating new universes of value in the milieus from which these subjectivities emerge.

Ecologies of Practice for Making More of Experience

Guattari can help us to think about the value of participating in processes of experimenting experience through therapeutic practices such as DMT. That is not to claim that DMT exemplifies exactly the therapeutic ethos advocated and affirmed by Guattari. But read through Guattari's therapeutic ethico-aesthetics, DMT can be grasped not so much as a technology of the self overcoded by the traditions from which it emerges but as an ecology of practices with the potential to generate modest variations in moving, feeling, and thinking.[64] The therapeutic spacetimes of DMT become consistent through the production of an affective transversality that holds together while also holding open the relations between moving bodies and their potential futures as part of the process of resingularizing subjectivities.

Critically, Guattari asks us to think about how the affective and ethico-aesthetic value of therapeutic interventions lies in their capacity to generate contexts for experimenting with the refrains of experience. On one level, they generate refrains that provide a degree of security — a way of moving, singing, relating that is sensed as the gathering of a familiar spacetime. On another level, these interventions open up such gatherings to the possibilities of moving otherwise. Interventions are therapeutic to the extent that they generate refrains as mutant temporalizations that give a degree of consistency to the heterogeneous components of subjectivities as existential territories while opening these up to resingularization. To take such claims seriously is to attend to the specificity of techniques, objects, and interventions that give a loose consistency to a practice like DMT. In this context, "a rigid neutrality or non-intervention would be negative."[65] Instead, as Guattari reminds us, in a therapeutic context it is important to "respond to the event as the potential bearer of new universes of reference"— to opt "for pragmatic interventions oriented towards the construction of subjectivities, towards the production of fields of virtualities."[66]

All this means that participatory experiments with an ecology of practices such as DMT require an openness to the possibility that such participation might make some qualitative difference to the sensibilities through which thinking takes place and through which experience comes to matter. Without this ethos of openness it would be difficult to claim that experience is in any way experimental. It would also be difficult to moderate the impulse to dismiss certain somatic therapies because they are entangled in traditions that might run counter to the currents of critical thinking that inform engagement with the politics of life and living in biopolitical modernities. Even if the conceptual basis for some of these therapies may be problematic in various respects, careful participation in their experimentalism can reveal possibilities for working through and with affective relations in ways that exceed their explicit framing by traditions of thinking with which one may be less comfortable.

The promise here, as John-David Dewsbury has written, is that "these relationships, these sensate ecologies, once revealed more explicitly, can be made to constructively make bodies feel the live present rather than the habituated past."[67] Equally, following Isabelle Stengers, whose own thinking also draws upon Guattari's enthusiasm for experimenting with refrains, we might think of the value of participatory experiment in DMT as part of a wider process of making ecologies of practices potentially available for transversal becomings. For Stengers, then, what matters here is how to "make present what causes practitioners to think and feel and act." As she continues, "this is a problem which may produce also an experimental togetherness among practices, a dynamics of pragmatic learning of what works and how. This is the kind of active, fostering 'milieu' that practices need in order to be able to answer challenges and experiment changes, that is to unfold their own force."[68] Understood thus, participatory experiments with elements of DMT might contribute to the tending of a milieu in which to cultivate practices whose affects circulate beyond the context in which they are enacted: and all as part of the amplification of a wider ethico-aesthetic ecology in which experience is, in Guattari's terms, always being remade through a myriad of modest experiments.

CHAPTER FIVE

Commentating

Semiconducting Affective Atmospheres

> On a level with conversation are the verbal improvisations of the radio commentator
> and the gossiping journalist. In exceptional moments they may begin to germinate the
> artistic phrase, but it is very rare indeed for them to produce forms of expression which
> are memorable. The words they toss off are only meant to be received and forgotten.
> — ROGER MANVELL, *On the Air: A Study of Broadcasting in Sound and Television*

The scenario may be familiar, yet it never ceases to irritate. The screen cuts to the upper torso and face of an athlete: a gold medalist at a major athletics championship; the captain of the victorious team of a fiercely contested football game; the scorer of the winning goal in the same game.[1] Sweating, beaming, animation: joy unconfined, obvious and palpable. And then the question: "What does it feel like?" "Wonderful, absolutely amazing, brilliant. I can't really believe it." And still the sweating, beaming animation: joy unconfined, obvious and palpable. Changing tack, the interviewer probes and presses for a little more detail, insight, reaction: "Talk us through that goal." Forced recollection of movement, patterning, connection. "To be honest, I didn't really think too much about it. I think Gary fed the ball to me and I cut inside and then just hit it as hard as I could. I connected with it really well and it flew into the top corner." And then a reaching for some sense of significance. "Could you tell us what this victory means to you?" "It means so much. I can't really put it into words." And still the sweating, beaming animation: joy unconfined, obvious and palpable. "So there we have it. Back to the studio for some detailed analysis."

The unease generated by this scenario has nothing to do with the manner in which sports interviewers conduct their own business: they have a job to do, after all. The unease arises because the scenario is so reminiscent of the ethos, style, and conduct of so much methodological work in the social sciences. At the risk of caricature, a great deal of this work operates through the logics of the postevent interview, albeit more formalized, more nuanced, and more concerned with issues such as ethics and rigor. Begin by observing things and events as they happen in the world. Interview participants in those events as a means of gleaning a partial account of how these participants made sense of what was happening. Convey the raw data to another site (the studio or the study) for detailed analysis and interpretation.

The continued attraction and appeal of this logic in the social sciences is a result of the residual assumption that rigor can be approximated and vagueness reduced only through the construction of a triangulated account of interpretive sense making. This way of thinking about and approaching the world is clearly of pragmatic value in many contexts. Yet what works for the sports reporter may be more problematic for those in the social sciences and humanities interested in thinking about and thinking within affective spacetimes. Perhaps most important, the tendency to proceed by going out into the world, reporting back, and then analyzing events is inadequate to the task of apprehending the affective and processual logics of the spacetimes in which moving bodies are generative participants. A sense of these spacetimes as events in process is lost through an emphasis on the requirement to capture postevent meaning as a necessary element of rigorous interpretive methodology. Clearly, the point is not to jettison postevent interviews. Nor to stop talking about events. However, when talking or writing about the affective spacetimes of moving bodies, it might be possible to refigure the relation between these spacetimes and forms and styles of talking and writing. It might be possible to move away from, or at the very least supplement, the logics of after-the-event sports reporting.

The proposition developed in this chapter is that the performative logics of "running commentary" on sporting events and, more specifically, on radio commentating on those events offer ways of stretching the relation between events and their expression. At first glance, radio commentating might seem of little promise in this respect. To focus on this practice could well appear a rather regressive move: radio is hardly at the forefront of contemporary experimental media ecologies.[2] And sport is always a difficult set of practices to harness as part of any ethico-aesthetic or political experiment. However, even if not always obviously avant-garde, radio remains an important participant in the "materialist energies" of contemporary technocultures and the atmospheric sensoria they generate: it operates very much in the familiar background of sonic cultures, part of the taken-for-granted and mediatized spacetimes of everyday life.[3] Paying attention to radio commentating is worthwhile, therefore, because it provides an important opportunity to think about how familiar forms of organized expression contain germinal opportunities for experimenting experience. To do so, however, requires understanding radio commentating less as a representational practice than as a technique of affective event amplification and transmission in which moving bodies participate. As a performative practice concerned with the event in passing, the distinctive rhythms, styles, and sensibilities of radio commentating draw together, or give consistency to, the lively spacetimes of affective atmospheres in which bodies move and are moved.

PLAYED ON A PITCH of approximately 137 × 82 meters between two teams of fifteen players, Gaelic football resembles a distinctive hybrid of association football, rugby, and Australian rules football. The game is played with a round leather ball slightly smaller than that used in soccer, and the goals are the same shape as those used in rugby. A goal (3 points) is scored by putting the ball under the cross-bar and a point is scored if the ball is put between the posts above the cross-bar. Players can score with feet or hands. Ball carrying is regulated in a distinctive way. When carrying the ball in hand, the player must — every four steps — bounce the ball or drop it onto the foot and catch it again with the hand (called a "solo"). Two bounces in a row are prohibited. Players cannot throw the ball to one another and instead must pass by kicking or by striking the ball with a hand or fist. The level of physical contact in the game is more than in soccer and less than in rugby: in effect, players are allowed shoulder contact but not to pull an opponent to the ground.

I stopped playing Gaelic football sometime around the age of nineteen or twenty. At that age I imagined there would be plenty of time to take up the game again at some point in the future. But moving first to the United

States and then to the United Kingdom meant that I had little opportunity to do so. Even when someone did mention the existence of a local game I never got around to making the effort. Indeed, I often shied away from it because the game can be a lot more physical and less effectively regulated at the local level when played abroad. Disclosing this prior participation here is not necessarily an act of positioning: the point instead is to signal the ongoing resonance of a relation-specific field of affective movement. As Michel Serres writes in *The Five Senses*, to have participated in a team sport is to have experienced a particular state of being "angelic," an experience that persists as the memory of "having passed without knowing how into another world, into a space without error or weakness, where the craziest plans were effortlessly successful, precise gestures, subtle movements, delicate and always accurate decisions." This experience leaves an "imperishable memory — of sport and one's body."[4] So even if I no longer participate as a player in Gaelic Athletic Association (GAA) games, the after-affects of involvement make their presence felt in various ways in an ongoing relation to a field of play, not least of which during those times when I listen to radio commentary upon Gaelic games, something made significantly easier by the availability of digital and Internet-based radio. The experience of listening to this commentary is shaped by a virtual reserve of somatic affects, the kind conjured so effectively by Seamus Heaney:

> and a cry from the touch-line
> to *Point her!* That spring
> and unhampered smash-through!
> Was it you
>
> or the ball that kept going
> beyond you, amazingly
> higher and higher
> and ruefully free?[5]

Clearly, the virtual memory of these movements is deeply infused with a melancholic affect. And, as a poet of the perceptive powers of Heaney is all too aware, the nostalgic refrain of this affect is always a potentially dangerous game, particularly so if it is part of an appeal to the territorial logics of a sport in which collective identities mark the ground around competitively charged affiliations to parish, county, and country. And yet as Heaney's own poetry also demonstrates, the refrain of these affects can become an occasion for thinking beyond the strictures of clear delineations of territory. One of the promises of poetry as commentary, to which I return in the conclusion to this chapter, is that its rhythms displace the certainties of territorial belonging, but not acidically so. Radio commentary offers a similar occasion for thinking. And this is particularly so if it becomes part of an attempt to think through how the affects of event-centered belonging are amplified and circulated in ways that disrupt the apparent coincidence of territory and identity. So while commentary can seem to sound the refrain of territories of belonging, venturing "from home" along the "sonorous" lines of the performance of commentating can become an occasion to explore alternative possibilities for thinking within the affective spacetimes of moving bodies.[6]

Radio's Affective Atmospherics

Steven Connor has argued that the emergence of radio in the early twentieth century can be understood in terms of the production of a novel type of experiential space, one that was "fluid, mobile, and voluminous," and one "in which the observer-observed duality and distinctions between separated points and planes" provided little purchase.[7] As Connor also suggests, the effort to make conceptual and aesthetic sense of this experiential space was often framed in terms of an atmospherics: that is, the invention of radio was bound up intimately with wider cultural imaginings of atmosphere as an ethereal medium through which forces and influences could travel and propagate, making their presences felt as if by some magical transubstantiation.[8] Radio's atmospheric associations did not necessarily depend upon the broadcast of clearly audible speech or music. Rather, before the presence of a voice that makes meaningful sense, the crackle and buzz of radio noise already provided a field of background vibratory potential from which a sense of other worldly presences could be felt.[9] Paul Carter puts it thus: "Like conspirators around an Ouija board we respond to radio's promise of presence even if it turns out to be saying nothing."[10] In short, radio seemed to crystallize, sonically, the atmospheric quality and generative potential of a field of affective materiality: what Michel Serres calls background "noise."[11] Radio's atmospherics provided the background from which the technologically mediated voice sounded the possibility of bodies moving and being moved across a distributed yet sensible field.[12]

This historical alignment between radio's experiential space and the production of an atmospheric sensorium speaks directly to more recent concerns with the question of how affects and emotions move across, between, and through bodies. On one level these concerns invite an exploration of spacetimes of proximity and encounter in which affectivity flows between bodies in all manner of tangibly intimate ways. Exemplified in practices like dance and sport, these spacetimes can be grasped as atmospheres generated through what the late Teresa Brennan calls the transmission of affect within and between bodies.[13] The intensity of these affective atmospheres consists of, and is modulated by, a range of processes including, for instance, facial expression, bodily stance, and relational gesture. But as radio demonstrates, affective atmospheres do not emerge between colocated or covisible bodies only. They also emerge between bodies at a distance: that is, between bodies that are not in any literal sense participants in shared affective spacetimes generated at a given geographical location.

The affective atmospherics of radio are not simply conjured into being by the mere existence of a certain kind of technological infrastructure, however crucial this infrastructure might be. Rather, these atmospherics are facilitated, sustained, and channeled through an assemblage of technique and technology. In this respect, radio does more than just provide for the broadcast of already existing practices: it also reworks these practices in subtle but important ways according to the technological requirements of the medium.[14] Singing is an obvious case in point: the technical capacities of early radio microphone and broadcast technology were especially suited to a softer mode of vocal delivery. As a result, "crooning" emerged as a distinctive style of singing that, by design or not, had the effect of generating a palpable atmosphere of intimacy through the technical and affective modulation of the broadcast voice. The appeal of this atmosphere differed, however: thus, what was popular in the United States failed to resonate — at least initially — in the United Kingdom, where the BBC remained suspicious of the artificial modulation of the singing voice. As Simon Frith has written, "the essence of the BBC case against crooning was that it was 'unnatural.' 'Legitimate' music hall or opera singers reached their concert hall audiences with the power of their voices alone; the sound of the crooners, by contrast, was artificial. Microphones enabled intimate sounds to take on a pseudo public presence, and, for the crooners' critics, technical dishonesty meant emotional dishonesty — hence terms like 'slushy.'"[15]

Such responses are reminders that radio's atmospheres are affectively differentiated. That is, radio's atmospheres are affective spacetimes within which intensities of feeling precipitate with variable strength and duration, and often as the result of deliberate intervention. Radio broadcast can thus be understood as a technology for engineering affective influence, not so much because it directs the action of listeners, but because it contributes to the generation of atmospheres that may, in certain contexts, shape the dispositional background from which action takes place.[16] It is one thing to make this claim about crooning, the affects of which, however "inauthentic," are relatively benign: radio has also obviously been used to engineer affects that are much more malign. Perhaps the most extreme example is the use of radio to incite hatred and violence: the radio broadcasts during the 1994 Rwandan genocide are a case in point.[17] Radio also works as a technology for generating and modulating "national" affective sensibilities. For instance, Danny Kaplan has argued that national radio in Israel is employed deliberately as a "mood-shifter." This process takes place through broadcasting policies that use music to "alter the public mood in response to national events." For Kaplan then, radio broadcasting acts as a sonic-geopolitical technology that extends "the function of the siren."[18] Equally, as Ben Anderson has written, radio can work as an affective technique for modulating morale during times of "total war."[19]

As these examples indicate, radio's atmospheres are implicated in the generation of affectively imbued imagined communities. The temporality and intensity of these communities is variable, depending upon the type of broadcast event in question, and the logics of the performative technique involved. Talk radio, for instance, facilitates the emergence of publics crystallizing around controversial events or issues. More specifically, talk radio is a technique for generating the promise of participation not only in public debate but in the amplification and circulation of collective feeling. As John Tebbutt has demonstrated through an investigation of the development of talk-back radio in Australia, "standards of contributions and styles of compering [are] ways of disciplining an audience, shaping it both as material form and in terms of affect. Station 'qualities' [are] reflected in the format and *performed* by the host, not simply communicated in messages, in the way hosts express[ed] themselves through voice and characterizations."[20]

More generally, the emergence of radio's atmospheric qualities foregrounded the spatiotemporality of attentiveness. As Susan Squier has written, "radio functioned as a powerful new site of cognitive activity in the twentieth century, linking different states of awareness, from passive reception to active listening; encouraging visual and spatial imaging in response to what we hear; activating basic brain structures that are then inflected differently by different cultural contexts."[21] Significant here is the distinction between listening and hearing, of which Jean-Luc Nancy reminds us.[22] Listening, for Nancy, is an active, corporeal orientation toward the voluminous spacing of noise and sound. Hearing is better understood as the effort to render sound meaningful. Both, of course, are implicated in attending to radio. And both involve the immanent affective modulation of the entire body in relation to whatever is being broadcast, to the immediate surroundings of the listener, and to the expansive temporality of radio's atmospheres.[23]

Listening, it should be remembered, also plays a role in the economy of rhythmic attentiveness and attunement outlined by Henri Lefebvre. For Lefebvre it is through listening that the rhythmanalyst takes up and is taken up by the rhythms of everyday life. As he puts it, the rhythmanalyst will "listen to the world, and above all to what are disdainfully called noises, which are said without meaning, and to murmurs [rumors], full of meaning — and finally he will listen to silences."[24] This mode of listening begins with the body — with attentiveness to its rhythms — before extending to prehend the rhythmic mobility of the surrounding environment, which includes the media, which "occupies" the day through a clamor of voices: "nocturnal voices, voices that are close to us, but also other voices (or images) that come from afar, from the devil, from sunny or cold and misty places. So many voices!"[25] Admittedly, these comments need to be qualified: in his writing Lefebvre is critical of the role played by media in shaping the spatio-temporal experience of everyday life. For Lefebvre the influence of popular media technologies is duplicitous: they shape experience without revealing the extent of their influence, and more profoundly, they diminish the importance of genuine dialogue in favor of the creation of a chattering background of voices. Acidic as this critique might be, it does not necessarily preclude efforts to approach everyday media practices as sources for cultivating the rhythmic attentiveness about which Lefebvre is also so enthusiastic. Rather, following Nancy and Lefebvre, tuning into practices that both are facilitated by and sustain radio's affective atmospheres might actually provide opportunities for experimenting experience in spacetimes of and for moving bodies.

Tuning In: Commentating

Radio commentary is a familiar element of the clamor of voices that provides the sonic background of everyday life. So much so, perhaps, that it is easy to forget how novel running commentary seemed when it emerged as a credible and technically feasible genre of expression in the later 1920s. In some ways, commentary merely extended radio's more general capacity to generate the experience of "liveness" for the listener: in the early years of radio, the production of liveness was one of the distinguishing features of the medium. As the comedian George Burns wryly put it, before radio, "the only way to see a performer was to see a performer."[26] Listening to someone crooning live in a studio was one thing: the relation here could easily be conceived and experienced as a relation of intimacy established between two individuals or, at the very least, between a small group of listeners and a singer. Listening to a major sporting or public event was something else entirely, generating a more expansive and intensive experience of liveness.[27] As Paddy Scannell has argued, in this context, radio commentary could offer the real sense of access to an event in its moment-by-moment unfolding. This *"presencing*, this re-présenting of a present occasion to an absent audience, can powerfully produce the effect of being-there, of being involved (caught up) in the here-and-now of the occasion."[28]

Precisely how radio commentary might best generate a sense of liveness was by no means self-evident, however, at least in the early years of its development. Indeed, early efforts by the BBC to "experiment" with commentary at a racecourse were considered a failure, in part because, as Mike Huggins has documented, rain "dampened hooves and spirits," and because the commentary itself failed to clearly convey the final result.[29] Other experiments, such as those involving a series of eyewitness accounts from spectators, were even less successful.[30] As an experimental technique for producing affective atmospheres then, the success of commentating was framed in terms of a number of stylistic and technical concerns germane to the question of how to allow the listener to feel present at a location whose sonic topography was much more complicated and chaotic than the insulated and controlled environment of the studio. One solution to this question was technological, and involved the effort to capture atmospheres through the careful positioning of microphones to pick up the noises and sounds of the crowd in ways that would convey with "dramatic intensity" the "pageant of sound" that circulated in the stands.[31] Richard Haynes describes this technical enterprise thus: "To create a sense of authenticity and actuality for the listener, [Outside Broadcasts] also utilized what were termed 'natural noises' to convey atmosphere. The roar of the crowd, still vital to contemporary football coverage, was faded in and out as required with the voice of the commentator. The production of these atmospheric sounds engaged the listener with the ups and downs of the match. These 'effects' gathered from the perimeter fences of football grounds proved an essential part of the OB."[32]

The technical infrastructure of commentating could only do so much: critical to the success of commentating was the vocal style of the commentator. In turn, this style consisted of both the nontechnical description of details and, perhaps equally importantly, the ability to take up and transmit a sense of the rhythms and movements of a field of activity. The latter required the commentator to modulate his own voice according to the rise and fall of the background atmosphere. As a BBC handbook put it, the point was to "convey only genuine excitement. For this the test is: does the pace and pitch of his delivery match the variation in the background of the roar of the crowd."[33] Commentating, in these terms, became a way of amplifying radio's atmospheric qualities, without necessarily exaggerating them, through employing a particular rhythm and economy of expression and description, with the emphasis on relatively simple language and lack of technical detail. In this respect radio commentating was and remains different from television commentating. As Andrew Crisell observes, "Its speed and style reflect the mood of the event and its language tends to be more explicit, creates its own context much more, than television commentating. It includes not simply a concrete description of the event but what has been described as 'associative material' — other sense-impressions such as the smell of new mown grass, the weather, and the human 'atmosphere'; and also the historical background, those facts and causes beyond the event."[34]

It may appear self-evident now, but as a distinctive form of "radio talk," commentating has its own codes and conventions of expression that were by no means inevitable, and which were shaped by the contexts within which they emerged.[35] In this respect it is worth noting that the extent to which the commentator became overtly emotional in his speech was a point of contention, one that reflected culturally specific conventions and styles of public address. For instance, where in the United States commentating was from its inception characterized by the expression of enthusiasm on the part of the commentator, the emotional identification of the individual with the affective intensity of the event was more frowned upon in the United Kingdom, at least initially, and for reasons similar to those that made crooning so problematic: overt enthusiasm raised the specter of emotional inauthenticity. It also made the commentator present in a way that, at least initially in the United Kingdom, was incompatible with the idea that commentating was first and foremost a form of public service in which one's duty was to the depiction of the event. The task was to convey a sense of this event, and its atmosphere, without necessarily revealing one's own participation in the generation and amplification of this atmosphere. The peculiar style and qualities of commentating therefore required the commentator to respond to the event in ways that did justice to it through forms of expression that made literal and affective sense in specific cultural and social contexts. This was further differentiated within national contexts along lines of class and gender. So in the United Kingdom, what sounded florid and indulgent to one educated ear was precisely what made commentating so appealing and involving to another.

If the question of how running commentary might convey the sense of events as they unfolded in time was addressed in different ways, so also was the implicit geography of the practice. On one level, this was manifest in concerns about the effect commentary might have on the behavior of audiences: for instance, in the early decades of its development in the United Kingdom, the suspicion was that commentary would discourage people from attending games, with obvious financial implications for professional sporting bodies. Furthermore, there were fears that commentary would render public events increasingly private as radio audiences listened to live broadcast in the comfort of their homes. The concern here was sometimes articulated in terms of the prospect of rendering audiences inactive and passive through the creation of a "fireside orchestra for sluggards."[36] As Paddy Scannell notes, this new geography of audiences also raised questions about whether or not listeners would respond appropriately during the broadcast of nationally significant events, and especially those involving the royal family.[37] The question here became how to guarantee that a radio audience listened with the proper degree of respect. Equally revealing were initial concerns about how listeners — rather than spectators — might make visual sense of events as they unfolded in a nonvisual space. This prompted some curious innovations. In the United Kingdom, the first live radio transmission of an association football game was broadcast in January 1927. Eager to ensure that listeners would be able to visualize what was unfolding on the pitch, the BBC published a special diagram of the pitch, divided into eight zones, in copies of the *Radio Times* during the week before the game. The broadcast itself involved two people. The commentator, Henry Blythe Thornill (Teddy) Wakelam, described the events on the pitch, while another broadcaster, C. A. Lewis, relayed to the audience which square the ball was in at any given moment.[38]

Conversely, if commentating involved an attempt to help audiences see events unfold, it also demanded that the commentator make imaginative sense of the audience to which his commentary was addressed. While commentating might well have been conceived as a public service, it is difficult to address such a diffuse and abstract entity as the public. Speaking into the void of a collective is potentially vertiginous. As one prominent Irish sports commentator, Michael O'Hehir, put it,

> One of the terrors of commentating is the feeling that you are talking to thousands and thousands of people. So in my early years of broadcasting I would picture in my mind's eye a place down in Ballycorrig and, up on a hill there, a man called Patrick Garry, who used to go to matches all over the country. For some years before I started broadcasting, he had been bedridden. So I'd imagine myself talking directly to him: this helped get rid of the feeling that I was addressing a multitude. In those formative years it was not the people of Ireland or anywhere I was speaking to, but to Patrick Garry, doing my best to tell him what was happening. That way I seemed to develop a style the radio audience seemed to like.[39]

O'Hehir's final point is justified. The journalist and writer Mary O'Malley puts it like this:

> Until we got our first television, when I was about thirteen or fourteen, I had never seen a proper hurling match. The game was not played locally at adult level. We used to listen, gathered around the radio on Sunday afternoons, entranced by the dramatic skill of the virtuoso commentator, Michael O'Hehir. Slowly he drew you in with a description of the crowd, the weather, the direction of the wind. Then there was the ritual naming of the teams, a few words of praise for each county, the entry onto the field of the Artane Boys Band. The teams would file out to cheers and applause. Then silence and the band played the national anthem.[40]

Such comments are obviously filtered through nostalgia. Yet they serve as reminders of the close association between familiar voices and the refrain of important public events. Equally, as these comments also suggest, commentating can become part of the mediatized performance of "banal nationalism" through the generation of an atmosphere of intimacy via a technologically mediated yet authentically authoritative voice.[41] But commentating can also be understood as technology of the voice through which the imagined community of the nation is affectively articulated through styles of moving and embodied practices. In this respect, Arjun Appadurai has argued that radio commentary on cricket in India worked as a technology of imaginative and bodily decolonization. For Appadurai, imagined communities are as much a matter of the cultivation of affectively imbued corporeal dispositions as about learning scripts and narratives about nationhood. And commentary facilitates this mixing of vocabulary and corporeal disposition. As he puts it, "vernacular commentary on radio (and later on television) provides the first step to the domestication of the vocabulary of cricket because it provides not just a contact vocabulary, but also a link between this vocabulary and the excitement of the heard or seen drama of the game, its strokes, its rhythm, its physical thrill. . . . The great stars of cricket are imitated, children are nicknamed after them, and the terminology of cricket, its strokes and its stars, its rules and its rhythms, becomes part of vernacular pragmatics and a sense of lived physical experience."[42]

In sum then, commentating is an affective technology of the voice through which the qualities of the live event are expressed and transmitted as part of the generation of radio's atmospheres. With the development of commentating, novel and distinctive spacetimes of affective experience emerge: spacetimes that are both intimate and distributed.

Voicing the National Event

Live commentary on Gaelic games has been a central element of broadcasting in Ireland since the early years of independence. The first Irish radio station, 2RN (later to become Radio Eireann and subsequently RTE) was established in 1926, four years after independence. From the outset, the station was intended to emphasize all that was understood to be unique and distinctive about Irish culture.[43] Douglas Hyde, the first Irish president, opened the station with a speech in which he suggested that "a nation cannot be made by an Act of Parliament; no, not even by a Treaty. A nation is made from inside itself; it is made first of all by its language, if it has one; by its music, songs, games, and customs."[44] The station 2RN was not, therefore, expected only to provide a forum for obviously artistic practices. It was also intended as a political technology through which to actively regenerate a range of activities as part of an effort to give spatiotemporal consistency to the nation-state. Radio was expected "to revive the speaking of Irish; to foster a taste for classical music; to revive Irish traditional music; to keep people on the farms; to sell goods and services of all kinds from sausages to sweep tickets; to provide a living and a career for writers and musicians; to reunite the Irish people at home with those overseas; to end partition."[45]

The GAA was one cultural organization that early on recognized the possibilities of radio. Founded in 1884 in Thurles, County Tipperary, the central aim of the association was and remains the cultivation and preservation of Gaelic games, including football, hurling, handball, athletics, and camogie. The establishment and growth of the organization can be situated in terms of the revival of discourses of Irish nationalism at the end of the nineteenth and beginning of the twentieth century.[46] Indeed, as Alan Bairner suggests, "Ireland's Gaelic Athletic Association is frequently offered as the best example of a sporting organisation formed for the precise purpose of producing and reproducing a sense of national identity."[47] With patronage by key figures in the Catholic Church and by notable supporters of constitutional Irish nationalism, the GAA also mobilized local parish-based communities and rivalries. While the founding of the GAA could be linked to the political project of reinvigorating Irish identity through the revival of cultural tradition, it also emerged from specific and genuine concerns for the corporeal basis of the Irish national character. On one hand this was born of a fear of the increasing popularity of English games — particularly association football, or soccer — which were seen as excessively effete when compared to the more muscular and vigorous nature of traditional Irish games. Yet at the same time the founders of the GAA — key among whom were Michael Cusack and Maurice Davin — were influenced heavily by Victorian ideas about the importance of cultivating (masculine) character through corporeal activity.[48] The GAA therefore offered a vehicle for the revival of national identity by drawing on a much wider concern with the necessity of reinvigorating domestic somatic culture.

The first live broadcast of a hurling match in Ireland, indeed the first live sporting broadcast in Europe, was the 1926 All-Ireland hurling final.[49]

Commentating on major Gaelic games has subsequently been an important part of the production and performative articulation of the imagined community of the Irish nation-state at different scales of belonging. As Luke Gibbons suggests, "far from passively relaying the activities of a thriving sporting body to an already captive audience," radio contributed significantly to the creation of a nationwide audience for Gaelic games.[50] This audience was also more than national — it extended to listeners comprising the Irish diaspora. In a strong sense, then, commentating on Gaelic games became a cultural-political "technology of the voice" through which intimacy and community were articulated together in an Irish context.[51]

As with other sports, one of the distinctive characteristics of commentating on Gaelic games has been and continues to be the relative dominance of a small number of commentators who become, de facto, the voice of these games and, given their popularity, the voice of national experience. Two figures stand out. The first is Michael O'Hehir, who broadcast actively from 1938 to 1985. In 1996, in the foreword to O'Hehir's biography, the then president of Ireland, Mary Robinson, captured his influence thus: "Very few people enter the subconscious of the nation. Micheal O'Hehir achieved this through his distinctive voice, telling the story of our national games."[52] While there have been other notable figures, including, for instance, Mick Dunne, O'Hehir's acknowledged successor was Mícheál Ó Muircheartaigh, whose commentating, like that of his predecessor, became very much part of the experience of Gaelic games until his retirement in September 2010. In a volume titled *Greetings to Our Friends in Brazil*, the Irish poet Paul Durcan captures a sense of the cultural resonance of Ó Muircheartaigh's commentating like this:

Getting good television pictures, we turned down the volume —
The diligent Ger Canning churning out clichés —
And, marrying radio sound to television picture
We tuned into the radio commentary
By the cordial Kerry Maestro Mícheál Ó Muicheartaig.
"We send greetings to you all from Djakarta down to Crossmolina
And the ball goes to Kenneth Mortimer having a great game
    for Mayo
He has a brother doing research work on the Porcupine Bank
But now it goes to Killian Burns of Kerry
The best accordion-playing cornerback in football today."[53]

It would be perfectly possible to understand both Gaelic games and commentating upon these games in terms of the ongoing discursive reproduction of spaces of identity and difference. Yet to do so is to remain wedded to a critical analytical position in which responding to a sporting activity is curiously uninflected by the affective field of potential in which this activity takes place. Instead, the relation between commentating and Gaelic games is better approached through the conceptual logics of the refrain of the event as a block of spacetime whose ongoing return is also a potentially sensed differential repetition. Clearly, the refrain of these events is territorializing. The periodicity of the All-Ireland final is inscribed in the national imagined community: football, hurling, and camogie finals are held on the same weekends every September. Furthermore, these events are also central to the imagined and affective drawing and redrawing of boundaries between counties, and to the rehearsal of a certain version of muscular nationalism that celebrates athleticism — and, importantly, amateurism — as part of a genuine commitment to the cause. So, for instance, the finals are preceded by the ritual marching of both teams around the field in quasi-militaristic fashion:

> Go raibh míle a mhaith agat, and the excitement is just unbelievable, down at the sideline all the way up to our level here in the third level of the Hogan Stand for the 115th All-Ireland Football Final, the first played away back in 1887 in a field called "the bank" in Clonskeagh, the 115th about to be played in Páirc Ui Chrócaigh, Dublin, Ireland, on today, as Uachtarain na hÉireann, Máire Mhic Ghiolla Íosa she's completed the walk in front of both teams, introduced to the Kerry team by the captain Darragh O'Shea, and then by Ciarain McGeeney, the Armagh captain, to the men of Armagh, as the Artane Boys Band, senior and junior, they're lined up in front of the Hogan stand to the right of the tunnel facing the canal side of the ground and the canal stand in preparation for the parade that will take them right around the field for a game that is due to start at half past three.[54]

Such commentating is obviously territorializing, taking up and being taken up by lines of segmentarity, rehearsing quasi-mythical narratives of nation and belonging. And yet Ó Muircheartaigh's radio commentating upon these events is much more subtle than the rehearsal of a national narrative. For one thing, the atmospheric field of the national event is deliberately individualized in this commentating, precipitating around details of individual spectators or players:

> Four on the score board to Ard Mhacha agus ta ceithre Chuilini go Chiarraí, agus sin co-scoir in any language, well there's a man called Pat Hanaway from Lislee up in Armagh, he's over 80 years of age and I was told when I was up in Armagh he'd be unable to travel to the game but he would be listening, good wishes to Pat Hanaway, and somebody who has travelled and I already mentioned, the people that are in Malawi, I know we have people all over the country, there's a man here today from Sneem in county Kerry, Fionnain O'Shea, he's watching his 76th consecutive final if you omit the Polo ground final of 1937.

Furthermore, Ó Muircheartaigh's commentating also opens onto a distributed, diasporic space, wandering beyond the clearly defined boundaries of the national territory. To be fair, the deliberate addressing of this audience has been a quality of commentating on Gaelic games for decades. The ease with which this audience can access such commentating has, however, been improved by developments in broadcast technology, particularly through the Web. The result is that the audience addressed by commentating occupies neither the same geographic territory nor the same time zone as the game itself.

The lines of this style of commentating clearly go in many directions, taking up the rhythms of different affiliations and delineating involvement in the event as an affectively shared spacetime. Rather than thinking of this process solely in terms of the performative rehearsal of spaces of identity, it is also possible to think of it as the becoming vocal of expressive territories. As Ronald Bogue, drawing on Deleuze and Guattari, suggests, this becoming vocal is a matter of the refrain because just "as birds sing their territory, so do humans speak or sing theirs."[55] Territories, in this sense, populated as they are by refrains, are always generative of incipient tendencies toward deterritorialization. Commentating is one way in which these tendencies become sonorous through the rhythms of the voice that takes up and is taken up by these tendencies. This should not be taken as a claim that the individual voice is expressive of a territory. While the voice of each commentator is unique, commentating also involves the voice becoming a participant in the event as a spacetime composed of colors, affects, noises, and sounds. In this way, commentating involves a "becoming-molecular in which the voice itself is instrumentalised" as part of the refrain of territorialized relations that are always also potentially open.[56]

To think commentating thus is to understand its relation with the affective field in which it participates in ways that go beyond questions of representation: it is to affirm commentating as a technique through which the becoming expressive of moving bodies as a field of play is transmitted as a sensible atmosphere. Brian Massumi's discussion of soccer as a field of relations provides some further orientation here. For Massumi, who draws in turn upon Michel Serres, the field of play is not necessarily defined as a collection of players, bodies, subjects, or objects. It is understood in relational terms — composed of "*modulations*, local modifications of potential that globally reconfigure (affects)."[57] The "potential" to which Massumi refers is "the immanence *of* the substantial elements of the mix to their own continual modulation. The field of immanence is not the elements in mixture. It is their becoming."[58] This is not to say that the players do not exist in any meaningful or material way on the pitch: of course they do. Rather, for the purposes of understanding the logics of the affective event, what is important is the distributed field in whose transformation the movement between players is always actively participating. Nor is it to suggest that soccer, and other team sports like Gaelic football, are enacted in isolation from social and cultural processes: however, to take these processes as the point of departure for any analysis of a field of play, at least according to Massumi, is to fail to grasp this field as a space of relational variation defined by a range of generative constraints — the ball, the lines of the pitch, and so on. Clearly, the emergence of the GAA can undoubtedly be understood as an exercise in cultural and corporeal codification: it involved the drawing up of certain rules and regulations that gave nascent protogames a particular structure and pattern of organization. But these rules did more than discipline bodies or regulate their movements. They also acted to generate spacetimes with affective potentiality. Put another way, drawing up rules, marking out lines, and codifying movement generates fields of play with the future potential for creative variation in the relations of which these fields are composed.

In the case of major sporting events, this field of affective modulation does not take place in a vacuum. For one thing, it bleeds into and receives feedback from the movements and noises of spectators in a process that may be either mutually reinforcing or mutually dampening. It is also amplified by a distributed becoming expressive, sensed as blocks of color glimpsed on houses, on bodies, and in the stadium itself (the lily-white of Kildare, the black and amber of Kilkenny, the red and white of Cork). It also bleeds into other fields of affective potentiality — particularly the home — without any feedback, through a process of media transmission. In describing this process, Massumi, perhaps understandably, concentrates on television. And, as a result, his focus is on how media transmission serves to capture and contain the complexity of the affective field of play. As he puts it, "media transmission [involves] event transitivity. . . . In the media interval, the event is a material but incorporeal immanence (an electron flow) moving through a dedicated technological milieu. When it is analogically re-expressed in televisual images, its conditions have drastically changed. Its substantial elements have been homogenized and reduced to fit sound speaker and screen."[59]

Radio broadcast participates in this process of event transmission, but it does so in a subtly different way from television: the event is not defined by the frame of the screen, but continues to "occupy" a voluminous space of variable intensity that expands and contracts, a space composed of noise, sound, voice. Clearly, the activity of commentating might be taken as a practice that qualifies this space, rendering it meaningful in words. That is, it would be easy to think of commentating as a practice that contracts a field of relational modulation into words and phrases in a process that is essentially one of representational capture. Radio commentating needs to be understood more generously than this, however: not so much as a gap or a break between affective fields (the stadium and the home, for instance), but as itself part of an ongoing field of affective modulation that moves, corporeally and incorporeally, between bodies. Radio commentating is part of the expressive quality of this distributed field. Remember again that expression is not the preserve of the subject. The subject does not express this field: rather, subjects and indeed bodies are particular modifications of this field. As Massumi, following Deleuze and Guattari, observes, the "force of expression strikes the body first, directly and unmediatedly. It passes transformatively through the flesh before being instantiated in subject-positions subsumed by a system of power. Its immediate effect is a differing. . . . The body, fresh in the throes of expression, incarnates not an already-formed system but a modification — a change. Expression is an event."[60] What the commentator does first then is to sense this differing, through being moved by the ongoing modulation of an affective field.[61]

Commentating is more than a matter of being moved: it also involves the capacity to pass on affects through a process that Michel Serres calls semi-conducting.[62] For Serres, semiconducting is associated with the vertiginous sense of the onrush of the world, a condition in which "the noises of space, the colours of the world are coming towards me. I am plunged here and now in colours and noises to the point of dizziness. Here and now means that a flux of noises and colours is coming at me. I am a semiconductor, I admit it, I am the demon, I pull among the multiplicity of directions the direction that, from some upstream, comes at me."[63] Put another way, the commentator leans into the virtual potential of affective spacetimes, becoming open to the immanence of the field of play. In doing so, commentary also edges the experience of listening/hearing with a sense of the virtual.[64] If radio is no less affective than any other technology in its capacity to draw out the powers of the virtual, commentating exemplifies its possibilities in this respect with particular force. And it does so not by mediating or representing a particular event or state of affairs: it does so through an on-going leaning into the flow of activity (sometimes understood as an ability to 'read' the game). In this sense the commentator performs the liveness of affective modulation by operating upon the virtual cusp of the event, the surprising "more" that in James's terms is always arriving. To commentate is to produce a sense of the openness of the "edged halo of expectation and anticipation" that marks an occasion as "an occasion, that makes it stand out as eventful":[65]

> Right now, the ball by Colin Moran for Dublin, Colin Moran sends it down again blocked by Alan Brogan, he slips it about, he's got the ball, he's inside the 50, he hops it, he's still inside it, he's now outside it, a neat little ball over to the right hand side, the ball is kicked by Collie Moran, yet again the man has done it, it's gone over the bar again, Collie Moran, no run, no dance, one foot on the 50, the other swinging in the air made contact and sent the ball from the 50 yard line with the citeog over the bar, 1–5 to Dublin, 4 points to the Meath men, what a round of applause these teams will get when they move off the field.[66]

Drawing upon Serres then, we might say that the good — or affective — commentator is a semiconductor in at least two senses of the word: in an electrical sense and in a musical sense. In an electrical sense, what the commentator semiconducts is affective modulation. To commentate is to pass on the incorporeal event through bodies. And in a musical sense the commentator semiconducts refrains: that is, he allows territorial refrains to become sonorous. Rhythm is crucial to this capacity for semiconducting. Indeed, Serres's semiconductor is also a rhythmanalyst in the sense described by Lefebvre. He takes up and is taken up by rhythms through a range of senses. He listens. And yet he also does so from a particular vantage point. In this respect the commentary box in the stadium becomes the window described by Lefebvre or, more accurately, it can be understood as a balcony, a site in which it is possible to be situated inside and outside. And like the rhythmanalyst, who avoids "gloomy courtyards" and "deserted lawns," what the commentator craves is activity: a field of movement.[67] But the commentator also takes up rhythms in a way that goes beyond the immediacy of the field of play — commentating involves the articulation of territorial style. In the case of commentating on Gaelic games, the style of commentating emerges within the context of and draws upon oral traditions with particular territorial associations. As Mary O'Malley suggests, the roots of Gaelic games, particularly hurling, "are deep in the linguistic structure that underpins what has become known as hiberno-English. There is a synchronisation between the action of an All-Ireland final and the accent and expression of the commentator that is undeniable."[68]

Commentating is a matter of the refrain insofar as it allows accent to become musical, to wander from home on sonorous lines. Crucially, the refrain of commentating is not strictly continuous. It is sustained by a pause, a pause that, through repetition, also keeps things going. This is expressed through style. For instance, a key element of Ó Muircheartaigh's style is his repetition of the name, a repetition that functions almost like a breath, through which movement is expressed in the gap between its coming and going:

> Thomas O'Shea going up on the right on the 70 yard line near the Cusack Stand line, trying to, smart ball away down, block by Dara Ó Cinnéide on the 50 yard line, Dara Ó Cinnéide lets it out to the wing, now moving on now is Eoghan Brosnan, Eoghan Brosnan trying to get inside, the ball sent out the wing moving on now to Liam Hassett, Liam Hassett on the ground gets the ball now to Dara Ó Cinnéide, shot from Dara Ó Cinnéide out the field, the ball goes in, Mike Frank Russell sends it over the bar, Mike Frank the player, but a good move.[69]

The repetitive pause is the suspension that also reveals the movement of a field that can never be reduced to the actuality of an individual body or actor. The repetitive pause is the expression of modulation as excessive of and yet immanent to speech. The refrain of the pause is a minor syncope, in which differing is sensed via a momentary deindividualization.[70] It is precisely this repetition that allows Ó Muircheartaigh to work on the cusp of the event. As he speaks, that about which he speaks has already happened — just about — but is still playing out. His task is to heighten the anticipatory experience of this aboutness: to find ways of enlivening the actuality of the listener with the potential of what might happen, the potential of the not yet. And by doing so he keeps things on the move by amplifying the affects of movement in a field of relations. This is something more than verbal redescription, something more than a recounting of that which has already taken place. For Ó Muircheartaigh does not commentate upon bodies: rather, he conducts and amplifies — through words but also through tone, speed, and rhythm — the sense in which a kick, a movement, a pass, potentially modulates the entire event-space of the field of play.

Calling Time: The Refrain of Commentating Events

In one of the few substantive reflections upon the topic, Andrew Crisell defines commentating as "the improvised description or word-picture of an event." The commentator, as Crisell continues, "is the mere purveyor of actuality. He is as self-effacing as possible, his primary duty is to events rather than to the listener, he is interested only in what is happening 'out there.'"[71] Crisell is correct in his observation that the primary duty of the commentator is to events rather than to the listener, or, rather, that his duty is to respond to the event as an affective spacetime in which the listener is a vicarious participant. Crisell is incorrect, however, when he writes that the commentator is a "mere purveyor of actuality." The radio commentator may well be concerned with the relaying of details, but also draws out or infuses the actual with a sense of the potential of the event. Commentating involves taking up, and being taken up in, the rhythms and refrains of affective spacetimes: it relies upon the capacity to affect and become affected by the movement of bodies; and it is enacted as an ongoing elicitation of the virtual as the sensed anticipation of what might happen. In consequence, commentating becomes a process of semiconducting rather than a technique of representational conveyance: a transductive technique of affective event expression that takes place via "an openness of bodies . . . in direct . . . channelling . . . to each other and to what they are not — the incorporeality of the event."[72] And while commentators have distinctive personalities, they do not express the event from a personal point of view. Rather, if successful, they express the more-than-personal expressive qualities of the event. Put another way, the voice, the most personal of modes of expression, is effectively instrumentalized and depersonalized, crossing a threshold of consistency that allows it to become synonymous with the affects of the event. The voice, while remaining caught up in the rhythms of territories, ventures from home on the thread of a tune.

In moving toward a conclusion, it is worth speculating upon how the logics of commentating might provide one technique for grasping the qualities of affective spacetimes in ways that move beyond the limits of the postevent interview. Here it is helpful to return to the relation between poetry and commentating, a relation hinted at earlier. The work of another Irish poet, Louis MacNeice, is especially instructive in this regard. On one level, this is because MacNeice's poetry displays a keen awareness of how the relation between bodies and spaces is never reducible to the misplaced concreteness of the immediate actuality of either. For MacNeice, bodies and spaces are grasped only in their passing. On another level, MacNeice is interesting because he is acutely sensitive to the peculiar experience associated with listening to commentary. Writing of his time before joining the BBC, MacNeice recalls: "I rarely listened to anything except concerts and running commentaries on sports events. These latter . . . gave me a pleasure distinct from that which lies in *seeing* a game or race."[73] MacNeice's own oeuvre also reveals how poetry works as commentary upon things and events in passing. His "Autumn Journal," for instance, can be read in this way, as an extended commentary upon — and perhaps even critique of — the movement of the everyday. For MacNeice, the point of such poetic work is less about eavesdropping on "great presences" than about producing a sense of the experience of things as they happen through the "splash of words in passing."[74] And it is precisely because of this that his poetry draws our attention to the importance of the refrain as that through which difference is sensed in repetition. As Neil Corcoran writes, in much of MacNeice's poetry, repetition and refrain function in a way "sensitively mimetic of the mind in progress — self-scrutinising, self-corrective, advancing hesitantly but keeping moving — while also, of course, sustaining an ear-delighting system of aural patterning."[75] It is not just the mind in progress, however, that is found here: it is the ongoing worlding of experience of which MacNeice's verse speaks. His style allows us to grasp how the differential repetition of the refrain functions as commentary, and at a range of scales and intensities. The repetition of an event, a name, the ongoing repetition of *and, and, and*: all these minor techniques allow differencing to be sensed in the ongoing movement between listening, hearing, and voicing.

Like poetry, the refrain of commentating provides a way of thinking and moving beyond the logics of the sports reporter model of social scientific research. In some respects the commentator might be understood as a kind of witness: the figure of the commentator, like that of the witness, acknowledges the ineffable prospect of the affective event. Yet the commentator, perhaps more so than the witness, affirms the possibility of moving in fields of expression that are always beyond the individual. The significance of commentating in this respect is that it refuses to indulge in the nostalgic affect that characterizes so much talking and writing about performance as disappearance. The movement of the field in which commentating participates is certainly always being lost, as with any performance. Yet commentating does not dwell upon this ontology of disappearance.[76] Instead, it voices affective spacetimes as an ongoing field of modulation, in which new relations are always arriving at what James called the "chromatic fringes" of experience. Certainly, commentating is inadequately understood as the "improvised description or word-picture of an event." More generously, if also more modestly, it might be better understood as a techique for semi-conducting the affective modulations of a field of potential in ways that speak of the capacity to move and be moved by bodies at a distance.[77] It is a mistake then to say that commentating involves commentary upon an event: rather, we might think instead in terms of commentating events. These commentating events are constrained by certain techniques and conventions but do not presuppose a separation from the affective atmospheres in which they are participating. Through the practiced enactment of specific technical, vocal, and ethical modalities, these commentating events encourage a commitment to becoming taken up in the rhythms of the affective atmospheres generated through and for moving bodies.

CHAPTER SIX

Moving Images
for Moving Bodies

August 2007, and I am in Montreal at a research-creation event.[1] After
the event I have a day to spare before a flight back to the United Kingdom.
In the morning I gaze awhile at the St. Lawrence River, before taking the
opportunity to visit the Montreal Museum of Modern Art, where there is
temporary exhibition of work by Bruce Nauman, perhaps most famous for
his creation of politically charged neon sculptures and installations. Even if
such work is interesting, it is not the neon, clownlike figures that grab my
attention most. What draws me in is a short piece of video art, called *Dance
or Exercise on the Perimeter of a Square* (1967–1968), in which Nauman side-
steps repetitively around and within a small square in metronomic fashion.
I sit and watch Nauman doing this for a number of cycles, captivated by
how he is marking time, making space — how he is drawing out the movement potentialized when lines are drawn on the ground.

Perhaps watching this video amplifies a heightened mood of responsiveness emerging from participation in the research-creation event — that sense of ongoing agitation that unsettles thinking through time. Perhaps it makes me more open to the value of lingering a while. Perhaps it makes me wonder more about what moving images might do. So just before leaving the museum I also decide to check out a rather unheralded exhibition in a room just off the museum bookstore, an exhibition I had noticed on the way in but had dismissed as of little interest. It is described thus: "As part of the Projection Series, we are offering a new program of music videos this summer. Amazingly inventive in their concepts and images, music video artists are constantly coming up with new ways of doing things, redefining cinematic creation and enriching the visual arts as a whole."[2]

My first response to such claims is a degree of cynicism: music videos? I notice, however, that "Losing My Religion" by R.E.M. is on the list, and, because I have a fond memory of the minor scandal it caused in early 1990s Ireland, I decide to sit in on the exhibition and let the wave of nostalgia wash over me. But I come in at the wrong time in the looped sequence of videos to see "Losing My Religion." And so I sit and wait in a darkened projection room watching a series of videos, until at some point "Losing My Religion" appears on the screen. And, while recognizing aspects of its inventiveness, I find myself a little embarrassed by its overwrought, mock anguish. That was you in the corner, once. Time spent waiting for "Losing My Religion" is by no means wasted, however. I watch other videos: some dimly remembered, some new. They include the videos for Grace Jones's "Slave to the Rhythm," OK Go's "Here It Goes Again," Fatboy Slim's "Praise You,"[3] and Gary Jules and Michael Andrews's cover version of Tears for Fears' "Mad World." Each of these videos is remarkably different. But one of the qualities they share is an emphasis on the deliberate organization and choreographing of moving bodies. And it is the movements of these bodies resonating with the songs they accompany that holds me fast for a good hour: these images begin deflating my initial incredulity, improving my mood, and, in the process, generate more responsiveness to the claim, made in the introduction to the exhibition, that music videos are tremendously inventive. In the darkened auditorium the affects and rhythms of music videos begin to participate in the modulation of the sensibility through which thinking takes place.

HOW MIGHT ENCOUNTERS with moving images of moving bodies become occasions for experimenting experience in contemporary economies and ecologies of image making? In pursuing answers to these questions, this chapter begins with the claim, increasingly well elaborated across a number of disciplines, that moving images have a nonrepresentational quality: that is, to grasp their participation in the generation of experience means understanding them as more than merely symbols whose effect registers primarily through and within processes of cognitive sense making. Over the past decade or so, scholars in film studies, philosophy, cultural studies, and the social sciences have become increasingly skeptical of the ability of what might be called a critical-representational model to grasp the power and force of moving images.[4] In terms of this model, moving images of moving bodies are considered important because they present preferred representations of bodies, representations that are always shaped by and shape the wider social and cultural fields within which they are made, thereby participating in the reproduction and contestation of ideologically and discursively constituted identities.[5]

It is easy to see, however, that this approach has some important limits. It is inattentive to the affective force of images, or to the power of images that might reside at least partially in something other than a capacity to stand in the place of something else. As such, this approach tends to reinforce a conception of culture that, because it is primarily symbolic, can often downplay the material participation of affect and sensation in everyday spacetimes, ignoring the way in which this participation enfolds the rhythmic relations of bodies, generating in the process opportunities for sensing difference in the making. As figures such as Vivian Sobchack, Laura Marks, and Steven Shaviro have convincingly argued at various points over the past two decades, moving images work by engaging the materiality of affect, perception, and sensation as much as they do by presenting particular narratives or scripts.[6] A great deal of work by these and other scholars has focused on the analysis of cinematic images. And yet, as Steven Shaviro has recently argued, the kinds of images that participate in the generation of affective spacetimes in contemporary capitalist societies has become rather more complex than the term "cinematic" can capture.[7] For Shaviro, then, the affective map of the present needs to be understood in terms of what he calls "postcinematic" affect, in which images are not only representational, but are better understood, following Deleuze and Guattari, as circulating blocks of expressive and symptomatic affects. Shaviro goes on to trace some of the qualities of this structure of feeling through a number of short films and music videos. In the process, he places the analysis of moving images at the center of attempts to understand the generation and circulation of value across bodies, screens, and the media ecologies in which they participate.

In this chapter I take up Shaviro's invitation to map, or diagram, the contours of postcinematic affect as part of the project of experimenting experience through the spacetimes of moving bodies. Shaviro's key claim is that to understand how the contemporary feels, we need a differentiated sense of how moving images participate in the generation of value through the production and circulation of affects. As the preamble to this chapter suggests, the scope of my contribution to this mapping is simultaneously more constrained and more expansive than Shaviro's analysis. Constrained, because my focus is on moving images of moving bodies; expansive, because I also want to consider images such as idents and advertisements as part of these media ecologies. Admittedly, I am wary of the term "postcinematic": to my mind it is a little too redolent of a kind of epoch-defining shift akin to that of such equally problematic terms such as posthuman or postmodern. Even if it is not Shaviro's intention, this term is also suggestive of a move from an engagement with full-length cinematic experiences to other kinds of filmic experience, particularly those of a shorter duration. Instead, I take the point emerging from Shaviro's analysis to be the importance of examining moving images of different durations: by doing this, it might also be possible to trace the way in which affects circulate across and between different images, amplifying or dampening the intensities of each other as they do.[8] At the same time, it also remains important to return periodically to cinematic images in order to examine how they contain nascent elements of the processes Shaviro characterizes as postcinematic.

This chapter explores possibilities for experimenting experience opened up by the structure of feeling Shaviro invites us to map, without necessarily agreeing with the claim that this structure involves the superseding of one kind of image (or affect) by another. It pursues answers to the question of how the significance of experimenting with moving images might be understood in the context of media ecologies that seem to have an endless capacity to derive value from every minor deviation or detour. At stake here is how any such experiment is not reincorporated entirely into the processes it seeks to problematize. One way to complicate this incorporation is to attend to the excessive qualities of affect. While affect is a central object target of contemporary forms of biopower, it always moves in excess of the technologies of capture and modulation through which biopower operates.[9] Because of this, moving images can be mobilized to modulate affect while also providing opportunities for the generation of occasions where the excess of affect can overfill experience through a process of minor experiment. Grasping the potential of such occasions requires more than the rehearsal of critical reading as a strategy of decoding: it involves instead finding ways of differentially modulating the speeds and affective energies of images as they move in order to provide opportunities for allowing these energies to participate in thinking.

Image Refrains

In *Matter and Memory*, Henri Bergson writes: "Matter, in our view, is an aggregate of 'images.' And by 'image' we mean a certain existence which is more than that which the idealist calls a *representation*, but less than that which the realist calls a *thing*."[10] For Bergson, then, images have a material force without ever being reducible to the status of a kind of object. And Bergson goes further: bodies themselves are distinctive kinds of images, subsisting amid an aggregate of worldly images. In effect, Bergson argues that bodies do not produce representations of themselves but are more-than-representational images circulating within experience as a precognitive sensibility. And what distinguishes bodies from other images is their capacity to select certain images from the aggregate in which they find themselves. Or, as Mark Hansen has put it, the body as image is a kind of worldly framing, a center of generativity rather than something framed, as it were, from without.[11]

This Bergsonist sense of bodies as more-than-representational images can be allied usefully with certain readings of Spinoza. Spinoza, as Deleuze reminds us, defines the body in terms of its capacity to affect and be affected by other bodies.[12] Furthermore, like Bergson, Spinoza complicates any sense of what the relation between bodies and images might be. This is because for the latter, anything that affects something else is a body. To take this claim seriously is, therefore, to cleave to the view that an image can be an affective body. Moreover, as Deleuze also suggests, the affective capacities of moving bodies can be mapped in terms of the intensive movements — or "speeds and slownesses"— of which they are composed and the affects of which they are capable. This definition of bodies complicates a narrowly phenomenological understanding of the affective relation between bodies and images. Importantly, however, it does not make it impossible to speak of human bodies, nor does it imply that they should be reduced to a quasi-mechanistic physics of force in terms of which Spinoza's philosophy is often characterized. Instead, as Brian Massumi has suggested, reading Bergson with Spinoza attunes us to the way in which moving bodies are always opening onto an affective field of potential movement.[13] Crucially, allying Bergson with Spinoza does not lead thinking out of this world, nor does it precipitate a privileging of the virtual over the actual. Instead, it requires us to think of how bodies are composed through the transformative actualizations of virtualities.

If moving images are not so much static snapshots that mark a withdrawal from a world of movement, they might be better understood, in the words of Deleuze and Guattari, as refrains or ritornellos. As we have already seen, in general terms the refrain is a block of affective spacetime with a degree of expressive consistency that also opens onto an outside. While this concept is articulated at great length in A Thousand Plateaus, it is also something about which Guattari writes in an essay called "Ritornellos and Existential Affects."[14] There, he makes it clear that the refrain engages multiple registers: sensory, expressive, enunciative, problematic, facial, and visual.[15] In developing this claim, he uses the example of the religious icon. As he puts it, "The primary purposiveness of an Icon of the Orthodox Church is not to represent a Saint, but to open an enunciative territory for the faithful, allowing them to enter into direct communication with the Saint. The facial [refrain] then derives its intensity from its intervening as a shifter — in the sense of a 'scene changer' — in the heart of the palimpsest superimposing the existential territories of the proper body."[16]

It is worth remarking upon a number of aspects of Guattari's description of the icon. First, he is explicit about the fact that the primary role of this kind of image is not representational. Rather, it is pragmatic: it opens up a dynamic-affective spacetime, a sensory world or "enunciative territory" that the faithful can potentially inhabit. So the importance of the image is as much about how it functions to generate or produce an affective spacetime as it is about an ability to stand in the place of something or someone else. Second, Guattari is obviously writing here about a still image, one that is not animated or moving in a kinetic sense. But such images are also "moving" images: as he suggests, the image (still or otherwise) moves by seizing or shifting — affectively — the scene in which the body of the faithful is a participant. So while the affects of this scene may well be read as incorporeal — such as spiritual transformation — they are nevertheless felt and experienced as corporeal modulations. In turn, this means the power of the image is only really grasped through its capacity to produce or catalyze affective transformations in the bodies of those who inhabit its scene — a scene that has an atmospheric quality. These transformations may of course be expressed in various ways: through often highly choreographed movements of the body, through the refrain of vocal enunciation, or, indeed, through the generation of a distinctive affective tonality. Finally, Guattari's use of the example of the icon is also a reminder that the affective capacity of images is not something new, and certainly not something that begins with the invention of obviously moving images through technologies such as cinema. Instead, the question of how moving images work as participants in world making begins more properly with openness to the capacity of those images to seize or shift bodies affectively.[17]

Moving Images and Affective Value

Guattari was acutely aware of the need to think about how images participate in the production and transmission of affective spacetimes in which subjectivities are reproduced under contemporary cultural and economic conditions. He was particularly interested in the role that television plays in this regard. For Guattari, the spacetime of the televisual experience functions like a refrain that closes in on itself, becoming a strange attractor seizing subjectivities in a process of deathly repetition. As he puts it, "When I watch television I exist at the intersection: 1. of a perceptual fascination provoked by the screen's luminous animation which borders on the hypnotic, 2. of a captive relation with the narrative content of the program, associated with a lateral awareness of surrounding events (water boiling on the stove, a child's cry, the telephone . . .), 3. of a world of fantasms occupying my day dreams. . . . It's a question of the refrain that fixes me in front of the screen, henceforth constituted as a projective existential node."[18]

Such a critique of television is nothing new. But Guattari's description of the spacetime of image-based experience as a refrain offers some purchase on the wider ecologies of image making in which television exists. Drawing upon Guattari, Maurizio Lazzarato has developed this claim in an essay called "Struggle, Event, Media."[19] Lazzarato's point of departure is the following question: "Why can the paradigm of representation not function in politics, nor in artistic modes of expression, and here especially in the production of works that employ moving images?"[20] For Lazzarato, grasping the real power of the moving image in contemporary capitalist societies goes beyond a critique of representation, however forceful. Attention is also required to the productive element of moving images: that is, to how moving images generate potentially inhabitable worlds as part of the immaterial labor through which value is created. Indeed, for Lazzarato, the power of capitalism is not so much its ability to produce objects or subjects, but to generate the valued worlds in which they move.

As Alberto Toscano has commented, the moving image receives particular attention from Lazzarato "because of the manner in which it can be seen to affect the brain without necessarily passing through explicit forms of representation: in other words, modulating the brain without necessarily functioning as an object for the mind."[21] The televisual image, and one of its exemplars, the advertisement, crystallizes this process. For Lazzarato the ad is not a representation but an event. This event consists of two elements. The first element is an incorporeal transformation producing shifts in value and sensibility. The second element of the advertisement is its realization in the affective and gestural economies of bodies: that is, the ad insinuates itself in and through ways of moving, living, relating, and so on. Any number of these ads exist, but some are more up-front about the importance of their affective qualities than others. As an example, take the "Joy" series of BMW ads, the script of one of which, voiced by Patrick Stewart, runs as follows: "Joy: that's who we answer to. Joy is youthful. Joy inspires works of art. It is collectible, and shapes the future. Joy has a fan club, it's contagious and it can even be counted. Joy is efficient, dynamic and unstoppable. We realized a long time ago that what you make people feel is just as important as what you make. And at BMW we don't just make cars, we make joy."[22] In another of these ads, for the BMW Z4, a car traces lines of paint across a vast canvas, accompanied by the hand-drawn patterns and lines of the artist Robin Rhode. These ads might well be seen as an effort to soften the rather hard edge of the BMW brand, making it more appealing to the family market. Regardless of how effective they might be, what is most interesting about these ads is perhaps the way in which they are so explicit about their intention to open up a particular kind of affectively inhabitable world: that is, they attempt to rewrite the history of BMW as a corporation concerned as much with generating certain ways of feeling as with producing objects.

Indeed, after watching these ads, one is tempted to remark that if Spinoza had driven a car, it might well have been a BMW.

For Lazzarato, the power of advertisements like this lies not in how they convey beliefs or ideologies. Instead, they work through the disclosive power of the example: the example as the disclosure of a possible world inhabited as an affectively felt orientation to a minor future. Furthermore, the power of such ads is also imitative: they encourage a degree of imitation in those who inhabit their scene-shifting potential. They circulate, in part, through the practices of imitation outlined so perceptively in the writing of Gabriel Tarde.[23] And it is here that the concept of the refrain does some more work. As Lazzarato puts it, "the design of an advertisement, the concatenation and rhythm of the images, the soundtrack are organized like a kind of 'ritornello' or a 'whirlwind.' There are advertisements that reverberate in us like a musical theme or a refrain."[24] The BMW ad can be seen as a refrain that attempts to recompose or resingularize the signature that is BMW. Another and perhaps better way of illustrating this process is through television ads and programs targeted at children. Anyone who has spent time with children will know how easily they take up and are taken up by these refrains, how they love to imitate them, and how they look to you to participate in this process of imitation, whether by singing along, by buying merchandise, or by looking at a DVD. These are the potentially inhabitable worlds of the affective image, and the endless repetition of the infectious tunes that accompany children's television performs their imitative transmission. In the process, the target audience actively reproduces the very affective spacetimes it is encouraged to inhabit.

Lazzarato's argument is powerful and suggestive. It is limited, however, insofar as it concentrates on the (admittedly important) medium of the televisual image: it needs to be supplemented with attention to the contemporary media ecologies that extend beyond television screens.[25] As various commentators, including Steven Shaviro, have argued, the screen itself is being reworked as mobile space through which moving images participate in the distribution and transmission of affective refrains for moving bodies: such screen-spaces stretch across TV, mobile devices, and the electronic billboards that cover more and more contemporary consumer space. The images moving in this media ecology need not be labeled explicitly as advertisements, or certainly not as product-specific advertisements. But the mobility of these moving images is such that they have become one of the defining affective experience events of contemporary liberal capitalism.

This analysis might seem rather bleak: it suggests that moving images are effortlessly incorporated in media ecologies that reinforce capitalist economies of value. A different take on this might be to pose the question of how encounters with moving images might be affirmed as occasions for experimenting experience but in ways that offer the potential for modifying these processes of incorporation. The possibility of this resides in the fact that refrains are not closed in on themselves: they are always potentially generative of creative excess, of lines of flight. As Lazzarato suggests, "a different possible world is always virtually present. The bifurcation of divergent series haunts contemporary capitalism. Incompatible worlds unfold in the same world. For this reason, the capitalist process of appropriation is never closed in itself, but is instead always uncertain, unpredictable, open."[26] Of course, there is no guarantee that these possible worlds might not be reincorporated — capitalism has a remarkable capacity to extract value from minor deviations. Nevertheless, this claim also reminds us of the significance of attending to and foregrounding moments when another potentially inhabitable world — however minor — becomes palpable through the excess of affect. Attending to these moments also requires the modification of critical habits of thinking about images through attention to the excessive affective energies catalyzed by moving images.[27] As William Connolly has argued, an affirmative critique of moving images might be imagined as an ethico-political disposition informed by an awareness of how moving images are implicated in problematic processes while simultaneously responsive to the possibility that these images might offer spacetimes for experimenting with the different layers of experience, especially insofar as they foreground attachments and dispositions already subsisting in the visceral and affective fields from which this experience emerges.[28]

By way of example, think of Jane Bennett's analysis of GAP TV commercials. Bennett's discussion is particularly instructive because it highlights just what is at stake — affectively and critically — in the effort to make more of moving images of moving bodies.[29] For Bennett, the moving bodies of the GAP ad draw our attention to and exemplify a condition of enchantment as a "mixed bodily state of joy and disturbance, a transitory sensuous condition dense and intense enough to stop you in your tracks and toss you onto new terrain, to move you from the actual world to its virtual possibilities."[30] The moving bodies of GAP ads have this potential insofar as they can catalyze affective refrains that resonate through thinking in a way that makes the distinction between critique and affirmation difficult to sustain. Crucially, the point Bennett is making here is not that critical thinking is suspended when looking at such ads; rather, in order to really appreciate what is going on when bodies sing and sway, even as part of the business of selling, the more acidic, judgmental tendencies of thinking in which demystification is primary need to be moderated.

Moving Images of Dancing Bodies

Bennett's analysis also serves as a useful example insofar as it addresses specific genres of moving image: those figuring the moving body in obvious ways as part of the articulation of a contemporary affective-kinesthetic structure of feeling that privileges the experience of movement.[31] This structure of feeling is, of course, not specific to the early twenty-first century. Its emergence can be traced through the development of the rhythmic kinesthetic outlined in chapter 2 and, more specifically, through attempts in the mid- to late nineteenth century to design practical technologies through which to explore the dynamic relations between moving images and moving bodies. Early efforts by Marey and Muybridge to capture movement through photo-chronographic techniques, for instance, were centered on the moving body as the object of analysis and vehicle for experimenting with moving images. The same can be said of early developments in cinema. Here is not the place to review or rehearse this history: it is enough to focus on the contemporary expression of this kinesthetic through particular kinds of moving images of moving bodies in order to outline briefly a diagram of their participation in the structure of feeling that Shaviro calls postcinematic affect.

One way to think of this diagram is in terms of moving images of insufficient length for the development of a sustained narrative, and in which the organized choreography of moving bodies takes precedence over dialogue. The best way to demonstrate this kind of image refrain is to exemplify it in a number of ways. The first and perhaps most obvious example is the music video. Often identified with late twentieth-century popular culture, the music video goes back in origin at least a century if a broader view of the relation between music and moving images is taken. Certainly, experiments using images to accompany the performance of music is something that began in the early twentieth century. The promotional film was also frequently used to accompany the release of songs throughout the latter half of the twentieth century. It was only in the early 1980s, with the emergence of networks such as MTV and VH1, that the music video became a crucial element of contemporary popular culture. Perhaps because it coincided with an engagement of elements of postmodern thinking, this popularity was understood initially within the social sciences and humanities through the lens of a critique that focused largely upon decoding text and symbols or, relatedly, on the role of the music video as a marketing tool in the commercial circuits of the entertainment business.[32] But the music video can better be understood in terms of the becoming musical of the televisual medium: that is, the point at which the affective capacity of television is more fully realized through the inventive choreography of sound, image, and moving bodies on screen. In these terms, music videos are understood as expanding the "spacious universe of affective possibilities surrounding a song," allowing television to became a more effective medium for producing refrains for moving bodies as affective image-events.[33]

As Michael Jackson's relationship with Pepsi demonstrated, the music video soon became indistinguishable from a second example of the images diagrammed here: the TV ad. Television-based ads featuring moving bodies are of course very common, but they can be usefully differentiated further. There are those, for instance, that play upon the choreographed fusion of bodies and technology in the production of joyous experiences, with the BMW ad being a case in point. Another example of this kind of ad was made for the Citroen C4 Hatchback. Produced by the London-based RSCG agency, it features a C4 that transforms into a dancing robot, all to the accompaniment of "Jack Your Body" by Les Rythmes Digitales. The movement of the robot is based upon a dance sequence developed by Justin Timberlake's choreographer, Marty Kudelka. Then there are those ads that play upon the dynamic relations between bodies and particular locations in such a way as to highlight the affective experience of being and becoming mobile in certain spaces. Consider, for instance, "Wrapshear," made by the California-based company Motion Theory for Reebok. It features a young man freerunning through a city constantly reconstructing itself and, in doing so, produces a video image in which transformations of the city, the brand, and the self seem to become indistinguishable. And there are those ads that foreground the durational experience of movement. Consider, for instance, the 1994 "Anticipation" ad, made for Guinness, in which a man appears to spontaneously invent a frantic dance while waiting for a pint of Guinness to settle. Guinness ads have often played — spectacularly — upon the experience of waiting and anticipation. More than this, their ads can be seen as deliberate efforts to animate, or create virtual memories for, the lost time of the experience of waiting.

An important element of the success of the "Anticipation" ad was the degree to which it prompted imitation. More generally, however, the imitative power of these ads is no longer restricted to television. It is also facilitated by Internet-based file-sharing platforms such as YouTube and by a range of mobile telecommunication devices. For instance, a 2009 ad for T-Mobile featured around 400 people appearing to burst spontaneously into dance in London's Liverpool Street Station. In February 2009, the station was forced to close temporarily as up to 12,000 people participated in the Liverpool Street Station Silent Dance in the same venue, imitating and parodying the T-Mobile ad. The latter event, of course, generated its own circulating refrains on countless screens. As such, it points to a third kind of image-event, one that can be co-opted by advertising but is not originally intended as such: the gratuitous, noncommercial dance-based video clip distributed on file-sharing websites. These video clips can feature individuals performing quirky or funny dance routines, or they can document collective events of movement including, for instance, so-called silent discos.

A fourth kind of image is the TV ident — those sequences used by networks to occupy the interval between programs. One of the most notable series of these idents in the United Kingdom ran from 2002 until 2006 on the BBC under the heading of "Rhythm and Movement." Each ident featured a different style of movement, from capoeira to ballet to tango. While apparently unpopular, the ident resonated with the reemergence of interest in the spectacle of dance in the United Kingdom, which is exemplified in the popularity of dance-based competitions broadcast on mainstream TV. A fifth and final type of moving image is the video game. While earlier commentary upon the video game tended to focus on how it rendered the body redundant, with all kinds of physical and moral implications, this position is increasingly difficult to sustain. Video games affectively engage the entire body, even among people who are merely observing others play.[34] And we know that video games are transforming in ways that demand active participation, with rhythm action games such as Dance Dance Revolution and Wii Fit being the most obvious, if somewhat dated, examples.[35]

Clearly, the examples just presented do not neatly add up to reveal a hidden ideological structure or discursive formation. Instead, they might be better understood as image refrains that participate in the production and circulation of the distinctive affective kinesthetic that Shaviro terms postcinematic. In this affective kinesthetic, the relation between moving images and moving bodies is a mutually constitutive one. Certainly, the moving images identified above do not just represent moving bodies — they generate circulating affective spacetimes that have the potential to affect other bodies. Furthermore, this process takes place and is enacted across a distributed screen space, in which, for instance, TV ads become available on the Internet and are played on portable media or communication devices. The process here is not best conceived as intertextuality: it is about the capacity of kinesthetic affects to flow between bodies, with those bodies acting as active relays in the flow.

OK Go

The videos shown as part of the Projection Series in Montreal can be situated squarely within this diagram of postcinematic kinesthetic affects.[36] For one reason or another, as I watched it in that darkened projection room, one of them stood out. It featured the four members of a band called OK Go performing a highly choreographed dance routine on exercise treadmills. Read through the terms of Guattari and Lazzarato, this music video can be understood as a kind of scene-shifting refrain — it has the capacity to move, to transport, by modifying the affective spacetimes of bodies. Clearly, this is most intense during the approximately three and a half minutes' running time, but it resounds beyond this measured time. And so it is not difficult to imagine how it might continue to circulate in thinking after the moment of watching.

On returning home I follow OK Go, dancing on the treadmills, through iTunes and YouTube. I am taken by the treadmill video. I have written about fitness machines before, but have never imagined they might be used in this way.[37] Treadmills, perhaps more so than other fitness technologies, seem to crystalize an image of the laboring body objectified, controlled, and regulated by technology according to the rhythms of capitalist temporalities. They symbolize the contraction of movement-space into a relentless, on-the-spot mobility for purely productive, self-serving ends. They foreground the embodied self as a project motivated by the dream of a healthier, happier, more well-toned you. As such, the treadmill is a technological platform for the reproduction of a diagram of fitness as a valued attribute of the biopolitical subject within forms of capitalism. In this diagram, effort is individualized to encourage the formation of more active consumer subjects that sustain the more general activity of capital-life across populations. It is easy, then, to read fitness machines and those using them as self-governing relays in the biopolitical assemblages of what Tim Luke has called "cyborg ecologies."[38]

As Felicia McCarren has demonstrated, there is a long tradition of choreographic fascination and experiment with technologies that, on the face of it, would seem to render the excessive expressiveness of dance redundant in favor of an economy of efficiency.[39] For instance, it was precisely the possibility of making industrial movement more efficient that motivated choreographer Rudolf Laban's study of effort. By decomposing effort, it would be possible, argued Laban, to choreograph movement in ways that eliminated extraneous or redundant efforts. It would also allow the body of the worker to move more efficiently within industrial machines.[40] In this context, the dancing machine occupies a rather ambiguous position, symptomatic of mechanization while also offering a way of developing a "critique of mechanization or its idealization, the staccato movement of bodies with machines or the stylization of their hybrid potential."[41] At the very least, then, the video for "Here It Goes Again" rehearses a tradition of choreographing hybrid or cyborg relations between bodies and machines. Indeed, read generously, it seems a remarkably inventive way of choreographing bodies using a technology often associated with repetitive, disciplined movement: an exuberant, if also gently subversive, take on the imperative to become fit through the development of intimate relations with technology. Read more critically, it celebrates and reproduces capitalist economies that endlessly generate value through emphasizing the importance of working upon and activating affective kinesthetic experience. The afterlife of this video is very instructive: its success generated a strange alliance between OK Go, iTunes, and Nike, in which the former supplied a thirty-minute soundtrack for a treadmill workout. The workout begins like this: "This is Damian Kulash from OK Go, and I'll be your coach for this Nike treadmill speed workout. Let's cut right to the chase — I am a treadmill God and you, well you are not. Luckily however I can help you with this. I can't promise you'll be ice-skating on that thing nor vaulting over it but at least we can work on your speed, your stamina, and your general fitness. The workout will be an alternating thing — you'll speed up, you'll slow down and I'll tell you when. So, to begin . . ."[42] In the process, the refrain of the video image "Here It Goes Again" becomes part of the field of refrains ("Just do it," the "swoosh," "Niketown," etc.) of which Nike is affectively and kinesthetically composed, resonating with Nike's investment in both "the depth of perception that is a person's bodily, affective memory and the cultural history of the perceptual mechanics of motion — the techno-artistic conceptions of speed and movement."[43]

Some months later I see a variation on this video used as part of the ad campaign for a heath supplement called Berocca, marketed on the basis that it provides a "hit of vitamins and minerals to help you have the best day possible. That sort of day when you catch that early train, make the lights, snatch the last parking space, get the phone number, nab the last one on sale, and score from your own half."[44] In the ad, four treadmills are located at a city intersection. Four passersby see the treadmills and begin to use them in a way that reprises the choreographed routine of OK Go's "Here It Goes Again," drawing a crowd in the process. It is easy, then, to see how the inventiveness of the OK Go video begins to circulate in a wider assemblage of techniques and technologies designed to produce distinctive spacetimes of experience in contemporary life. Furthermore, as OK Go's alliance with Nike and iTunes suggests, it is very easy for such refrains to be mobilized in efforts to generate and cultivate certain propensities to act-work-consume as part of what Friedrich von Borries calls a "corporate situationism."[45] In some respects, then, the video for "Here It Goes Again" might be understood as an exemplar of one of the many refrains of and through which contemporary biopolitical economies reproduce and resingularize themselves, generating attention, value, and interest in the process. The experience of viewing it might well become part of the process through which existential territories — or subjectivities — become circumscribed by the affects of the screen, "reframed in terms of both its (increasingly capitalized) sub-representational, bodily and biological dimension and of its abstract participation in machinic assemblages of enunciation, technological dispositifs and informational circuits."[46]

Any initial enthusiasm for the "Here It Goes Again" video might therefore be dampened and modified such that a different affect emerges: disappointment. The alliance between OK Go and Nike might be taken as evidence of a certain selling out, of a deliberate complicity with a range of contemporary biopolitical regimes designed to engineer the fit and healthy self. It may be that a moment of inventiveness has been reincorporated into a system of corporeal and affective capital-value. But any critical disappointment that emerged could still be interrupted periodically by the exuberant affirmative energies of the movement of the video every time it is viewed. And so, understood thus, it might be possible work to rebalance that initial response to OK Go on the treadmills. Clearly, it is implicated in the production and reproduction of certain kinetic imperatives; it also exemplifies, however, a certain inventiveness with respect to the relation between bodies and machines. In keeping this inventiveness front and center, even the most constraining machines — in this case treadmills — might become platforms for experimenting with the affective excess of moving bodies. And in this way video images such as "Here It Goes Again" might become refrains for opening up other potentially inhabitable worlds.

Odd Coupling

How, then, to pursue this possibility as part of the cultivation of an affirmative critique of moving images of moving bodies? One way might be to juxtapose different image refrains, not so much to complicate their meanings as to modify their affective energies. It might be possible to do this by juxtaposing "Here It Goes Again" with a range of other images of moving bodies that circulate through the diagram of postcinematic affect. In my case, this possibility emerges — unintentionally — during encounters with older films that feature moving bodies. While these films might not be immediately sensed as postcinematic, subsisting with their narratively structured cinematic experiences are images with the postcinematic affects of which Shaviro writes. Indeed, as film theorist Amy Herzog has argued, "looking even at the most hackneyed, clichéd films, the attentive, inventive thinker might see within their stutterings and pauses waves of affect that move against the prevailing current."[47]

Consider, for instance, some of the films that I sometimes watch as a form of affective self-modulation: that is, I watch them in the same way I might listen to a favorite track on a long-loved album. Among such films are some by Stan Laurel and Oliver Hardy. As a comedy duo Laurel and Hardy are interesting in many ways, not least because they exemplify a tradition of odd couples and strange attractors across a range of cultural practices and performances.[48] Equally, Laurel and Hardy can be conceived of as an affective complex composed of multiple refrains that have crossed what Guattari calls a "threshold of consistency": that playground jingle introduction; Stan running his fingers through his hair while puckering his face and whimpering; Ollie's face as he turns toward the camera with a look of knowing exasperation—can you believe this guy? And, of course, Ollie declaring, "That's another nice mess you've gotten me into." These refrains cohere, hold together, without necessarily precipitating a held, an object. And each of these elements, even if encountered in isolation, functions as a catalytic trigger for the affective complex that is Laurel and Hardy, in the same way that the swoosh functions as a trigger for the affective complex that is Nike, a light saber for *Star Wars*, and "Feck" for *Father Ted*. Furthermore, this affective complex is composed of other refrains that have come to circulate beyond their positioning within the narrative structures of feature-length cinematic adventures. Two scenes from *Way Out West* (1937), one of Laurel and Hardy's most famous films, are exemplary in this respect. The plot, as in all their films, is straightforward. Our two heroes are charged with the task of delivering to a young woman in a Western town the deeds to a lucrative goldmine that she has (unknowingly) inherited. Just before Stan and Ollie can complete this task, they are tricked into handing the deeds over to the wrong person. They spend the rest of the film trying to return them to their rightful owner. Along the way they have various mishaps, adventures, and awkward encounters.

The film features two equally famous scenes, each of which has post-cinematic tendencies. The first takes place shortly after Laurel and Hardy arrive in the town. After an angry confrontation with one of the locals, Stan and Ollie walk up to a saloon, on the steps of which a band is playing. As they watch the band, they both begin to sway, ever so slightly, before beginning to dance in unison, a dance that gradually becomes more elaborate, ending with a final flourish as they enter the saloon. The second scene comes a little later, as Stan and Ollie wait at the bar. Overhearing the musicians outside, they begin to sing the words to "The Trail of the Lonesome Pine," with Stan's voice shifting dramatically from low to high pitch midway through their rendition. These scenes add nothing to the narrative and were not in the original script. But it is precisely the gratuitous and gently interruptive quality of their affective duration that has allowed both scenes to circulate in a way that the films within which they were originally produced cannot. They have a mobility that is transversal to the narrative structures within which they sit. And because of this mobility, they are particularly interesting examples of refrains that move in ways that anticipate the qualities of the postcinematic diagram outlined by Shaviro.

Indeed, both scenes can be understood as prototypical music videos. More accurately, they can be situated within a long tradition, traceable through the twentieth century, of combining music with images in order to expand the affective spacetimes of both. This tradition, and its many formats, can easily be dismissed insofar as it seems to offer little in the way of critical commentary upon the social or political conditions in which it was made. In this respect, Laurel and Hardy can sometimes suffer in comparison with other stars of the earlier decades of popular cinema, especially Charlie Chaplin, who, as Henri Lefebvre observed, offered a critique of capitalism by providing encounters with its "reverse-image": "an image of everyday reality, taken in its totality or as a fragment, reflecting that reality in all its depth through people, ideas and things which are apparently quite different from everyday experience, and therefore exceptional, deviant, abnormal."[49] It is Chaplin who, in *Modern Times*, demonstrates how the affective body is caught up in the machinic choreographies of capitalism. If Laurel and Hardy do anything approximating this, it is in a watered-down, derivative manner. They can hardly be deployed as figures of critical resistance in the same way that Lefebvre deploys Chaplin. Furthermore, they are not nearly as inventive or original as, say, Buster Keaton. It is not in terms of critique or originality that Laurel and Hardy should be judged, however. Instead, perhaps it is in terms of their affective capacity: that is, their capacity to affect and be affected by the movement of other bodies in a way that is excessive of any straightforward political reading. Both clips outlined here exemplify this. In these scenes, what Stan and Ollie do is demonstrate the capacity to take up and be taken up by rhythms, to be moved by the affective modulations of music, to wander from home on the thread of a tune. And what both clips also produce are affective energies that have the potential to move in a similar way to more recent moving images such as music videos or file-shared clips.

Experimenting Refrains for Moving Images

Two moving images, two blocks of spacetime, multiple refrains: OK Go on the treadmills and Laurel and Hardy dancing in front of a saloon. How to experiment with these moving images in ways that foreground their affective energies as much as their complicity with various discursive or representational practices? It is one thing to let waves of affect-imbued images wash over you, and to allow them to modulate the sensibility through which thinking takes place. Such active passivity is an important element of the cultivation of an affirmative critique. But it might also be possible to go beyond this, to work more actively with the affective energies of image refrains. How then to contribute to an affirmative critique that, with respect to the moving image, "uses it, manipulates it, edits it in order to generate situations, instead of contemplating or merely watching it"?[50]

Consider, then, the following scenario. You receive an invitation to present a research seminar. You decide to use the occasion as an opportunity to gather together ideas about how moving images of moving bodies might afford opportunities for experimenting experience. Initially you think that both scenes just discussed might be useful in illustrating how moving images work as affective refrains, how they work with and against one another. And you choreograph a presentation, playing around with the sequence of slides in ways that might help you demonstrate your point. And at some point you may wonder what might happen if you played the music from one refrain over the images of another. And so you juxtapose the visual scene-shifting refrain of OK Go on the treadmills and the soundtrack that accompanies Laurel and Hardy's dance scene. You play the OK Go video with the volume turned down and instead turn up the sound on Laurel and Hardy. And what you get is a modified affective refrain whose constructive interference links the pratfalls of the music hall with those of the contemporary music video. With the help of Laurel and Hardy, OK Go slow down, no longer so expressive of a powered-up kinetic capitalism. A gentle interruption modifies the affects of both clips, producing a subtle variation in a minor refrain, a modest event of scene shifting.

Why do this? On one level, to throw into sharp relief the particular role that moving images play in the knowledge practices and events of academic knowledge. Intervening in the rhythms and affects of these events might provide ways of reworking the act of presentation as a process of experience and experiment. Presenting a presentation is a way of experimenting experience as much as anything else: as valuable and as potentially powerful a technique for thinking with images as watching or making a film. So experimenting with moving images might generate minor complications in the presentational economies of academic knowledge and pedagogical practice insofar as it foregrounds the refrain of experience as something always in the making. In the process, it opens up the image such that it generates opportunities to become more attuned to the role that affect and perception play in the process of thinking. As Alberto Toscano, following Lazzarato, writes, to experiment in this way is valuable precisely because "working in real time on the matter of perception — delaying, contracting, accelerating — translates fluxes inaccessible to human perception into images, but in turn also allows human agents access to aesthetic dimensions hitherto unavailable for manipulation."[51]

On another level, and second, such modest experiments draw attention to the wider processes through which refrains get mixed up and modified in all kinds of ways across a range of screens. Indeed, a search on YouTube for *Way Out West* throws up a myriad of such experiments with this refrain. It is accompanied by, among others, Soft Cell's "Tainted Love," Santana's "Oye Como Va," and the Gap Band's "Party Train." These videos do more than modify the meaning of images or sounds. They resingularize refrains, and rework the affective materials of which these refrains are composed. Running refrains together is a matter of exploring how the rhythms and affective energies of one modify those of another and how in the process a new refrain might emerge. This process, to be sure, is caught up in the techniques of imitation about which Lazzarato, drawing upon Gabriel Tarde, writes. But it is also a matter of invention insofar as it is about adapting forces and combining them with others in order that both are modulated.[52]

In turn and third, this opens up opportunities for intervening in the contemporary affective economies of which Guattari and Lazzarato write. As they both suggest, refrains are never closed in on themselves. They always open other potential worlds. The inventive production, or what Isabelle Stengers calls the "fabrication," of these refrains can be understood as part of the work needed to resingularize the affective spacetimes of contemporary biopolitical life.[53] In this respect the work of critique might be more powerful if allied with affective refrains that have the capacity to scene shift by modulating and modifying moods, affects, feelings, and emotions. The wager here is that the affective refrain of one register of experience and experiment can fold into and inflect the other as part of an ecology of practices composed of multiple refrains, some of which work, some of which don't; some of which cross a threshold of consistency, some of which don't. This ecology is underpinned by what Guattari calls an ethico-aesthetic: an affirmative disposition toward the potential of experience and experiment. What makes this disposition aesthetic is that it engages matters of expression across ecologies of practice (actual and virtual). Any number of obviously "aesthetic" practices can provide opportunities for catalyzing such refrains: literature, art, cinema, dance. Regardless of the source, the trick is not to be exclusive: aesthetic does not here name a threshold of judgment above or over which practices need to cross. It refers, rather, to a certain kind of organization of expressivity, one that is never only a matter of individual self-creation. So an ethico-aesthetic sensibility refuses the tendency for judgment — or taste — to work as a kind of somatic marker: a memory-imbued disposition to foreclose generosity toward other practices. Nor does it necessarily cringe or wince at country music, line dancing, Cajun dancing, river dancing, corn, or treadmill running.[54] And this sensibility is ethical, in the sense that it provides not tools or guidelines for living but opportunities for the generation of novel refrains through an ongoing process of experiment.

Another Fine Mess

In *Difference and Repetition*, Gilles Deleuze writes that the "conditions of a true critique and a true creation are the same: the destruction of an image of thought which presupposes itself and the genesis of the act of thinking in thought itself."[55] Influenced in part by Deleuze, much has been written about the destruction and failure of a representational image of thought in Western philosophy and culture. Yet as Deleuze's own work suggests, to engage in a critique of this image of thought is not to claim that we no longer need to or indeed that we cannot think about and with images. His point, one also made by Bergson, is that we need to rethink the question of how images — as blocks of spacetime — participate in the materiality of thinking. To foreground the affective dimensions of experience does not so much involve the acidic dismissal of images as it reconfigures the terms of their use: it is about thinking through how moving images are participants in the experiential tissue of a world that moves us before we ever have time to affirm its presence through representational modes of thought. Clearly, moving images fail to capture movement — this failure is inevitable. But this does not preclude affirming the necessity of the manipulation and modification of moving images as affective refrains: refrains that circulate as alluring spacetimes.

The success of any experiment involving running two refrains together might not necessarily be the degree to which it critically subverts codified meanings. It is also about how far this effort succeeds in "determining an agreement between forces not by the means of a *mediation* or *convention* but by establishing a *new plane of immanence* where the forces co-produce new 'modulations' of their relations and discover a 'way not yet paved' that permits them to use themselves reciprocally."[56] Deleuze and Guattari knew the value of this style of thinking as part of the process of sensing difference differing.[57] So, in their own way, did Stan and Ollie.[58] The second of these odd couples reveal as much in another of their films, *The Flying Deuces* (1939). In that film they attempt a reprise of the kind of dance scene featured in *Way Out West*, albeit with less success. Earlier in the film, however, they remind us that the affective spacetimes in which moving images participate never close in on themselves: they also have the capacity to disclose the inventive potential of difference in repetition. The scene finds Stan and Ollie in Paris, on the banks of the Seine. Having been rejected by a woman with whom he had become infatuated, Ollie is about to end it all by jumping into the river. He has roped (metaphorically and literally) Stan into this act, arguing that his companion could not possibly want to go on without him. Stan seems convinced. They say their goodbyes, but just as they are about to jump, Stan interrupts:

STAN: Ollie?

OLLIE: What?

STAN: I just thought of something. Listen, do you remember once you were telling me that when we passed away we'd come back on this earth in some other form? Like a bird or a dog or horse or something?

OLLIE: Oh you mean reincarnation.

STAN: Yeah, yeah, that's it. Well, now that we're going to go, what would you like to be when you come back?

OLLIE: I don't know, I've never given it much thought. [Pauses] I like horses. I guess I'd like to come back as a horse. What would you like to be when you come back?

STAN: Oh I'd rather come back as my self. I always got along swell with me.

OLLIE: [Exasperated] You can't come back as yourself. Now come on, and stop wasting my time![59]

You can never come back as yourself. Not just in any life to follow, whatever that might be, but in this life, with all of its variations. As Maurizio Lazzarato suggests, "to exist means to differ," and this differentiation is "newly uncertain, unpredictable and risky each time."[60] Of course it is possible to overdo this claim, to celebrate differentiation as a given. The point here, however, is to affirm the possibility of participating in the generation of difference such that it complicates problematic tendencies in contemporary forms of life. Moving images participate in these forms of life. They can, admittedly, capture difference within the territorializing power of refrains that reinforce certain values. But such capture is never complete. As the kinds of image refrains discussed in this chapter exemplify, moving images can provide sources for sensing and amplifying the affects of the contemporary kinesthetic structure of feeling, and in ways that might disclose possibilities for modulating and modifying these affects anew.

CHAPTER SEVEN

Choreographing Lived
Abstractions

How, and in what ways, should the relation between abstraction, space, and moving bodies best be understood? It is not unfair to say that answers to this question within the social sciences and humanities have for the most part tended to cast abstraction as something that works against the critical or creative apprehension of the lived, affective spacetimes of moving bodies. That is, abstraction has often been understood as both a process and device through which the differentiated meaning and lively materialities of moving bodies are incorporated within philosophical, technical, and political frameworks that reduce and constrain this difference and life.

The charges leveled against abstraction in this regard are by now reasonably well rehearsed. Most obviously perhaps, abstraction is often framed as an epistemological process through which the rational mind, facilitated by the terms of the Cartesian mind-body split, withdraws itself from the lively, chaotic, and unpredictable energies of the sensate world in order to better understand this world from a distance. Here, abstraction becomes synonymous with the elision and denigration — in thought at least — of lived corporeal difference.[1] That is, abstraction figures as a central cornerstone of a philosophical and sociopolitical tradition that allows the recognition of difference only to the extent that a range of bodies — female, insane, nonwhite, and so on — are perceived to have the capacity to undertake abstract thinking. The position of abstraction is downgraded further when it is considered as a generalized set of techniques of alienation existing beyond philosophical thinking: that is, when understood through the myriad practices by which subjects come to understand themselves as necessarily distanced from the immediacy of their lived, embodied, and affective experience in different spheres of life.

Abstraction has also been subject to critique insofar as it underpins the production and distribution of particular models of bodily regulation and comportment that, having been separated from lived experience, are then used to generate practices and technologies through which to harness the surplus energetic value of real, fleshy bodies in multiple contexts. Put another way, the same modes of thinking that allowed Descartes to conduct hypothetical experiments in self-mutilation in support of his philosophical arguments also allow the affective energies of bodies to be captured and mobilized to productive ends, most obviously through time and motion studies applied to industrial and ergonomic systems.[2] In short then, abstraction has become a placeholder for a more general critique of certain aspects of Western thought and political life including, but not limited to, disembodied habits of thinking, techniques of value generation through alienation, and a failure to recognize the lived reality of everyday corporeal difference as it is experienced.[3]

This critique of abstraction continues to provide purchase on a range of aspects of contemporary life. But what remains of abstraction for thinking in the wake of this critique? More specifically, how, and in what ways, does it remain possible to affirm abstraction, albeit in a qualified manner, as part of the process of thinking through and experimenting with the affective spacetimes of moving bodies? This chapter explores answers to this question by examining the role abstraction plays in choreographic techniques and technologies, the aim of which is to sensitize bodies to their capacities for movement and to facilitate experiment with this movement.[4] Encounters with these choreographic techniques and technologies can encourage the development of a differentiated sense of abstraction that refuses to allow some of the acknowledged problems with abstraction to prevent its cautious affirmation in certain relation-specific contexts as something that provides opportunities for making more, not less, of the affective capacities of moving bodies.

Thinking Through Abstraction

Where then to begin thinking through abstraction, space, and moving bodies in ways that open up possibilities for affirming the relations between these terms? A particularly providential point of departure in this regard is the writing of Henri Lefebvre. And this is not least because of Lefebvre's interest in the centrality of bodies in Western philosophical, political, and cultural conceptions of space. Particularly in his later work, Lefebvre repeatedly claims that bodies do not simply occupy space in a passive manner — instead, spaces and bodies are actively produced together in a generative relation. There is, then, an "immediate relationship between the body and its space."[5] As he puts it, "each living body *is* space and *has* its space: it produces itself in space and it also produces that space. This is a truly remarkable relationship: the body with the energies at its disposal, the living body, creates or produces its own space."[6] Clearly, by space Lefebvre does not just mean some three-dimensional Euclidean container for the body, but an animated, affective field of modulation. Admittedly, at various points in his writing Lefebvre would seem to suggest that the spacetimes of everyday life are generated from within bodies where the latter are discrete, already existing entities separate from the spaces within which they move: in this respect it is worth recalling that bodies, for Lefebvre, are always composed of rhythms, and these rhythms interact in ways that give a certain consistency to the spacetimes of bodies. So, read generously, for Lefebvre neither bodies nor spaces are already given in advance of one another but are matters in generative co-formation.

It is in this context that Lefebvre's critique of abstraction, and particularly his claims about abstraction in *The Production of Space*, must be understood. There, Lefebvre outlines the contours of what he calls abstract space. As detailed by Lefebvre, abstract space emerges through the alignment of the political imperatives of the modern state, the concerns of Western philosophy, and the representational technologies shaping everyday experience. It is composed of three elements, or "formants." The first of these formants — the geometrical — is underpinned by the absolutism of Euclidean space, and is demonstrated every time three-dimensional realities are reduced to two dimensions through drawing, mapping, or graphing. The second formant discloses the process by which the visual becomes the dominant and privileged mode of sensory engagement in Western societies. The phallic formant refers to the masculinist imperative to symbolically or physically occupy space. Taken together, the elements of abstract space enact an erasure of the difference of everyday life in which Lefebvre invests so much ethical, political, and aesthetic potential. They are also fundamentally duplicitous inasmuch as they conceal the real forces shaping everyday life behind the appearance of homogeneity. Abstract space is not homogeneous, however: as Lefebvre observes, "it simply has homogeneity as its goal, its orientation, its 'lens.'"[7] Most damning of all, however, is the claim that abstraction is intrinsically violent and "repressive in essence."[8] The violence and repression of abstraction take place physically and symbolically though the hierarchical positioning and identification of bodies within particular spaces.

Abstraction is therefore anything but an inconsequential conceptual technique of thinking: it is transformative and destructive, and is — in Lefebvre's terms — a "brutal spatial practice."[9] Abstraction's power reveals itself in the planning or development of urban environments and through the operation and logics of systems that render everyday life a calculable and manageable set of processes.[10] This critique of abstraction as technical instrumentalism is linked closely with its importance to the reproduction of forms of capitalist life. The abstractions of capitalism are inherently alienating, turning "[man] into a thing himself, just another commodity, an object to be bought and sold."[11] Crucially, these abstractions are thoroughly embedded in and constitutive of the fabric of lived experience, circulating through processes of exchange, accumulation, growth, calculation, planning, and programming that have a "social existence."[12]

These ideas frame Lefebvre's understanding of the relation between space, bodies, and abstraction in The Production of Space. There he is concerned especially with how the concrete violence and homogenizing tendencies of abstraction frame relations between space and bodies such that lived experience has been transported "outside itself in a paradoxical state of alienation."[13] In this way, abstraction is thoroughly implicated in the betrayal, denial, and abandonment of the body by rendering it an object.[14] As he puts it: "Abstract space functions 'objectally,' as a set of things/signs and their formal relationships: glass and stone, concrete and steel, angles and curves, full and empty. Formal and quantitative, it erases distinctions, as much those which derive from nature and (historical) time as those which originate in the body (age, sex, ethnicity)."[15] It might seem then that the corollary of Lefebvre's critique of abstract space is the affirmation of the primacy of the phenomenological body in relation to its generative participation in lived space. Certainly, one of his aims — both in *The Production of Space* and elsewhere — is the cultivation of a style of thinking that takes account of and affirms the capacities of the body to exceed the reductive logics of abstract space. This is a "practical and fleshy body" always involved in an intimate and generative relation with spatiotemporality.[16] Going further, Lefebvre's project can be read as resonating with phenomenological accounts of embodiment, especially with the earlier work of Maurice Merleau-Ponty.[17] At the very least, both figures support an affirmation of the lived body as the locus of any critical or creative analysis of the spacetimes of everyday life. It is easy to overstate this claim, however, not least because of the complexity of what counts as the lived as it evolves within Merleau-Ponty's later work. Equally, it needs to be remembered that Lefebvre distinguishes his own work from that of Merleau-Ponty on the basis that the latter fails to develop a critique of lived experience designed to identify the conditions for change in this experience.[18]

The question of lived experience is also complicated further in Lefebvre's work because he himself acknowledges the value — indeed the necessity — of abstraction in grasping elements of this experience. As he puts it in the second volume of his *Critique of Everyday Life*, "we are proceeding via abstraction, using analysis on the plane of the imaginary, because the operation requires a kind of imagination if it is to delve into the hidden life of visible and tangible human beings." Abstraction in this sense is necessary precisely because it "reaches something which psychological or sociological evidence does not reveal."[19] Put another way, abstraction does not so much offer a technique through which thinking withdraws from a world of lived experience: rather, it is a process of drawing out something of this world that would otherwise be unavailable to thought. In affirming abstraction in this way, Lefebvre therefore complicates any appeal to the preconceptual or pretheoretical immediacy of lived experience as the self-sufficient grounds for a critique of everyday life. Indeed, as Lefebvre, following Marx, puts it, "if the senses themselves become theoreticians, theory will indeed reveal the meaning of the sensory realms."[20] In some ways this is precisely what rhythmanalysis exemplifies. While it does not begin with "generalities found in abstractions," it nevertheless proceeds via a speculative empiricism that moves between the abstract (in the shape of concepts) and the concrete-practical. The key point is that concepts, as abstractions, are for Lefebvre derived from the "experience and knowledge of the body."[21] The upshot here is that Lefebvre's thinking can support a critique of abstract space while simultaneously affirming abstraction as part of any effort to think through lived experience. This is hardly surprising given Lefebvre's claim that abstract space is at "once lived and represented, at once the expression and foundation of a practice, at once stimulating and constraining."[22]

The fraught place of abstraction in Lefebvre's thinking can also be grasped in some of his comments on the architectonics of space, particularly those that draw upon his reading of theories of geometry. Thus, in *The Production of Space*, he writes that "the laws of space, which is to say the laws of discrimination in space, also govern the living body and the deployment of its energies."[23] What are these laws? Here Lefebvre draws upon the work of the mathematician Herman Weyl, whose interest in the ontology of space and time was influenced in turn by the phenomenological writings of Edmund Husserl.[24] Weyl's 1918 book, *Space, Time, Matter*, proposed a post-Euclidean geometry in light of Einstein's discoveries.[25] More specifically, however, for Lefebvre, Weyl's ideas about symmetry provide a way of thinking about the space of moving bodies in terms of an architectural geometry that is not imposed from without, but is already implicated within the dynamic trajectories of movement. It is worth quoting Lefebvre at length on this point:

> In nature, whether organic or inorganic, symmetries (in a plane or about an axis) exist wherever there is bilaterality or duality, left and right, "reflection," or rotation (in space); these symmetries are not properties external to bodies, however. Though definable in "purely" mathematical terms — as applications, operations, transformations or functions — they are not imposed upon material bodies, as many philosophers suppose, by prior thought. Bodies — deployments of energy — produce space and produce themselves, along with their motions, according to the laws of space. And this remains true, Weyl argues, whether we are concerned with corpuscles or planets, crystals, electromagnetic fields, cell division, shells, or architectural

forms, to which last Weyl attributes great importance. Here then we have a route from abstract to concrete which has the great virtue of demonstrating their reciprocal inherence.[26]

On one level, this would seem to position moving bodies squarely within the abstract geometry about which Lefebvre is elsewhere so critical. And yet, as this passage suggests, Weyl points Lefebvre toward a generative sense of abstraction: where abstraction is not a form existing external to bodies, but a mode of emergent organization implicated in the active and generative occupation of space, and expressed through symmetries and rotations. This is not the occupation by a body of an already existing space: rather, it is "an occupation which would need to be understood genetically — that is, according to the sequence of productive operations involved."[27]

This genetic process is the expression neither of a transcendent plan nor of an intentional mind but a dynamic process of abstraction that cuts across any division between the internal space of the body and the external space of the environment. Lefebvre, drawing upon Marx, uses the spider's web to exemplify the generative occupation of space as part of the "productive secretion of a 'residence.'"[28] The spider is interesting in this respect precisely because, for all its "lowliness," it is capable of "demarcating space and orienting itself on the basis of angles. It can create networks and links, symmetries and asymmetries. It is able to project beyond its own body those *dualities* which help constitute that body."[29] The movements through which the web takes shape are transversal to body and environment, emerging neither internally nor externally. In the process, the spider reveals a preintentional capacity to mark space as lived before the assumed primacy of the subject. It reveals an "internal rationality" to lived geometry existing prior to its being subsumed to the logic of the creative, intentional agent: this is a zone of "virtual or deferred tensions," the "locus of potentiality" through which bodies emerge as a series of pathways.[30] What Lefebvre seems to be suggesting here is that movement is a technology of abstraction for producing lived worlds prior to any separation of the natural — or lived — and the abstract. This is a process involving the deployment of energies in relation to a milieu apprehended through the transformative operations of symmetries and rotations. It is a process disclosing geometries of moving involvement — a choreography of worldly arrangement expressive of rather than reductive of difference. Thus, "the actions of each individual involve his multiple affiliations and basic constitution, with its dual aspect: first, the axes and planes of symmetry, which govern the movements of the legs, hands and limbs in general; secondly, the rotations and the gyrations which govern all sorts of movements of trunk or head — the circular, spiral, 'figures of eight,' and so on."[31] "Govern" is of course a strong word in this context. Here it might be understood as something akin to a necessary constraint through which the generation of difference is actualized in the production of spaces. The broader point to be made here is that Lefebvre affirms a dynamic, generative sense of abstraction as a means with which to grasp the process through which movements become bodies or, put another way, through which lived worlds are produced via the movements of which they are composed. And, in doing so, he encourages exploration of practices and techniques that foreground abstraction as part of the process of thinking through the spaces of moving bodies, while simultaneously remaining attentive to some of the problems of abstraction.

Choreographing Kinesthetic Architectures

Consider the following scenario. It happens along the following lines. One morning, early in the week, we are standing and talking in the narrow, white-walled corridor and stairwell of the Chisenhale Dance Space. Someone says: "Let's just begin by moving." A mildly worrying proposition if you don't take your own capacity to "just begin by moving" for granted. In that confined space we begin to encounter the walls, the stairs, and, from time to time, each other. We stretch along surfaces, explore corners. Continue for a while and then, without saying anything, stop: stop because it is not obvious what to do next. Talk for a while about ideas, before trying again. Another injunction — "Just begin by moving." The difficulty, some kind of ineffable blockage, remains. It is as if the effort gets in the way of the movement: nothing comes only from within. I wander about aimlessly, self-consciously. Stop again, and ask for some help, something to give a degree of loose consistency to such tentative grasping: some facilitating orientation.

A suggestion, an intervention: extend your kinesphere to its farthest point. "Kinesphere" is a term developed by Austro-Hungarian movement artist Rudolf Laban (1879–1958) as part of the elaboration of a system of choreographic movement analysis. Laban describes the kinesphere as

> the sphere around the body whose periphery can be reached by easily extended limbs without stepping away from that place which is the point of support when standing on one foot, which we shall call

the "stance" (also sometimes called "place"). We are able to outline the boundary of this imaginary sphere with our feet as well as with our hands. In this way any part of the kinesphere can be reached. When we move out of the limits of our original kinesphere we create a new stance, and transport the kinesphere to a new place. We never, of course, leave our movement sphere but carry it always with us, like an aura.[32]

Standing in the corridor, I make a big cross with my arms and legs outstretched. It seems to me that the effort is obvious.

"No, *really* extend your kinesphere."

Try again.

"No, extend it further."

Finally, muscles straining, I sense the approach of some tangible limit to that kinespheric space traced out by my movement: an imagined bubble, or sphere of sorts, surrounding the body as a zone of potential movement. I allow the effort to fully occupy this space and the quasi-geometric shapes this effort produces to give some orientation to my movement. The effort becomes a way of moving in a more architectural, more angular fashion. I begin playing around with the points at which kinespheric space intersects the lines and planes of the corridor. Before long I no longer simply trace arcs in a self-contained kinespheric space: lines of movement emerge somewhere between my orientations and the cold geometries of the white-walled corridor and staircase.

A MINOR MOMENT, of course, but one that serves as a point of departure for an exploration of the possibilities contained in the work of Laban and, equally, the degree to which this work articulates some of the questions precipitated by an encounter with the writing of Lefebvre. Inasmuch as Lefebvre's work exemplifies both the promise and possibility of abstraction for thinking philosophically about everyday life, Laban's work provides an equally apt point of departure for examining how abstraction participates in efforts to make sense of and experiment with the spacetimes of moving bodies through choreographic techniques.

At the outset, it is also worth noting that Laban's work can be situated in relation to the kinesthetic structure of feeling outlined in chapter 2. Like Dalcroze's experiments with cultivating musical sensibility through rhythmic movement, Laban's interest in the primacy of movement resonated with a range of cultural, aesthetic, and technological concerns.[33] Indeed, Laban was among the many notable visitors to Dalcroze's eurhythmics institute at Hellerau. Beyond an interest in the transformative possibilities of movement, these two figures also share something else: an uneasy implication in the choreographic politics of European corporeal cultures in the first half of the twentieth century. Laban's position in this regard is potentially even more problematic than that of Dalcroze.[34] As a major figure in German dance circles, Laban worked for a time under the patronage of the Nazi regime. His vision of "movement choirs," in which groups of people would move together in sympathetic expression, seemed to embody the corporeal aesthetic that appealed to this regime. Yet Laban's efforts to produce mass choreographic events were precisely what led him to fall out of favor with the Nazis — he left Germany after a choreographic spectacular planned for the 1936 Olympics was viewed unfavorably by Joseph Goebbels.[35]

The work of Dalcroze and Laban diverged in an important respect, however. Where Dalcroze argued that dancers, no less than musicians, had to submit themselves to the rhythms of music in order to properly cultivate aesthetic sensibility, Laban believed movement to be an expressive force in itself: if anything, movement needed to be unshackled from the tyranny of music. This is because movement for Laban is a metasense, which unlike other senses is not concentrated in "any one particular part of the body": it is not organ specific but is distributed throughout the body, allowing the individual to negotiate the totality of the immediate environment.[36] Movement is thus the way in which bodies are situated in a wider universe of motion.

Laban's writing and work is complex and eclectic, combining an interest in mysticism and the quasi-spiritual nature of movement, with an attraction to the value of abstraction and geometry as elements of movement analysis. At the heart of this system is a vision of the movement of bodies in terms of a dynamic geometrical architecture.[37] This relation between architecture and movement is crucial to Laban's work — indeed, he considered them to be the "two basic arts from which the others derive."[38] As an energetic space simultaneously generated and occupied by bodies, the kinesphere serves as the point of departure for this architecture. For Laban, movements within (and to some extent beyond) the kinesphere are "trace-forms," dynamic trajectories akin to organically unfolding pathways in space. The goal of the movement analyst is to render these trace-forms visible but also, in doing so, to increase the capacity of the dancer to invent new trace-forms in the dynamic space of the kinesphere. Echoing Lefebvre's interest in the genetic laws that determine the generative relation between bodies and space, Laban's analysis of movement in kinespheric space — or what he calls choreutics — is informed by his ideas about a crystalline architecture of movement. As Laban puts it, movement is "a continuous creation of fragments of polyhedral forms. The body itself, in its anatomical or crystalline structure, is built up according to the laws of dynamic crystallisation."[39]

In contrast to Lefebvre, Laban's ideas are more obviously informed by a Platonic understanding of ideal abstract forms such as the cube, sphere, and triangle. Of these forms, for Laban the icosahedron provides the most "natural and harmonious tracks for [bodily] movements." As a twenty-faced structural midpoint between a cube and sphere, the icosahedron contains "a rich series of inner and outer trace-lines with dimensional connections provoking 'stable,' i.e. easily equilibrated, movements as well as diagonal connections."[40] This geometrical shape can also accommodate within its structure the three-dimensional planes used by Laban as further orientations for the body in space — high-low, forward-backward, and right-left. Clearly, Laban's appeal to Platonic ideal forms sits uncomfortably with Lefebvre's critique of the imposition of abstraction upon bodies: these ideal forms seem to capture precisely the tendency of abstract space to transcend the generative processuality of bodies. Nevertheless, this geometry did not translate into a strict mechanical rationalism. As Colin Counsell suggests, this is one of the key ways in which Laban's choreographic experiments exemplify the wider structure of feeling in which his work emerged. Specifically, the impulse to transcendence represented not just a nostalgic return to an earlier geometric idealism: it also spoke of the tendency for abstraction in modernism to provide a vaguely mystical window onto the infinite as a zone that exceeded the mechanical geometries of rationalism.[41]

The prominence of abstraction in Laban's work is also revealed by his interest in developing a comprehensive system of graphic movement notation. The most elaborate manifestation of this is Labanotation, but it can also be illustrated through some of his other work. Consider, for instance, effort shape graphs. Effort for Laban was the manifestation through movement of an inner affective-psychological impulse, and could be discerned in the variation of weight, emphasis, intensity, and so on, of this movement.[42] As he puts it, a person's efforts may be both "unconscious and involuntary, but they are always present in any movement; otherwise they could not be perceived by others, or become effectual in the external surroundings of the moving person."[43] Effort was therefore the external manifestation — through movement — of something internal to the body.

Effort graphs were developed by Laban — in collaboration with management consultant Frank Lawrence — as schematic diagrams providing a quick and consistent representation of the force and direction of individual movements.[44] There are clear parallels here with the time and motion studies of F. W. Taylor — which had been introduced to wartime Britain in order to improve productivity — and with the work of Frank and Lillian Gilbreth to improve the efficiency of industrial processes. In Manchester, Laban and Lawrence employed their shared interests to improve the ability of women to lift heavy objects, encouraging them to introduce a swing or lilt into the rhythm of their movements, thereby generating sufficient momentum. Like the work of Taylor and the Gilbreths, Laban's movement analysis was a technology for extracting — through abstraction — the value of movement through the lines of graphic or diagrammatic representation.[45] As such, it is complicit with the wider incorporation of bodily movement into the abstract spaces about which Lefebvre is so critical. As he writes, "unfortunately [this] is the space of blank sheets of paper, drawing boards, plans, sections, elevations, scale models, geometrical projections, and the like." For Lefebvre the problem here is that "a narrow and desiccated rationality of this kind overlooks the core and foundation of space, the total body, the brain, gestures, and so forth. It forgets that space does not consist in the projection of an intellectual representation, does not arise from the visible-readable realm, but that it is first of all *heard* (listened to) and *enacted* (through physical gestures and movements)."[46]

And yet, as with Lefebvre's own writing, the question of abstraction in Laban's work is not so easily reduced to the terms of this critique. Laban is fully aware of the limits of his architectural models and graphic renderings: they fail to capture what he took to be the underlying continuity of movement. In terms that have certain sympathy with the ideas of Bergson, Laban suggests, "Forms of objects and living beings, when in quietude, may suggest a 'standstill' in the big unceasing stream of movement in which we exist and take part. This illusion of a standstill is based on the snapshot-like perception of the mind which is able to receive only a single phase of the uninterrupted flux. It is our memory which tends to perpetuate the illusion created by the 'snapshots'; and the memory itself waxes, changes and vanishes."[47] The choreutic shapes devised by Laban only make sense as part of a "living architecture created by human movements and made up of pathways tracing shapes in space."[48] As abstractions, these shapes have to be experienced through movement — through the actual occupation and generation of space in a dynamic sequence of gestures.[49] And as abstractions, they serve the purpose of cultivating kinesthetic sensibility and, over time, for facilitating improvisation in movement. Thus, for Laban, "getting the 'feel' of a movement gives real understanding of it. To achieve an integral understanding, which is of the highest importance, a synthesis of a vital impulse with its performance by the body is indispensable. This performance need not be on a large scale. It can be so small that it is almost imperceptible to other people. It can, at times, approach pure meditation leaving the body apparently quiet."[50] Equally, Laban's choreutic geometry does not necessarily determine movement; rather, it only specifies certain directions and orientations that can then facilitate improvisation. Understanding it thus — as a pragmatic technique through which to cultivate kinesthetic sensibility — it becomes possible to appreciate how and why Laban's kinesthetic architecture continues to be used, and in contexts that do not necessarily privilege ideal models of embodiment.

Petra Kuppers — one of the co-collaborators at the Chisenhale — provides a useful illustration of how Laban's work can be deployed. In some of her performance and movement-based community work, Kuppers draws upon elements of Laban's geometries "as a scaffold to construct varieties of physical expression." As Kuppers suggests, the kinesphere and dynamosphere are "maps that can be located and explored in participants' own bodies, and through them performers can feel their own extension in their environment."[51] How does this work? Kuppers offers the following example: "For instance, when we are engaged in visualisations of breath filling our bodies, we focus on the body's extension backward and forward. When we are standing up, we focus on the body's location in the pull of gravity and the muscle's force. . . . We have to train ourselves to attend to the motility of our bodies through an increasing awareness of minute movement possibilities."[52] By mobilizing elements of Laban's kinesthetic architecture thus, Kuppers's research practice points to the possibility that this architecture does not inevitably privilege an ideal form of able-embodiment, despite emerging from a Platonic idealism. Rather, it can become entangled in partial and minor ways in specific enactments of relational movement offering possibilities for expression at different scales and intensities. And it is precisely in this way that Laban's work is employed in the Chisenhale.

In their shared interest in the development of a dynamic architecture immanent to the generation of spaces, both Lefebvre and Laban foreground the complex relation between bodies, space, and abstraction. They also both affirm abstraction as a necessary element of experimenting in movement and thinking.[53] This makes it difficult to use Lefebvre in any straightforward way to critique Laban's work insofar as the latter mobilizes abstraction. The real problems with the latter are not necessarily to do with abstraction per se, but lie elsewhere. First, Laban's kinesthetic architecture tends to privilege and valorize as aesthetic only certain styles of movement: specifically, those that are harmonious, and those which appear to unfold organically. In the final analysis, for Laban, "movement makes sense only if it progresses organically and this means the phases which follow each other in a natural succession must be chosen."[54] The significance of this emphasis needs to be seen in terms of how it could inform a corporeal and choreographic politics of community, embodied in Laban's enthusiasm for movement choirs as events of collective celebration and joy: these are exactly the choreographic forms that make his relation with interwar German choreographic politics problematic. For Laban then, movement is only truly aesthetic if — through the deliberate effort of the individual (albeit in concert with others) — it realizes the harmonious continuity of the kinesthetic rhythms of space and time. The upshot is a micropolitics of spatial apprehension based on an ethics and aesthetics of movement between kinespherically centered subjects.

A second problem with Laban's work is the extent to which it remains dependent upon the claim that movement emerges from within the individual. Insofar as it is meaningful, movement in Laban's work is centered on the primacy of the phenomenological subject acting in a world. Moreover, this claim is implicated in a division between an internal space of emotional expression and an external space into which that expression extends. In these terms, abstraction tends to be external to the moving body, a kind of scaffolding — albeit an incredibly dynamic one — erected around the center point of the kinesphere. In some sense, then, Laban's choreographic architectures are almost not abstract enough because they keep abstraction external to movement by remaining wedded too closely to the claim that movement emerges from within bodies and finds its expression in a space external to bodies. A more adequate account might necessarily consider movement to already be partially abstract before any scaffolding is added to it.

It is, however, worth remarking that there are hints in Laban's work of other ways of thinking movement and abstraction. Thus, at one level there are hints of ways of thinking about how kinesthetic architectures might be disaggregated, destabilized, and disrupted. For instance, at points Laban alludes to a choreographic version of cinematic montage, in which movement becomes a matter of "unexpected jumps, breaks, gaps, and repetitions," and where dynamic architectures are full of fantastic, surprising discontinuities. Furthermore, at the center of his kinesthetic architecture are lines that seem to want to break free from kinespheric center points, to fly off in other directions and in ways that complicate an overarching logic of spatial harmony premised on the intentional subject as the source of movement. These are transversal lines. Within the three-dimensional geometry of this kinesthetic thinking, transversal lines are defined as those traversing the icosahedral choreutic scaffolding without intersecting at its center.[55] Such lines suggest the possibilities of choreographing movements without taking an intentional phenomenological subject as a point of departure. Put another way, even if they remain incorporated within the scaffolding of Euclidean geometry, there are hints of other geometries in Laban's choreographic work, hints of other ways of thinking and affirming abstraction.

Choreographing Abstraction

Laban's choreographic experiments only take us so far in thinking through possibilities for affirming abstraction in relation to moving bodies. These possibilities might be pursued further through dwelling a little on the notion of line and, more specifically, on the relation between lines and movement. Under the terms of the standard critique of abstraction, the lines of which Laban's architectural geometries are composed are static representations of movement: reductive attempts to capture the complexity of movement in two-dimensional forms. In turn, if read selectively through aspects of Lefebvre's work, these same lines are manifestations of a wider culture of abstraction that inhibits and extracts the energies of the body.

Other choreographic experiments might allow for a more affirmative stance to be taken here, however. The American-born, Frankfurt-based choreographer William Forsythe offers some useful orientation in this respect. In recent years, Forsythe's Ballet Frankfurt has made extensive use of the performance space at Hellerau in Dresden. Even if it by no means rehearses the vision of aesthetic experiment outlined by Appia, let alone the rhythmic exercises of Dalcroze, the presence of the company at Hellerau is an important marker of the ongoing significance and potential of this architectural space as a site for facilitating experiment with moving bodies. More immediately important here, however, is how Forsythe thinks of and deploys the line in a process of abstraction that facilitates choreographic improvisation in ways that both echo and go beyond Laban's work. On one level, for Forsythe, like Laban, choreography is fundamentally about "organizing bodies in space." As Forsythe suggests, when you are doing choreography "you're organizing bodies with other bodies, or a body with other bodies in an environment that is organized."[56] And in some respects, elements of Laban's work offer points of departure for Forsythe's work.[57] However, Forsythe actively departs from the Euclidean geometries of Laban's phenomenologically centered architecture, multiplying and decentering it in ways that open a range of creative possibilities. Crucially, where for Laban there is one kinespheric center point, around and through which movement pivots, for Forsythe there are multiple — indeed an infinite number of — kinespheric centers. This means that any number of points of departure for movement exist. In effect, Forsythe remains faithful to the principle that movement is architectural, but in the process also foregrounds the generative possibility of losing balance, of disorientation, and of disequilibrium, in ways that work against the ethico-aesthetics of harmony underpinning Laban's subject-centered geometrical forms.

Forsythe dismantles the architecture developed by Laban while nevertheless making more — not less — of the potential for experimenting movement in terms of lines and planes as choreographic abstraction. He does this in a way that departs from any sense of an original or universal architectural geometry of movement-space: his point is not to devise choreographic works that adhere to Platonic geometrical forms. Rather, the architectural geometries of Forsythe's choreographic work are generative in the manner that Lefebvre understands abstraction — experiments with abstraction for producing novel possibilities for moving. This affirmation of abstraction informs the choreographic work of Forsythe's dance company. He actively encourages dancers to understand movement as a series of transformations along various lines and planes. Unlike Laban's work, these architectures do not precede movement — they emerge through movement. The dancer works with lines in a way that "does not depict any concrete or existing space, but rather a *potential* space — as the piece forms, an architecture emerges."[58] These lines are thus not representations external to movement but are transformative operators, part of the more-than-human assemblage of agency through which movement sequences emerge. They function as intuitive orientations for potential improvisation rather than modes of withdrawal from an assumed self-presence. Equally, and crucially, these architectural abstractions do not revolve around a self-contained body. Instead, for Forsythe the moving body emerges through a series of almost tangential trajectories: put another way, body is the process, rather than the initiator of a process external to it.[59]

A movement architecture composed of lines is therefore not so much a technology for constraining the body in a prefigured space of abstraction: it is about exploring potentials for residing through abstraction as a process of drawing out worlds. As Lefebvre reminds us, the distinction between housing and residing is an important one: the former is a functional abstraction whereas the latter is a mode or style of occupying and producing spaces. More generally, Lefebvre's ideas are in sympathy with Forsythe's choreographic experiments as a process of generative abstraction: that is, abstraction as the capacity to produce the differential repetition of body spaces. Clearly, architectural form can induce difference through repetition as a superficial adornment. But it also has the potential to produce a differential space akin to the way in which Forsythe's choreographic work does, and in ways that suggest a baroque sensibility — a sequence of self-differential curves and spirals. As Lefebvre puts it: "To build a few blocks of flats that are spiral in form by adding a handful of curves to the usual concrete angularities is not an entirely negligible achievement — but neither does it amount to very much. To take inspiration from Andalucia, and demonstrate a sensual use of curvatures, spirals, arabesques and inflexions of all kinds, so achieving a truly voluptuous space, would be a different matter altogether."[60] The question for Lefebvre then is this: "Why should spaces created by virtue of human understanding be any less varied as works, or products, than those produced by nature, than landscapes or living beings?"[61]

Perhaps the most direct illustration of how Forsythe uses lines as choreographic operators through which to produce variations in movement is in *Improvisation Technologies: A Tool for the Analytical Dance Eye*. This CD-ROM–based work was produced to allow dancers to understand Forsythe's approach to choreographic improvisation. In this work Forsythe offers multiple examples of how movement sequences can be constructed using a series of progressively more complex operative processes and transformations. At the heart of *Improvisation Technologies* is an injunction to develop and experiment playfully with a kinesthetic vocabulary in the form of choreographic line drawing. Playing with the generative possibilities of lines is at the center of this process. As he puts it,

> You can establish a line with a gesture. . . . I can establish a line by making a crumbling gesture. I can establish a line on the floor with little hops. I can establish it by rubbing it into the floor . . . by making little tiny dots, or between two dots. . . . I could probably smear it, slide it, tap it, swat it, kick it. A line or a point is there in space and how you establish it or how you manifest it is really up to you. It is very important that this part of the process remain extremely playful and extremely imaginative. Don't restrict yourself to strict drawing of lines like you're drawing with a knife or a pen for that matter. You have to use the surface of your body and your imagination about how lines could form and how you could manifest these things with your body.[62]

Forsythe's choreographic operators are not limited to lines: his use of lines does however serve as a reminder of the centrality of abstraction as a transformative operation within his work. To draw a line in the way Forsythe suggests is not to frame the body, or to constrain it in a predetermined space. It is an invitation to use abstraction as a technology for generating bodies through movement. So, while Forsythe claims that a line or a point is "there in space," it would be wrong to think this means it preexists the movements of which it is composed. It lurks as unformed potential rather than as a preformed possibility. As Erin Manning has written, Forsythe does not so much ask or instruct dancers to look for trace-forms already existing in space. Rather, he develops a series of propositions eliciting "action in an environment of change in which choreography is a multiplying ecology governed by the specificity of a co-constituting environment."[63]

Reaffirming Abstraction

How do these brief encounters with the work of figures such as Lefebvre, Laban, and Forsythe inform understandings of the relation between abstraction and moving bodies? In the first place, they offer an important reminder that abstraction is differentiated. Abstraction can be a static form withdrawn from the dynamism of matter. It is easy to see how this sense of abstraction provides purchase on a range of practices and techniques, including choreography. Read thus, elements of Laban's choreographic geometry rehearse this kind of abstraction insofar as it imposes a Platonic idealism upon moving bodies. But if the relation between moving bodies and abstraction is limited to these terms, then it will always remain impossible to affirm the latter in relation to the former. If moving bodies are always assumed to exist prior to abstraction, then it is clearly inevitable that any process of abstraction, including choreography, will be understood narrowly as visiting violence upon these bodies. And any form of argument or matter of expression that mobilizes abstraction in pursuit of thinking or experimenting with moving bodies will be dismissed as inattentive to bodily difference.

There is another way of thinking abstraction in relation to moving bodies. This is hinted at in the work of Lefebvre — a sense of abstraction immanent to movement rather than imposed from without. Thus, while Lefebvre's work can and has often been used to reinforce a critique of abstraction in relation to the lived spaces of moving bodies, his treatment of abstraction is actually more complex: in fact, Lefebvre remains dependent upon the promise of abstraction as a technique for thinking and experimenting with movement. He encourages examination of how abstraction is mobilized in different ways in practices for experimenting experience. This is also exactly the value of Forsythe's choreographic work: what emerges through this work is an appreciation of a second kind of abstraction. As an immanent process rather than an ideal form, this second kind of abstraction is a process through which to draw out a set of virtual tendencies abroad in the world. These tendencies are virtual in the sense of a real but abstract condition of potentiality for change. As Brian Massumi has suggested, this sense of the virtual as potential has important implications for thinking moving bodies: "In motion, a body is in an immediate, unfolding relation to its own non-present potential to vary. That relation, to borrow a phrase from Gilles Deleuze, is real but abstract. . . . Here, abstract means: never present in position, only ever in passing. There is an abstractness pertaining to the transitional immediacy of a real relation — that of a body to its own indeterminacy (its openness to an elsewhere and otherwise than it is, in any here and now)."[64]

As Massumi argues, abstract virtuality is the very potential for change in bodies. To take this claim seriously means that the moving space — or spacing — of the body is always composed of a multiplicity of abstract virtualities as much as it is a matter of a singular, lived actuality against which abstraction in the first sense is counterposed. Hence Massumi's claim that the issue is not that our ways of thinking moving bodies are too abstract, but that they are not abstract enough to grasp the real abstractness of any potential for change and variation. Such an argument for the necessity of abstraction complicates any phenomenological claims about the actuality of the lived as self-coincident presence.[65] But it also encourages revision of the critique of choreographic operators such as lines. It suggests that kinesthetic architectures composed of lines, while appearing to be defined in relation to a geometric Platonic idealism, are already always potentially open to the processual potential of abstraction existing prior to this idealism. And this is what Forsythe's choreographic work reminds us of: by deforming abstraction of the first kind, he provides conditional constraints through which abstraction of a second kind opens bodies up to their own ongoing process of transition. If the first kind of abstraction opens onto a space of possibility — the realization of forms already determined — the second kind of abstraction opens onto a space of potential — of indeterminate yet actualizable tendencies. As the architectural theorist and critic John Rajchman — drawing upon Deleuze — observes, "For as long as one thinks of the *abs-tractus* as form withdrawn from matter, one thinks in terms of possibilities and their realizations (or later transcendental or dialectical conditions of such possibility). . . . But once one allows for a world that is disunified, incongruous, composed of multiple divergent paths, one can think in terms of abstract virtualities that, in contrast to such abstract possibilities, are quite real, even though they are not actualised."[66] This distinction is critical insofar as it holds open the spacetimes of choreographic abstraction to the potential for their own mutation and multiplication. It is a reminder of the value of allowing thinking to become responsive to techniques and technologies, such as those found in certain choreographic practices, through which the distinction between the lived and the abstract no longer serves as a stable point of orientation for critique but an invitation to experiment further with the promise of this relation.

All this points to the importance, indeed the necessity, of revising the terms of the critique that has informed efforts to think through abstraction. In *Adventures of Ideas*, the philosopher Alfred North Whitehead remarks that "you cannot think without abstractions; accordingly, it is of the utmost importance to be vigilant in critically revising your modes of abstraction."[67] Isabelle Stengers has reminded us of the importance of Whitehead's claims about abstraction.[68] On one level, abstractions for Whitehead allow thought patterns to "succeed in holding together and in maintaining themselves" in the manner that societies do.[69] Yet for Whitehead, Western thinking has tended to privilege abstractions whose origin is no longer clear. An awareness of this fact should not, claims Whitehead, lead inevitably to the disavowal of abstraction in favor of an appeal to the immediacy of experience. We critique abstraction in order to correct a fundamental misunderstanding of what abstractions do. As Stengers observes, Whitehead's abstractions "are not 'abstract forms' that determine what we feel, perceive and think, nor are they 'abstracted from' something more concrete, and, finally, they are not generalizations." Rather, abstractions have a positive role insofar as they "act as 'lures,' drawing attention toward 'something that matters,' vectorizing concrete experience."[70]

Whitehead therefore calls our attention to the importance of cultivating an affirmative critique of abstraction — as simultaneously process, concept, and technique — for moving bodies. A critique of abstraction for moving bodies is affirmative if it does not allow an awareness of some of the potential problems with abstraction to foreclose the possibility that abstraction might generate novelty in thinking and moving. An affirmative critique of abstraction for thinking with moving bodies refuses to engage in the misplaced apprehension of the lived, the experiential, or the concrete as categories that go beyond the abstract. It seeks instead to explore how abstraction is always part of thinking through moving bodies. And it understands abstraction as something providing pathways for sensing difference, rather than something erasing it. This is precisely the point on which Lefebvre's critique of abstraction is in most need of the kind of revision outlined above. In *The Production of Space*, Lefebvre contrasts abstract space with what he calls differential space — a space of difference and creativity. As he writes toward the end of that book, "in the misapprehended space of the body, a space that is both close by and distant, this paradoxical junction of repetitive and differential — this most basic form of 'production' — is forever occurring."[71] For Lefebvre, abstraction makes this difference difficult to grasp, rendering the relation between difference and repetition "more antagonistic" through its reductionist and homogenizing tendencies: difference becomes something already calculable or definable in relation to a prefabricated set of possibilities.[72] It is the difference excessive of abstraction that Lefebvre wants to affirm. And yet Lefebvre himself appeals to abstraction in his efforts to develop a system of thinking through the spatial generativity of bodies. Lefebvre's mistake is that by failing to develop a sufficiently differentiated sense of abstraction he cannot fully grasp how abstraction might actually be a necessary element of thinking through the differential space he is so eager to affirm.[73] The task of an affirmative critique of abstraction for moving bodies, therefore, is to experiment with abstraction such that it acts as a lure through which to generate potential futures that complicate the "bad abstractions" about which Lefebvre is sometimes so scathingly critical. In this way abstraction facilitates experiment with moving through inducing "empirically felt variations in the way our experience matters."[74] Choreographic experiments remind us of this fact insofar as they affirm choreography as a technology for drawing out multiple pathways of movement that are not always given in advance. Laban points us in this direction, but his work remains far too beholden to movement as the product of an intentional agent navigating a kinesthetic architecture whose scaffolding has already been prefigured. Forsythe, on the other hand, shows us how choreography relies upon a vocabulary of quasi-architectonic shapes in order to provide the generative conditions for new lines of movement to emerge. In making more of these lines, choreography does not necessarily alienate the body from its own movement; rather, choreographic abstraction, as it is exemplified in the work of Forsythe in particular, facilitates the experimental generation of affective spacetimes through movement.

CHAPTER EIGHT

Promising Participation

The promise of participation is an extremely alluring one in the social sciences and humanities. And participation is often understood as an immersive engagement in activities at a research site with the view to gaining a more fine-grained insight into how these activities are organized and experienced. Moreover, participation is also often aligned with the idea of the participatory: that is, with an imperative to go beyond the confines of the academy to make a difference in the world through a range of techniques of involvement.[1] Framed in this way, the participatory foregrounds a sense of participation that is avowedly critical and political. It affirms participation as an indicator of worldly engagement.

But the relation between participation and the possibility of making a difference within the world is by no means reducible to the participatory, however laudable the latter may be. This is because to speak of participation is not only to ask how thinking might be transformed such that it partici-pates in a world from which it is assumed to be distant because of abstrac-tion. It is also to ask how the world participates in the process of thinking, and how we might learn to be affected by this participation.[2] To ask these questions is to be open to the possibility that participation therefore always begins before the decision to participate is taken. Participation is, as Brian Massumi argues, always taking place, in part, prior to cognition.[3] Rendered in affective terms, it is the feeling of something happening before reflective thought kicks in — what, following William James, we might call a feeling of tendency. The affects of participation can sneak up on you, their influ-ence only becoming evident in retrospect. Equally, participation is never reducible to the intentional act of an individual human actor. Participation takes place through relational assemblages of bodies, materials, concepts, and affects: participation in these terms is always a cofabrication, a copro-duction that involves more than the individual human participant.

The question of participation always therefore begins with the potential abroad in the world. This potential may well remain virtual even though it can also be actualized in any number of ways, some of which will be acci-dental. But this process can also be initiated by something: a crystal or seed that might provide opportunities for drawing out the potential of partici-pation. A seed can take many forms: a gesture, an act, a proposition. It can also take place as a call, a cry, or a refrain. As Isabelle Stengers has argued, perhaps one of the more important challenges facing the social sciences and humanities is the production of new refrains for experimenting expe-rience.[4] Stengers is interested in experimenting refrains as a cosmopolitical process; that is, she is calling for refrains offering opportunities for glimps-ing or hearing the multivarious worlds in which we are some of the many coparticipants, worlds that do not obey the traditional ontological, episte-mological, and ethico-political reference points of nature and culture. The importance of such refrains is that they draw together or give consistency to territories, providing a necessary constraint for experimenting with po-tentially inhabitable futures. But the success of these refrains also depends upon a commitment to respond to their call with a degree of generosity. As Stengers also suggests, the milieus from, across, and into which the call of a refrain is articulated may well be too toxic to sustain that refrain: it can all too easily perish, not just because of a grand gesture of dismissal, but also through myriad minor acts that work to dampen its affects. Refrains for participation are therefore fragile. The cultivation of a disposition that would seek to foster refrains that might open up worlds for experimenting experience is therefore crucial.

Calling for the Event

One way to produce new refrains for participation is to call for different kinds of events. This point requires some initial qualification. At present, when the event is invoked in the humanities and social sciences, it is often glossed either by an otherworldly sense (the event as an impossible, incorporeal transformation) or by a kind of heroic decisionism (the event as that spatiotemporal conjuncture that calls forth and demands an ethical subject).[5] Yet the social sciences and humanities reproduce themselves, at least in part, through much more mundane, earthly events at which nothing much often seems to happen and few decisions are taken, despite the sheer volume of people and papers present: annual conferences, one-day symposia, seminars. These kinds of events do matter, of course. Yet what is most (un)remarkable about such events is their predictability and the fact that often, much of the really interesting activity actually takes place outside of or interstitial to the presentations: in corridors, for instance. Indeed, one wonders, following William James, if it might not be better to build conference spaces composed entirely of corridors, where people would mill about, bump into one another, and then leave, having had a series of interesting and fairly open-ended conversations: spaces defined by the cultivation of an "attitude of orientation" rather than any particular "result."[6]

One of the obstacles to producing and affirming this kind of corridor work as part of the serious business of thinking is the fact that the nature of participation, and the sites at which such participation is assumed to take place, are so often already prefigured by the deathly repetition of a very familiar refrain: that call for participation — submit your abstract. Prepare to present and be present at a given time and place. And in the face of that call, what are you going to do? The process of generating a novel refrain for experimenting experience might therefore be as deceptively straightforward as introducing a note of variation on the familiar call for participation. And to offer this kind of call might become a way of producing another kind of event for experimenting experience. It might, in the words of Stengers, become a cosmopolitical act that opens up possible worlds, albeit in modest and minor ways. This not to claim that the format of any such event would be absolutely novel: instead, it might draw upon techniques for thinking and moving that already circulate across multiple sites.

So, in late 2005, I am forwarded a call for participation in an event to be held in Montreal.[7] The name of this event is Dancing the Virtual, and it is described thus: "We would like to challenge the dichotomy between creation and thought/research by establishing a working environment in which the emphasis will be placed on the ways in which research-creation reinvents collaboration and on the new modes of thought and action this makes possible. . . . To engage actively in research-creation is not only to create movements of thought, it is also to instantiate new platforms of experimentation. This project proposes to create such a platform of experimentation."[8] The themes outlined in this call are compelling, and they seem to resonate with my own work: movement, abstraction, the virtual, research-creation. The key thing, however, is that this is a call for participation, not for papers. It may not seem like much, but this minor shift disturbs, however subtly, that well-ingrained habit of thinking — the production of an abstract for a paper presentation. And I wonder — what can we do (as academics) at such gatherings if we don't present? So a response to a call for participation becomes an opportunity to reflect upon the ethos through which one tends to act into gatherings. And it becomes an opportunity to think upon how to act into a situation without anticipating too rigidly the outcomes: how to provide some orientation without refiguring the relation to come. So I respond, outlining not so much a plan. Instead I frame my potential participation by posing three broad questions that might provide some constraint while opening into the concerns of the event:

- First, what conceptual devices allow us to enact a thinking-space in terms of forces of movement and affect?
- Second, how do we enact and construct a relational and experimental movement-space?
- Third, what techniques best facilitate the refiguring of research as a movement of thought?

In preparation for the event I read the suggested reading for participants.[9] And I take notes, identifying passages that seem to move and resonate with the concerns of the event to come.

When it happens, the event itself takes place in a large, bare studio space populated by a range of materials designed to facilitate forms of relational interaction, where again, these relations involve concepts, affects, and percepts: things in transition and things in the making. As things turn out, a great deal is afforded by this thinking-space: relational movement, conceptual speed dating, dancing with José Gil.[10] Indeed, so much happens that I am drawn back, the following year, for a similar kind of event, albeit one with a different name — Housing the Body. In preparation for the second event, I read some more.[11] And even if the second time around this kind of event is no longer as novel, it still has the capacity to generate surprises.

A third call appears in 2008, for an event to take place in May 2009: A Society of Molecules. This event is much more distributed: the aim is for a series of molecules to generate possibilities for relational experimentation at a multiplicity of sites. The themes of the event are inspired in part by the work of Félix Guattari and in particular his ideas about the possibility of producing new ecologies of thinking that operate transversally to hegemonic structures and values. For Guattari, these ecologies are ethico-aesthetic in orientation — they work to recast systems of value and, in doing so, create new possibilities for life, new subjectivities. As in much of his writing, Guattari's claims mix wild optimism, conceptual abstraction, and the earthly affirmation of the value of experimenting experience. Yet even if his writings are sometimes heroic in tone, Guattari's life and work remind us that when it comes to experimenting experience, the key question is a profoundly pragmatic one: what sites, techniques, and concepts provide opportunities for expanding horizons of potential, for providing new "universes of virtuality" through which to recast subjectivities, if only modestly? Guattari, in other words, affirms participation in the wi(l)dest possible sense of the word.

So, shaped in part by the promise of Guattari's writing, I begin responding to this call for participation by thinking with another of the participants at one of the earlier events, Housing the Body: Sarah Rubidge, a researcher and choreographer. Together we devise a response to this call for participation in the form of the following question: How to diagram a thinking space between geography and choreography? The question itself operates like a refrain: holding together ethico-aesthetic territories while also holding these territories open. The aim from the outset, if that point could ever have been identified with any real degree of precision, is to try to generate a distributed thinking-space within which to explore and experiment with the relations between questions of the geographic and questions of the choreographic.[12] There are, of course, various matters of concern shared by both questions and the traditions of thinking from which they emerge. They share a concern with the relations between bodies and spaces, where neither are given in advance, and with how these relations can be articulated and organized through various processes: representational, social and cultural, or affectual. More specifically, they share a concern with the generative quality of the relations between bodies and spaces — with the question of how bodies and spaces are mutually implicated in a process through which novel ways of moving can be produced. And they also share an interest in the kinds of techniques that might facilitate this generative activity: techniques that encourage improvisation and experimentation.

Against the context of these shared concerns, the overall aim in preparing for this event is rather loosely defined and not in any way delimited. In part, this is an effort to avoid closing down at the outset how either geography or choreography is understood: at most, the aim is to diagram a thinking-space in which to experiment with the possible overlaps between elements of these traditions of thinking. In the process the hope is that variations in concepts, affects, and percepts might emerge in ways that allow you to make more of the gathering of these elements.

Milieus

The question of how to think between the geographic and the choreographic begins to be explored at a number of locations (including Oxford, London, Chichester) through the activities of various event particles generating materials as contributions for an event to come. These event particles compose different and sometimes divergent trajectories. For each of these event particles, participation begins taking place through the milieu in which it moves. In an essay called "What Children Say," Deleuze writes that "a milieu is made up of qualities, substances, powers, and events: the street, for example, with its materials (paving stones), its noises (the cries of merchants), its animals (harnessed horses) or its dramas (a horse slips, a horse falls down, a horse is beaten)."[13] Deleuze makes this claim in the context of a critique of the tendency of psychoanalysis to interpret the movements and behaviors of children through the referential coordinates of parents. In the process, he suggests, psychoanalysis finds it difficult to grasp the dynamic affective cartographies generated through the movements and activities of children. This cartographic activity is coterminous with the milieus in which children are participants: as he suggests, "there is never a moment when children are not already plunged into an actual milieu in which they are moving about." Deleuze's point here is not to suggest that parents are unimportant. Instead parents themselves become "a milieu that children travel through: they pass on through its qualities and powers and make a map of them. They take on a personal and parental form only as the representatives of one milieu within another." At the same time, parents often "simply play the role of openers or closers of doors, guardians of thresholds, connectors or disconnectors of zones." This even applies to infants, the parents of whom, for Deleuze, are defined in relation to a "continent-bed, as agents along the child's route."[14] Deleuze's essay does require some qualification. It is not just about what children say: it might have been better to call it "What Children Do," or, more precisely, what they do when they draw out affective territories, part of which involves saying. Nevertheless, it represents perhaps the most emphatically cartographic statement in his writing, pointing as it does to the possibility of thinking of mapping as the processual generation of affective cartographies composed of trajectories. The key to these cartographic trajectories is that they exceed the interpretive work of recognition. Indeed, for Deleuze, as soon as they are subjected to interpretation they lose a sense of affective dynamism.

As it happens, my own event particle takes shape in the middle of participation in the milieu of which parenthood consists. The milieu consists of various predictable activities: eating, excreting, sleeping. And it consists of equally predictable spaces: cots, car seats, baths, and strollers.[15] The milieu of parenting involves an ongoing movement between these activities and spaces. In the thick of it, sometimes life seems to consist of nothing more than these activities and spaces, and universes of value, horizons of potential, seem to be contracting, shrinking, closing in on themselves. But there are always possibilities for making connections with other milieus, for drawing relations between them that open affective trajectories. Take one example: sleep. Sleep is a trajectory or becoming as much as an activity in which physical displacement of the body is more obvious. One goes to, or falls, asleep. Or one is taken by sleep. The question of agency is not an important one here: the fact remains that sleep is a becoming. For an infant, however, this trajectory is by no means an inevitable one, and it is not always easy. Much of what the milieu of the parent consists in involves the continual effort to facilitate this trajectory. It involves an ongoing series of pragmatic experiments with and within rhythmic territories. Walking up and down the room, pacing. Walking up and down a garden, hoping that movement, repetitive but never too regular, will lull. Certain devices participate: rockers, baby carriers, cars, and strollers. Seeking out the right kind of surface over which to move. Gently bumpy, but not so much as to make sleepiness become wakefulness: an ongoing soothing disturbance of ground.

So my participation in an event of research-creation organized around the aim of diagramming movement is inflected by the need to walk with a stroller on moderately bumpy ground while trying to facilitate sleep. As it turns out, the most useful piece of such ground close to hand is a playing field, part of which is marked out with the lines of two soccer pitches. It can be difficult to wander around a very clearly defined space. So these markings provide lines of orientation. In the process, the dynamic affective trajectory of a child-parent milieu is expressed: this "trajectory merges not only with the subjectivity of those who travel through a milieu, but also with the subjectivity of the milieu itself, insofar as it is reflected in those who travel through it. The map expresses the identity of the journey and what one journeys through. It merges with its object, when the object itself is movement."[16] Through sheer repetition, the movement within and through this milieu generates occasions for thinking, for generating questions: how might the trajectories of this milieu participate in an experiment to diagram the relations between the geographic and the choreographic?

As one way of thinking through this question, I decide to draw out these trajectories. Draw lines. Borrow a basic GPS device. Lots of lines. Lines that trace a certain wandering from home (fig. 8.1). These lines do not so much represent one milieu and the trajectories of which it consists: instead, just like the stroller, they work to allow milieus to connect. They facilitate movement across and between milieus precisely through connective abstraction. In this case, the child-parent milieu becomes articulated through the diagramming movement milieu, and vice versa. Such traces recall the abstractions of geography and, more specifically, of time geography. Emerging in the 1970s, time geography consisted, at least in part, of an effort to capture in diagrammatic form the time-space paths of everyday lives. In Torsten Hägerstrand's work, the diagram became a technique for drawing out — abstracting — these paths.[17] As a contribution to a renewed interest in what Parkes and Thrift called a "chronogeographic perspective," these diagrams provided a technique for describing and notating the dynamic constitution of the trajectories of everyday life.[18] Yet it was precisely this tendency toward

FIGURE 8.1

abstraction that some observers found so problematic.[19] The consequences of these tendencies were especially problematic for feminist scholars: the abstractions of time geography underpinned what Gillian Rose argued was the erasure of lived, bodily, and emotional difference through conceiving of space and agency in the image of the white master-subject.[20] There is certainly something of substance to these critiques. However, the rendering of the time geographic diagram as essentially static can and is being revised.[21] As Nigel Thrift has observed, these diagrams were, in part, a very situated "attempt to describe the pragmatics of events," in a way that also foregrounded the complexity of the nonhuman in everyday life.[22] Indeed, these diagrams were anything but static. As Thrift continues, "time geographic diagrams draw you in through a quietist creativity, trapping you in their nets. What they represent is a dynamic world in a world."[23] Seen thus, time geography enacts a diagrammatic aesthetic that anticipates more recent cartographic and choreographic efforts to draw out the movement of the world.

The traces of GPS devices can be understood similarly. They are not so much representations of movement as abstractions that draw out the lines and trajectories of which milieus are composed. Moreover, insofar as they become participants in the preparation for the event to come, these traces are not so much outlines of possible action as speculative lures for moving bodies. In a sense these traces are versions of what William Forsythe calls choreographic objects, even if this takes that term beyond its original usage by Forsythe. As Forsythe puts it, a choreographic object is a "model of potential transition from one state to another in any space imaginable. An example of a similar transition already exists in another time-based art practice: the musical score. A score represents the potential of perceptual phenomena to instigate action, the result of which can be perceived by a sense of a different order: a transition via the body from the visual to the aural. A choreographic object, or score, is by nature open to a full palette of phenomenological instigations because it acknowledges the body as wholly designed to persistently read every signal from its environment."[24] Importantly, choreographic objects do not necessarily need to be defined in terms of their relation to dance: as Forsythe reminds us, choreography and dance are not the same things, and the activity of choreography is not coterminous with the activity of dancing. Instead, to think with choreographic objects is to explore "alternative sites for the understanding of potential instigation and organization of action to reside."[25]

Generating Materials for the Event to Come

Reaffirming lines as choreographic objects opens up a series of possibilities for thinking about how the relation between the geographic and the choreographic might be experimented. And it feeds forward into the preparation for a collaborative event of research to come. It becomes entangled in a series of propositions for activity that might sustain this collaborative activity: these propositions include speculative materials, microactivities, operations, and objects. For my part these include the following:

- Generate directions for improvising with the aim of producing small acts of repair. These directions can be a combination of cartography and gesture. For instance: do you want to know the way to Montreal? Place a compass on the ground and help people to orient themselves in the direction of that city. Invite them to give directions to an object, experience, place, or person they would want themselves or someone else to take.

- Produce a form of abstract movement writing. Think of this as a kind of abstract skywriting, one that is not height or medium specific. The drawing point might be the kinesphere, or any other point for that matter.
- Write on the back of the maps of Montreal, Berlin, Madrid, and so on.
- Ask people to imagine stories for abstract traces.
- Bring maps of each of the Society of Molecules locations, including Montreal, London, Berlin, Ottawa, Tijuana, Toronto, Boston, New York, Amsterdam, Tunisia, Naples, Weimar, Sydney, Melbourne, In-between.
- Devise a compass for disorientation.
- Devise a device for perambulating.

Mixing and Mapping

On May 23, 2009, these ingredients and others are mixed at the Siobhan Davies Dance Studios in London. We have been preparing for this event for quite some time: undertaking sorties, fieldwork, and minor journeys. Much of this preparatory activity has been documented and detailed: notes, maps, photographs, films, drawings, writing. The ingredients contributed by the other participants include:

- An attempt to deliberately reclaim hitchhiking as a technique of relational movement (Joe Gerlach and Thomas Jellis)
- A series of walks along lines in Berlin (Gill Clarke) and three video fragments in response to the seed sent by emissary Jaime del Val (from Cuerpo Común, Madrid molecule)
- GPS traces of a walk in the woods, a rural environment, and graphic representations of a written "score" for an urban walk (Sarah Rubidge and Alan Stones)
- Coordinates for an ethico-aesthetic intervention in Chichester (Andrew Wilford)
- GPS traces of child-parent trajectories in a local milieu (Derek McCormack)
- A sense of what other molecules might be doing

In the morning of the twenty-third we sit and share these ingredients, exploring possible areas of overlap. The aim in doing so is not so much to reduce them to a simple or single theme as to mix them in ways that might be understood as a mutual modification of maps, where maps are composed of trajectories. The encounter between the different ingredients on the table is experimental insofar as "each map" has the potential to find "itself modified in the following map."[26] Rather than searching for a point of origin between the choreographic and geographic, an experimental space might be produced whose success could be evaluated on the basis of what kinds of "displacements" it facilitates between "mapping and movement."[27]

In the afternoon, another displacement takes place: maps are superimposed and modified again when we move to the main dance space of the Siobhan Davies Dance Studios, a bare and empty room that waits. That same sense of anticipatory anxiety: how to begin moving? Anxiety framed also by the echo of a certain disciplinary imperative: how to begin participating as a geographer?

As it has been before, the short answer to this question is a map. A large laminated map of the world is placed in the middle of the empty space of the dance studio (fig. 8.2).

FIGURE 8.2

Placed thus, it seems to operate as a kind of crystal, or seed, potentializing the room without prefiguring it, in the same way that putting a football on a grassy field or on tarmac potentializes that empty space. Very quickly, and without much discussion, an improvised geography begins to take shape around this map. Locations materialize at different real and imagined distances in the form of names on sheets of paper: Montreal, Berlin, Sydney, Ottawa, Tijuana, Melbourne, Madrid, Amsterdam, New York,

Boston, Tunisia, In-Between. Many of these locations are the sites at which other molecular events are taking place. Others represent who knows what.

At the same time, lines also appear in various forms (Post-its, notes, and seeds), sometimes running between possible destinations, sometimes veering off as tangents (fig. 8.3).

FIGURE 8.3

Using whatever is ready to hand in the room (including benches of various lengths), we begin furnishing a territory, producing differences in elevation, affording opportunities for minor inflections in our trajectories.[28] That this furnishing is central to our activity is not incidental. As Bernard Cache suggests, furniture is "that object that is directly connected to our bodies. For our most intimate or most abstract endeavours, whether they occur in bed or on a chair, furniture supplies the immediate physical environment in which our bodies act and react; for us, urban animals, furniture is thus our primary territory. Architecture, object, geography — furniture is that image where forms are fused together."[29] To furnish a room in this way is therefore to produce a "procedural architecture."[30] In some respects of course this is very similar to what Adolphe Appia had in mind when he imagined a performance space full of mobile furniture or modules that could be reconfigured in order to facilitate generative relations between spaces, music, and moving bodies. For Appia the rhythm of moving bodies would in some sense be animated by contrast with the lines and angles of this furniture. In the context of the work emerging here in this studio space, the question of juxtaposition is not so important. It is more a matter of generating a relational procedural architecture that is both the product of experimentation and the context within which that experimentation takes place. And it is not only furniture that participates in this generative process. Ideas, notes, sounds, and traces generated in advance also do. The GPS traces become projected into the space in a process of superimposition. We can think of the introduction of these materials as part of a process of multiplying what Arakawa and Gins call perceptual and kinesthetic landing sites.[31] Each offers surfaces of variation that might prompt thinking to take place. Each affords an opportunity for thinking and moving.

As we continue, something is emerging. Something is being produced.[32] If this is a work, or installation, it is no piece of "monumental or commemorative art." Yes, it is composed in part of physical objects. But it is composed of much more. It can best be understood as a relation-specific cartographic and choreographic milieu "made up of qualities, substances, powers, and events," a milieu offering opportunities for minor experimentation within and between bodies. It is a milieu composed of pathways and trajectories internal and external to it. And the real pathways we lay down are "intertwined with the virtual paths that give [this milieu] new courses or trajectories." This milieu is a "map of virtualities, drawn up by art, . . . superimposed onto the real map, whose distances [*parcours*] it transforms."[33] It emerges, at least in part, through the realisation described in figure 8.4.

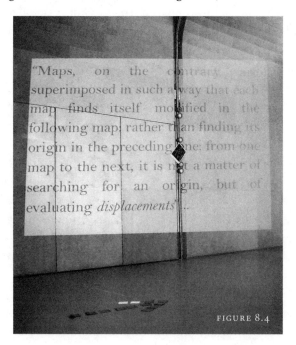

"Maps, on the contrary superimposed in such a way that each map finds itself modified in the following map rather than finding its origin in the preceding one: from one map to the next, it is not a matter of searching for an origin, but of evaluating *displacements*" . .

FIGURE 8.4

Then, at some point late in the afternoon, steps are retraced. Furniture is returned to the sides of the room. Notes, Post-its, paper are all removed. What takes place is a deliberate decomposition that is also, of necessity, an ongoing collaborative generation. It continues, until at some point only the map remains. Finally, that is also rolled up and removed.

Diagramming Value

What emerges from this kind of activity, from its paths, trajectories, and displacements? As before: a diverse set of divergent tendencies, affects, percepts, and possible concepts that find their way into other sites and events, being drawn out in diverse ways, beginning to participate in ways that have yet to be realized. But something else also emerges, something with a little more organizational consistency: a machine, a "strange contraption" for reaffirming the relation between choreography and geography. A device for organizing bodies in ways that allow them to experiment with spacetimes of experience.

Equipment

- A map of the world, preferably laminated
- A set of blank destination signs
- A set of blank instruction signs
- Pens and paper
- Local furniture: artificial or natural

Directions

- Find a location ripe for revalorization.
- Place the map.
- Distribute the blank destination signs and invite participants to write destinations, real or imagined, on the signs. Ask them to place the destinations on the ground.
- Distribute the blank signs and invite participants to devise simple instructions for traveling between destinations.
- For instance, explore how long it takes to move between two places. Travel between destination A and B in exactly 3 minutes and 25 seconds but don't use a watch.

- Pick a destination and point yourself in its direction. Close your eyes and then try to find your way to this destination.
- Pick up a traveler on your way to somewhere else.
- Become a concept venturing from home on the thread of a tune.
- Write postcards documenting your trajectories.
- Devise impossible destinations, speeds, or modes of traveling.
- Replace destinations with favorite quotes, micropolitical activities, or techniques of thinking.
- After a given period of time, disassemble signs and remove the map.

In retrospect, we might think of this game as a kind of ritornello or refrain game: an ethico-aesthetic machine for resingularizing relations between the cartographic and the choreographic such that any given site might become a relation-specific opportunity for reworking the value of geography.[34] Think of it as an alternative to the board game Monopoly. Monopoly in its current form is a perfect diagram for the reproduction of capitalist value. Accumulate sites, build property, and collect rent. And continue, around and around, until you dominate: relentlessly. Domination or bust are the only end points. Or at least this is the way in which the story is usually told. The origins of the game are rather more complicated, however. In the early years of the twentieth century, the Quaker Elisabeth Magie devised a board-based game called the Landlord's Game as a way of illuminating "the nexus connecting land laws, property rights and social injustice."[35] Later, during the 1930s, Monopoly was based on Magie's game, but without its reformist vision. In some ways what emerged through our experiment in the dance studio is a relation-specific game that short-circuits the axes of Monopoly by foregrounding how movement between events creates opportunities for generating universes of value that are not defined by site-specific capital accumulation. The work in the dance studio therefore becomes an eventful spacetime within which to devise a machine for making more of the value of geographies distributed across and between bodies in process. The game that emerges can therefore be understood as a modest diagram for facilitating what Stephen Bottoms and Matthew Ghoulish call "small acts of repair" in everyday spacetimes.[36] These small acts of repair offer opportunities for intervening in and reworking, on however modest a scale, economies and ecologies of value, and for differentiating trajectories of thinking and moving.

The Promising Geographies of Refrains for Moving Bodies

In the course of an interview about Leibniz's concept of the fold, Gilles Deleuze suggests that it is "not beginnings and ends that count, but middles. Things and thoughts advance or grow out from the middle, and that's where you have to get to work, that's where everything unfolds." For Deleuze, things and events are composed of lines. Thinking can be understood as a kind of "multilinear complex" that can "fold back on itself with intersections and inflections" like so "many twists in the path of something moving through space."[37] *Refrains for Moving Bodies* makes a case for experimenting with experience in the middle of these kinds of multilinear complexes: events composed of many lines of thinking, feeling, and moving, events that fold and refold themselves at various points. But it departs from Deleuze's claim in one important respect: these event-full complexes do not so much move "through spaces"; instead, they can be understood as generative spacetimes in the middle of which are opportunities for experimenting with affective experience. These spacetimes emerge through a kind of transversal organization whose form, duration, and intensity are facilitated by but not prefigured by preparation. While they are facilitated by certain sites, these spacetimes are not site specific: thus, while the activities at the Siobhan Davies Dance Studio are a crucial element of the process, they do not so much mark the point at which participation in a collaborative event finally begins. Rather, this daylong event is a relation-specific materialization of divergent lines and trajectories that participate in ways that run across and between — transversally — to established or obvious interests.

It is difficult to say where this kind of participation begins. It might begin much earlier, in other spacetimes. It might begin in the corridor and stairwell of the Chisenhale, as so many minor variations in sensibility generated by rhythmic movement up and down a corridor. It might begin within session after session of dance movement therapy, through the attempt to attend to and through the movement of others. It might begin during minor experiments within the affective territories of the 5 Rhythms, experiments that are successful insofar as they act as an encouragement to wander from home on lines of movement. Participation begins — or commences taking place — in the middle of each of these and so many other affective spacetimes. And the sense of participation emerging thus persists in a range of interrelated ways through encounters and events that also work to sustain this sense. It persists as a kind of ethos of "presumptive generosity" toward the question of how thinking takes place.[38] It persists as a kind of critically affirmative responsiveness to situations and events that do not immediately present clearly defined outcomes or outputs. And it persists as a reminder of the importance of a version of the Spinozist claim that one never knows in advance what bodies can do. Here the claim becomes something like the following: one never knows in advance what kind of affective spacetimes moving bodies might help generate, nor what opportunities for experimenting with experience might be afforded by these spacetimes. That is not to say that anything is possible, but that the question of what might happen is never prefigured fully in advance.

Making sense of and making more of the question of what it might mean to think of and enact logics of participation in these spacetimes is central to the affirmation of an experimental view of experience. Indeed it is often precisely through such logics of participation that the sensibilities through which thinking takes place are rendered more tangible and palpable, with the consequence that they become more available for modification or alteration. The example of abstraction is a case in point: an interest in the relation between movement and affectivity that emerges in part as a response to a critique of abstraction becomes, through encounters with movement practices, an opportunity for revising and revisiting the terms of this critique.

REFRAINS FOR MOVING bodies are generative spacetimes sensed as gatherings of intensity in the shapes of worldly arrangements. Refrains hold bodies in certain worldly arrangements at the same time as they open up other ways in which bodies can generate worlds and the values that sustain them. Refrains for moving bodies give a palpable consistency to the processual immediacy of the present while always opening that present onto the futures that edge it. Sometimes these refrains are shapes that won't let you go, while on other occasions they are creative variations in the tissue of experience.

Refrains for moving bodies are abroad in the world and are felt as such. As thinkers including Jane Bennett and Kathleen Stewart have argued, these refrains are the ways in which the worlding of the world is felt as a calling forth of the powers and capacities of bodies and their many possible arrangements.[39] As I have been arguing in this book, the capacity to modulate and perhaps invent these refrains can be cultivated in the privileged experimental constraints provided by the relation specificity of particular practices, from sports commentating to choreography. These practices furnish opportunities for working on and modulating the affective spacetimes of moving bodies through what Franco "Bifo" Berardi calls "perceptive tunings."[40]

To participate in the generative refrains of affective spacetimes is to trace a geography of sorts. The production of this geography is not about constructing an abode, or a dwelling place in which refrains are reduced to familiar names, gestures, or gatherings, although there is nothing inherently wrong about these kinds of refrains: rather, the participation toward which this book is working is about tracing a set of trajectories through which bodies emerge as the shapes of worldly participation.

This geography is always errant, unruly, concerned with surfaces of variation along which movement remains prior to any sense of site, location, or position. This geography, emerging as a more or less than disciplinary involvement in research-creation, is a transductive sensing of the processuality of spacetimes. Its inclination is to become affirmative in and of transition: affirmative of experience as both the target of critique and the necessary condition for going beyond critique; and affirmative of situations of experimental empiricism from which new refrains might emerge in a "tentative constructing toward a holding in place."[41] It is a geography that works hard to respond generously to events, practices, and situations that offer possibilities for holding open futures, however modestly. Put another way, this geography is about stretching out the spacetimes of empirical moments in ways that allow these spacetimes to become intervals of potential that percolate in thinking, feeling, and moving. One never knows what might emerge from these intervals. This doesn't mean that anything is possible: it means that while working within a given set of relation-specific constraints, even within a given set of disciplinary habits of thinking, one never knows what might happen, what kinds of refrains might be generative of what kinds of worlds, however minor, and what new ways and relations of becoming ethico-political, however modest, might emerge as part of the inventive production of what Whitehead calls "novel togetherness."[42]

Preface

1. Brian Friel, *Dancing at Lughnasa* (London: Faber, 1990).

2. See, for example, Declan Kiberd, "Dancing at Lughnasa," *Irish Review* 27 (2001): 18–23; Anna McMullan, "'In Touch with Some Otherness': Gender, Authority and the Body in 'Dancing at Lughnasa,'" *Irish University Review* 29, no. 1 (1999): 90–100. Perhaps most significant here is McMullan's observation that Friel's narrator, Michael, ends up reproducing the figure of the male narrator as distanced observer of emotional female bodies. Equally, the centrality of nostalgia in the play has also been subject to some criticism. My preface obviously runs the risk of rehearsing some of these problems.

3. Friel, *Dancing at Lughnasa*, 71.

4. My aim in this book is not to rehearse an overview of nonrepresentational theory. Nigel Thrift, *Non-representational Theory: Space, Politics, Affect* (London: Routledge, 2008); and Ben Anderson and Paul Harrison, eds., *Taking-Place: Non-representational Theories and Geography* (Farnham, U.K.: Ashgate, 2010), already perform this role very well. I would echo Anderson and Harrison's observation that this work is best understood as a diverse assemblage of theories and not one overarching approach. Equally, it is also worth noting that while this work continues to generate a range of critical responses, the point of *Refrains for Moving Bodies* is not necessarily to mount a defense of nonrepresentational theories that addresses these responses directly. For sympathetic overviews of some of the key questions posed to and about nonrepresentational theories, see Hayden Lorimer, "Progress in Cultural Geography: Non-representational Conditions and Concerns," *Progress in Human Geography* 32, no. 4 (2008): 551–559; Tim Cresswell, "Review Essay. Non-representational Theory and Me: Notes of an Interested Sceptic," *Environment and Planning D: Society and Space* 30, no. 1 (2012): 96–105; Eric Laurier and Chris Philo, "Possible Geographies: A Passing Encounter in a Café," *Area* 38, no. 4 (2006): 353–363. For a rather stronger critique, especially of the

emphasis on affect in much of this work, see Clive Barnett, "Political Affects in Public Space: Normative Blind-Spots in Non-representational Ontologies," *Transactions of the Institute of British Geographers* 33, no. 2 (2008): 186–200. Another potential "blind spot" in this book is close attention to the relation between gender, bodies, and non-representational thinking. For a discussion of the generative tensions between strands of feminist thinking and nonrepresentational theory, see Rachel Colls, "Feminism, Bodily Difference and Non-representational Geographies," *Transactions of the Institute of British Geographers* 37, no. 3 (2012): 430–445. Needless to say, I don't think that anything about which I write in this book precludes attention to such issues.

5. As will become clear throughout this book, this conceptual approach owes a particular debt to the radical empiricism outlined by William James. See William James, *Essays in Radical Empiricism* (Lincoln: University of Nebraska Press, 1996).

6. That said, the terms of political engagement in this book are limited in important ways. *Refrains for Moving Bodies* does not engage in any sustained way, for instance, with the processes through which the affective spaces of moving bodies become implicated in the politics of race and ethnicity. For affectively imbued accounts of these issues, see Arun Saldanha, *Psychedelic White: Goa Trance and the Viscosity of Race* (Minneapolis: University of Minnesota Press, 2007); Ash Amin, *Land of Strangers* (Cambridge: Polity, 2012); Dan Swanton, "Flesh, Metal, Road: Tracing the Machinic Geographies of Race," *Environment and Planning D: Society and Space* 28, no. 3 (2010): 447–446. At the same time, as chapter 6 demonstrates, my aim here is also to cultivate opportunities for a certain minor politics, by, for instance, identifying opportunities for developing nonterritorial affective techniques from within the midst of territorializing practices.

7. I draw the idea of relation-specificity from the work of Brian Massumi and Erin Manning. See Brian Massumi, "Urban Appointment: A Possible Rendez-Vous with the City," in *Making Art out of Databases*, ed. Joke Brouwer and Arjen Mulder, 28–55 (Rotterdam: V2 Organisatie/Dutch Architecture Institute, 2003); and Erin Manning, *Relationscapes: Movement, Art, Philosophy* (Cambridge, MA: MIT Press, 2009).

8. As Ben Anderson and Paul Harrison have argued, this kind of affirmative critique is central to the promise of nonrepresentational theories and is exemplified in the work of figures such as Jane Bennett and William Connolly. See Anderson and Harrison, *Taking-Place*.

Introduction

1. This, of course, is one of the key insights emerging from the so-called mobilities turn across the social sciences and humanities. For overviews see Tim Cresswell, *On the Move: Mobility in the Western World* (New York: Routledge, 2006); John Urry, *Mobilities* (Cambridge, MA: Polity Press, 2007); Peter Adey, *Mobility* (London: Routledge, 2010). There are obvious resonances between the project of the present book and the conceptual and empirical trajectories that scholars working on questions of mobility are pursuing, not least through the question of how the affective qualities of moving bodies are organized through various techniques and technologies. At the same time,

while this book deliberately emphasizes the affective capacities of moving bodies, it should be clear, I hope, that this emphasis is not intended to naively champion or privilege the intentional, active body. Nor does it preclude or undervalue the conceptual, empirical, or ethico-political significance of stillness. See, for instance, the wonderful collection of essays in David Bissell and Gillian Fuller, eds., *Stillness in a Mobile World* (London: Routledge, 2010).

2. Erin Manning, *Politics of Touch: Movement, Sense, Sovereignty* (Minneapolis: University of Minnesota Press, 2007).

3. For an overview see Sebastian Abrahamsson and Paul Simpson, "The Limits of the Body: Boundaries, Capacities, Thresholds," *Social and Cultural Geography* 12, no. 4 (2011): 331–338.

4. There is an extensive literature on thinking spacetime in relational terms. See, for example, Doreen Massey, *For Space* (London: Sage, 2005); Nigel Thrift, "Space," *Theory, Culture and Society* 23, no. 2–3 (2006): 21–35.

5. Henri Lefebvre, *The Production of Space*, trans. Donald Nicholson Smith (Oxford: Blackwell, 1991). José Gil understands this relation in a similarly useful way. For Gil, bodies in movement do more than simply occupy space: they are also always creating a space of potential akin to an aura. Gil describes this process as one of exfoliation. Gil's use of the term "exfoliation" captures a sense of how bodies are always giving off space. As such, it is suggestive of a process akin to shedding dead skin, which for me does not quite capture the lively, animated qualities of the spacetimes of which moving bodies are generative. José Gil, *Metamorphoses of the Body*, trans. Stephen Muecke (Minneapolis: University of Minnesota Press, 1998).

6. I borrow the term "attunement" from Kathleen Stewart: "Atmospheric Attunements," *Environment and Planning D: Society and Space* 39, no. 3 (2011): 445–453.

7. See Patricia Clough and Jean Halley, eds., *The Affective Turn: Theorizing the Social* (Durham, NC: Duke University Press, 2007); Melissa Gregg and Gregory Seigworth, eds., *The Affect Theory Reader* (Durham, NC: Duke University Press, 2010). Within the discipline with which I am most familiar, human geography, this affective turn has its own fissures, which have opened up around distinctions between terms such as affect and emotion. Somehow, in the process, these fissures have been artificially expanded by various commentators to form an unbridgeable gap, which these same commentators then try to help us all cross. Despite how it may seem, I have always been more interested in cultivating an affective empiricism through a kind of conceptual differentiation than in engaging in a tired critique that assumes concepts are part of some strange zero-sum empirical and political game.

8. See Brian Massumi, *Parables for the Virtual: Movement, Affect, Sensation* (Durham, NC: Duke University Press, 2002); Ben Anderson, "Becoming and Being Hopeful: Towards a Theory of Affect," *Environment and Planning D: Society and Space* 24, no. 5 (2006): 733–752.

9. Kathleen Stewart, *Ordinary Affects* (Durham, NC: Duke University Press, 2007).

10. For a persuasive critique of this emphasis on the relational, see Paul Harrison, "'How Shall I Say It . . . ?': Relating the Nonrelational," *Environment and Planning A* 39, no. 1 (2007): 590–608.

11. This project has by now taken on a life of its own. Important contributions include Nigel Thrift, *Non-representational Theory: Space, Politics, Affect* (London: Routledge, 2008); Anderson, "Becoming and Being Hopeful"; John-David Dewsbury, "Witnessing Space: 'Knowledge without Contemplation,'" *Environment and Planning A* 35, no. 11 (2003): 1907–1932.

12. A critique of space and spatiality has often been integral to philosophical arguments about the necessity and difficulty of affirming the reality of movement and becoming. The writing of Henri Bergson has had a notable influence here. Famously, for Bergson our habits of perception tend to spatialize movement, reducing it to a series of discrete points on a line of extension. We think movement in the manner of cinematic perception, and by doing this we lose a sense of the real duration of movement in itself. Similarly, for Alfred North Whitehead, thinking the reality of process is badly served by what he called the fallacy of misplaced concreteness, through which the dynamic becoming of actual entities is misapprehended. See Alfred North Whitehead, *The Concept of Nature* (New York: Prometheus Books, 2004) and Alfred North Whitehead, *Process and Reality*, rev. ed. (New York: Free Press, 1978). The force of the influential critiques by Bergson and Whitehead would seem to work against the naive affirmation of space and spatiality as part of the effort to grasp the participation of moving bodies in the processual nature of kinesthetic and affective experience. Certainly, Bergson suggests that in order to understand duration we need to "separate from the mind the space in which it is so at home"; Henri Bergson, *The Creative Mind: An Introduction to Metaphysics* (New York: Dover, 2007), 29. But the real upshot of philosophical attempts to think movement and process is not necessarily a dismissal of space per se, nor the affirmation of a form of thinking that is determinedly aspatial. Rather, the respective works of Bergson and Whitehead might better be understood as incessant reminders of the problems that arise when we conceive of space and time as separate ontological dimensions. Importantly, they also encourage the development of modes of thinking that take spacetime seriously as an ontogenetic process: a process generative of ongoing differentiation. This is precisely why it is important to experiment with concepts like rhythm, atmosphere, and refrain as part of the process of thinking and generating spacetimes.

13. Giorgio Agamben, *The Man without Content*, trans. Lisa Albert (Stanford, CA: Stanford University Press, 1999), 101. The gendering of these claims is, of course, problematic.

14. For an overview of the geographies of rhythm, see the introduction to Jon May and Nigel Thrift, eds., *TimeSpace: Geographies of Temporality* (New York: Routledge, 2001); and Tim Edensor, ed., *Geographies of Rhythm* (Farnham, U.K.: Ashgate, 2010).

15. See, for instance, Derek P. McCormack, "Engineering Affective Atmospheres: On the Moving Geographies of the 1897 Andrée Expedition," *Cultural Geographies* 15, no. 4 (2008): 413–430; Ben Anderson, "Affective Atmospheres," *Emotion, Space, and Society* 2, no. 2 (2009): 77–81; David Bissell, "Passenger Mobilities: Affective Atmospheres and the Sociality of Public Transport," *Environment and Planning D: Society and Space* 28, no. 2 (2010): 270–289.

16. Anderson, "Affective Atmospheres," 80.

17. Gernot Böhme, "The Art of the Stage Set as a Paradigm for Aesthetic Atmospheres," 189, contribution to a colloquium, Cresson, accessed September 28, 2010, www.cresson.archi.fr. In some sense Böhme does not go far enough here because he assumes that the things between which atmospheres float are relatively well defined.

18. Böhme writes that "the making of atmospheres is therefore confined to setting the conditions in which the atmosphere appears. We refer to these conditions as generators" (Böhme, "The Art of the Stage Set," 189).

19. Their most explicit treatment of this concept is in Gilles Deleuze and Félix Guattari, *A Thousand Plateaus*, trans. Brian Massumi (London: Athlone, 1988).

20. Félix Guattari, "Ritornellos and Existential Affects," in *The Guattari Reader*, ed. Gary Genosko, 158–171 (Oxford: Blackwell, 1996), 158.

21. See Elizabeth Grosz, *Chaos, Territory, Art: Deleuze and the Framing of the Earth* (New York: Columbia University Press, 2010).

22. Guattari, "Ritornellos," 158. For a discussion of the refrain in relation to how such territories can be mapped through the wider affective contours of the contemporary conjuncture in Western societies and economies, see Lawrence Grossberg, *Cultural Studies in the Future Tense* (Durham, NC: Duke University Press, 2010).

23. The creation of concepts is not akin to a one-off Eureka moment. Instead, it is a process of re-creating, in which concepts are remade every time they are put to work. This is a process that has the potential to modify both concepts and the situation in which they participate.

24. Isabelle Stengers, "A Constructivist Reading of *Process and Reality*," *Theory, Culture and Society* 25, no. 4 (2008): 91–110.

25. By learning to be affected, I mean something similar to Bruno Latour's use of that term as a way of pointing to the importance of being moved by the humans and nonhumans that compose a field of enquiry and involvement. See Bruno Latour, "How to Talk about the Body: The Normative Dimension of Science Studies," *Body and Society* 10, no. 2–3 (2004): 205–229.

26. Thrift, *Non-representational Theory*; Jane Bennett, *The Enchantment of Modern Life: Attachments, Crossings, Ethics* (Princeton, NJ: Princeton University Press, 2001); William Connolly, *Neuropolitics: Thinking, Culture, Speed* (Minneapolis: University of Minnesota Press, 2001); Erin Manning, *Relationscapes: Movement, Art, Philosophy* (Cambridge, MA: MIT Press, 2009); Massumi, *Parables for the Virtual*.

27. See the introduction to Ben Anderson and Paul Harrison, eds., *Taking-Place: Non-representational Theories and Geography* (Farnham, U.K.: Ashgate, 2010).

28. See Michel Foucault, *Ethics, Subjectivity and Truth: Essential Works of Foucault 1954–1984*, ed. Paul Rabinow (London: Penguin, 1997), 132.

29. See, for example, John-David Dewsbury, "Performativity and the Event: Enacting a Philosophy of Difference," *Environment and Planning D: Society and Space* 18, no. 4 (2000): 473–496; and Nigel Thrift, "Afterwords," *Environment and Planning D: Society and Space* 18, no. 3 (2000): 213–255.

30. There are parallels here with other reworkings of experiment as part of the reimagining of urban materialities and ecologies. See Steve Hinchliffe, Matthew Kearnes, Monica Degen, and Sarah Whatmore, "Urban Wild Things:

A Cosmo-political Experiment," *Environment and Planning D: Society and Space* 23, no. 5 (2005): 643–658.

31. For an exemplary demonstration of anthropological fieldwork that captures this sense of the field through ethnography, see Yael Navarro-Yashin, *The Make-Believe Space: Affective Geography in a Postwar Polity* (Durham, NC: Duke University Press, 2012). My project here is similar in the sense that it is open to the affects of different agencies, but different in the sense that it is not overly indebted to a particular view of what counts as ethnography.

32. For an overview, see John-David Dewsbury and Simon Naylor, "Practising Geographical Knowledge: Fields, Bodies and Dissemination," *Area* 34, no. 3 (2003): 253–260; Hayden Lorimer, "The Geographical Fieldcourse as Active Archive," *Cultural Geographies* 10, no. 3 (2003): 278–308; Richard Powell, "Becoming a Geographical Scientist: Oral Histories of Arctic Fieldwork," *Transactions of the Institute of British Geographers* 33, no. 4 (2008): 548–565. For discussion of the wider philosophical and empirical recasting of the field and fieldwork, see Bruno Latour, *Pandora's Hope* (Cambridge, MA: Harvard University Press, 2002); Michael Pryke, Gillian Rose, and Sarah Whatmore, eds., *Using Social Theory: Thinking through Research* (London: Sage, 2003).

33. For exemplary performances of how geographies might be narrated as an art of experimental address that gathers the fragments of experience without letting them settle, see the work of John Wylie: "Smoothlands: Fragments/Landscapes/Fragments," *Cultural Geographies* 13, no. 3 (2006): 458–465; and "Landscape, Absence and the Geographies of Love," *Transactions of the Institute of British Geographers* 34, no. 3 (2009): 275–289.

34. In this respect I have been fortunate to begin my career as an academic geographer at a time when such experimentalism has been actively encouraged, not least through the exemplary influence of Nigel Thrift. For exemplars of this narrative experimentalism, see the essays in Anderson and Harrison, *Taking-Place*. Equally, one might make a more general point here: that disciplines, if they are alive, consist of an ongoing series of experiments with what counts as an experiment. This is by no means a new claim, albeit one that has been made for different reasons. See Isaiah Bowman, "Geography in the Creative Experiment," *Geographical Review* 28, no.1 (1938): 1–19. For a more recent review of how ideas and practices of experiment frame geographical research, see Angela Last, "Experimental Geographies," *Geography Compass* 6, no. 12 (2012): 706–724; and Richard Powell and Alex Vasudevan, "Geographies of Experiment," *Environment and Planning A* 39, no. 8 (2007): 1790–1793.

35. See Massumi, *Parables for the Virtual*.

36. See Lauren Berlant, "On the Case," *Critical Enquiry* 33, no. 4 (2002): 663–672, 663.

37. Gregory Bateson, *Mind and Nature: A Necessary Unity* (New York: E. P. Dutton, 1979). Charles Sanders Peirce, *The Collected Papers of Charles S. Peirce*, 8 vols., ed. Charles Hartshorne, Paul Weiss, and Arthur Burks (Cambridge, MA: Harvard University Press, 1931–1958).

38. See Andrew Barry, "Political Situations: Knowledge Controversies in Transnational Governance," *Critical Policy Studies* 6, no. 3 (2012): 324–336.

39. See William James, *Essays in Radical Empiricism* (Lincoln: University of Nebraska Press, 1996), 57.

40. Steven Shaviro, "Post-cinematic Affect: On Grace Jones, *Boarding Gate* and *Southland Tales*," *Film-Philosophy* 14, no. 1 (2010): 1–102.

Chapter One. Transitions

Parts of this chapter appeared in Derek P. McCormack, "Drawing Out the Lines of the Event," *Cultural Geographies* 11, no. 2 (2004): 212–220.

1. For an account of the architectural and cultural history of the corridor, see Mark Jarzombek, "Corridor Spaces," *Critical Inquiry* 36 (summer 2010): 728–770.

2. George Perec, *Species of Spaces and Other Pieces* (London: Penguin, 1999).

3. See Petra Kuppers, *Disability and Contemporary Performance: Bodies on Edge* (London: Routledge, 2003).

4. For a parallel account see Petra Kuppers, "Landscaping: Spacings," *Women and Performance: A Journal of Feminist Theory* 13, no. 2 (2003): 41–56.

5. Established in the early 1980s by an artist's collective, the Chisenhale exists to provide an environment in which dancers, movement artists, and others can explore and engage in collaborative work. See www.chisenhaledancespace.co.uk.

6. See Nick Kaye, *Site Specific Art: Performance, Place, and Documentation* (London: Routledge, 2000).

7. Kuppers, "Landscaping," 41.

8. See Kanta Kochhar-Lindgren, *Hearing Difference: The Third Ear in Experimental, Deaf, and Multicultural Theater* (Washington, DC: Gallaudet University Press, 2006).

9. Elizabeth Bishop, *Complete Poems* (London: Chatto and Windus, 1991), 3.

10. See Henri Bergson, *The Two Sources of Morality and Religion*, trans. R. Ashley Audra and Cloudesley Brereton, with the assistance of W. Horsfall Carter (Notre Dame, IN: University of Notre Dame Press, 1977).

11. Giorgio Agamben, *Infancy and History: On the Destruction of Experience*, trans. Lisa Heron (London: Verso, 2007).

12. See Ben Anderson, "Affect and Biopower: Towards a Politics of Life," *Transactions of the Institute of British Geographers* 37, no. 1 (2012): 28–43.

13. See, for instance, Michel Foucault, "Technologies of the Self," in *The Essential Works of Michel Foucault, 1954–1984*, vol. 1, ed. Paul Rabinow and Nikolas Rose, 145–169 (New York: New York University Press, 2003).

14. As Claire Blencowe has argued, in Foucault's work biopolitics "should be understood as a historically specific formulation of experience and embodiment." See Claire Blencowe, *Biopolitical Experience: Foucault, Power, and Positive Critique* (Basingstoke: Palgrave Macmillan, 2011), 1. Foucault is therefore concerned with the history of the positivity of modernity and the forms of experience, life, and value that it produces.

15. Raymond Williams, *Keywords* (London: Flamingo, 1984).

16. John Dewey, *Art as Experience* (New York: Minton Balch, 1958), 4.

17. William James, *Essays in Radical Empiricism* (Lincoln: University of Nebraska Press, 1996), 4.

18. James, *Essays in Radical Empiricism*, 26.

19. James, *Essays in Radical Empiricism*, 23.

20. Dewey, *Art as Experience*, 23.

21. John Dewey, "The Need for a Recovery of Philosophy," in *The Philosophy of John Dewey*, ed. John McDermott, 59–97 (Chicago: University of Chicago Press, 1981), 63.

22. Dewey, "The Need for a Recovery of Philosophy," 65.

23. James, *Essays in Radical Empiricism*.

24. Dewey, "The Need for a Recovery," 64.

25. James, *Essays in Radical Empiricism*, 69.

26. James, *Essays in Radical Empiricism*, 71.

27. Dewey, "The Need for a Recovery," 91.

28. Dewey, "The Need for a Recovery," 63.

29. Dewey, "The Need for a Recovery," 91.

30. For a similar argument, albeit one influenced by a reading of Deleuze on the event, see John-David Dewsbury, "Performativity and the Event: Enacting a Philosophy of Difference," *Environment and Planning D: Society and Space* 18, no. 4 (2000): 473–496.

31. See Isabelle Stengers, "A Constructivist Reading of *Process and Reality*," *Theory, Culture and Society* 25, no. 4 (2008): 109.

32. Following Erin Manning, I take generative constraints to mean parameters of possibility that gather together participants in specific ways precisely to provide conditions for going beyond these parameters. See Erin Manning, *Relationscapes: Movement, Art, Philosophy* (Cambridge, MA: MIT Press, 2009).

33. Richard Shusterman, *Body Consciousness: A Philosophy of Mindfulness and Somaesthetics* (Cambridge: Cambridge University Press, 2008), 139.

34. William James, "The Energies of Men," *Science N.S.* 25, no. 635 (1907): 321–332.

35. Cited in F. Matthias Alexander, *The Alexander Technique: The Essential Writings of F. Matthias Alexander*, selected and introduced by Edward Maisal (New York: Carol Communications, 1989), 171–172.

36. Cited in Alexander, *The Alexander Technique*, 171–172.

37. See William Connolly, *Neuropolitics: Thinking, Culture, Speed* (Minneapolis: University of Minnesota Press, 2001).

38. See William Connolly, *A World of Becoming* (Durham, NC: Duke University Press, 2011).

39. See Jason Kosnoski, "Artful Discussion: John Dewey's Classroom as a Model of Deliberative Association," *Political Theory* 33, no. 5 (2005): 654–677.

40. Kosnoski, "Artful Discussion," 667.

41. Kosnoski, "Artful Discussion," 669.

42. Francesca Bordogna, *William James at the Boundaries: Philosophy, Science, and the Geography of Knowledge* (Chicago: University of Chicago Press, 2008), 256.

43. William James, *Pragmatism* (Indianapolis: Hackett, 1981), 29.

44. See Bordogna, *William James at the Boundaries*, 257.

45. Jarzombek, "Corridor Spaces," 263.

46. As an architectural space, the precise origins of the cloister are rather unclear. As Walter Horn argues, the cloister seems to have emerged primarily for a range of economic and social reasons, not least of which was the need for a degree of uniformity in the structure and organization of monastic life. In addition, it seems that the cloister borrowed from the design of certain notable Mediterranean villas. See Walter Horn, "On the Origins of the Medieval Cloister," *Gesta* 12, no. 1–2 (1973): 13–52. The historian Mary Carruthers has also argued that the cloister played a particular function in the performance of memory work. As she puts it, "the cloister became, by the eleventh century, the pre-eminent place of meditational memory work, where monks read and prayed and also where novices were instructed." For Carruthers the cloister is therefore not so much a "cryptogram, but rather a tool, a machine for thinking," one in which the craft of memory is performed. Crucially, insofar as the cloister functions as this kind of thinking-space, it is not reducible to the physical or architectural attributes of its design — it is composed instead as a space through which the gestural and the symbolic, the localized and the infinite, are coemergent. See Mary Carruthers, *The Craft of Thought: Meditation, Rhetoric, and the Making of Images, 400–1200* (Cambridge: Cambridge University Press, 2000), 272–273.

47. Henri Lefebvre, *The Production of Space*, trans. Donald Nicholson Smith (Oxford: Blackwell, 1991), 216.

48. Lefebvre, *The Production of Space*, 217. For a more developed discussion of how some of Lefebvre's ideas can illuminate the microspaces of religious practice and performance, see Darlene Brooks Hedstrom, "The Geography of the Monastic Cell in Early Egyptian Monastic Literature," *Church History* 78, no. 4 (2009): 756–791.

49. Lefebvre indicates that gesture is not merely a feature of human movement: "'Gesture' should be taken here in a broad sense, so that a turning around may be considered a gesture, one which modifies a person's orientation and points of reference. The word is preferable to 'behaviour,' for a gestural action has goal or aim (which is not, of course, to imply some immanent teleology). A spider moving around on its web or a shellfish emerging from its shell are performing gestures in this sense" (*The Production of Space*, 174).

50. Lefebvre, *The Production of Space*, 216.

51. Michel Serres, *The Five Senses: A Philosophy of Mingled Bodies*, trans. Margaret Sankey and Peter Cowley (London: Athlone, 2008).

52. Kuppers, "Landscaping," 52.

53. On this understanding of affect, see Brian Massumi, *Parables for the Virtual: Movement, Affect, Sensation* (Durham, NC: Duke University Press, 2002).

54. Elizabeth Shouse, "Feeling, Emotion, Affect," *M/C Journal* 8, no. 6 (2005); Ben Anderson, "Becoming and Being Hopeful: Towards a Theory of Affect," *Environment and Planning D: Society and Space* 24, no. 5 (2006): 733–752.

55. William James, *The Principles of Psychology*, vol. 1 (New York: Dover, 1950), 254.

56. James, *Principles of Psychology*, 255.

57. James, *Principles of Psychology*, 255.

58. James, *Principles of Psychology*, 255–256.

59. Kaye, *Site Specific Art*, 1.

60. See Brian Massumi, "Urban Appointment: A Possible Rendez-vous with the City," in *Making Art out of Databases*, ed. Joke Brouwer and Arjen Mulder, 28–55 (Rotterdam: v2 Organisatie / Dutch Architecture Institute, 2003).

61. William James, *A Pluralistic Universe* (Lincoln: University of Nebraska Press, 1996), 321.

62. James, *A Pluralistic Universe*, 97.

63. Robert Irwin, *Being and Circumstance* (San Francisco: Lapis, 1985), 27.

64. Mike Pearson and Michael Shanks, *Theatre/Archaeology* (London: Routledge, 2001), 24.

65. Pearson and Shanks, *Theatre/Archaeology*, 24.

Chapter Two. Rhythmic Bodies and Affective Atmospheres

This chapter builds upon ideas first developed in Derek P. McCormack, "Diagramming Practice and Performance," *Environment and Planning D: Society and Space* 23, no. 1 (2005): 119–147.

1. The English term seems to have originated with John Harvey in Birmingham, who derived it from the Platonic idea of eurhythmia. Dalcroze himself used the term *La rythmique*. See Clark Rogers, "Dalcroze Eurhythmics," *Southern Communication Journal* 35, no. 3 (1970): 225–226.

2. See Francis Steegmuller, *Cocteau: A Biography* (London: Macmillan, 1970); Modris Eksteins, *Rites of Spring: The Great War and the Birth of the Modern Age* (New York: First Mariner Books, 2000).

3. John Dewey, *Art as Experience* (New York: Minton Balch, 1958), 155.

4. Dewey, *Art as Experience*, 155.

5. Dewey, *Art as Experience*, 155, emphasis in original.

6. Dewey, *Art as Experience*, 147.

7. Dewey, *Art as Experience*, 15.

8. Lefebvre is critical of pragmatism's focus on individual experience at the expense of breadth of theoretical vision and a concern with the problems and dialectical conflicts in everyday life. See Henri Lefebvre, *Critique of Everyday Life*, vol. 2, trans. John Moore (London: Verso, 2008), 232–234. For a discussion of some of the overlaps between Lefebvre and Dewey see Ben Highmore, "Homework," *Cultural Studies* 18, no. 2 (2004): 306–327; Mary McCloud, "Introduction," in *The Pragmatist Imagination: Thinking about Things in the Making*, ed. Joan Ockman, 170–175 (Princeton, NJ: Princeton Architectural Press, 2000).

9. Lefebvre's ideas about rhythmanalysis are developed over a number of publications. See Henri Lefebvre, *The Production of Space*, trans. Donald Nicholson Smith (Oxford: Blackwell, 1991); *Critique of Everyday Life*, vol. 2; *Critique of Everyday Life*, vol. 3, trans. Gregory Elliot (London: Verso, 2008); *Elements of Rhythmanalysis: Space, Time, and Everyday Life*, trans. Stuart Elden and Gerald Moore (London: Continuum, 2004).

10. "Rhythmanalysis" is also a term used by Gaston Bachelard. However, the term

is neither Bachelard's nor Lefebvre's but is derived from M. Pinheiro dos Santos, who taught at the University of Porto in Brazil. As outlined by Bachelard, Dos Santos's rhythmanalysis involves a study of "the phenomenology of rhythm from three points of view: material, biological, and psychological." See Gaston Bachelard, *The Dialectic of Duration*, trans. Mary McAllester Jones (Manchester: Clinamen Press, 2000), 38.

11. Lefebvre, *Elements of Rhythmanalysis*, 42.

12. Lefebvre, *The Production of Space*, 207.

13. This invitation has been taken up in different ways. See, for example, Ian Borden, *Skateboarding, Space and the City* (Oxford: Berg, 2001); Gregory Seigworth and Michael Gardiner, "Rethinking Everyday Life: And Then Nothing Turns Itself Inside Out," *Cultural Studies* 18, no. 2–3 (2004): 139–159; Paul Simpson, "Chronic Everyday Life: Rhythmanalysing Street Performance," *Social and Cultural Geography* 9, no. 7 (2008): 807–829.

14. Lefebvre, *The Production of Space*, 406.

15. Lefebvre, *The Production of Space*, 205–206.

16. Lefebvre, *Elements of Rhythmanalysis*, 66.

17. Hillel Schwartz, "Torque: The New Kinaesthetic of the Twentieth Century," in *Incorporations*, ed. Jonathan Crary and Sandford Kwinter, 71–126 (New York: Zone Books, 1991). This kinesthetic was also expressed through the context-specific cultural formations of particular cities and places. For an example, see Alexander Vasudevan's account of forms of experimental embodiment in Weimar Germany, in "Symptomatic Acts, Experimental Embodiments: Theatres of Scientific Protest in Interwar Germany," *Environment and Planning A* 39, no. 8 (2007): 1812–1837.

18. For illuminating accounts see Anson Rabinbach, *The Human Motor: Energy, Fatigue and the Origins of Modernity* (Berkeley: University of California Press, 1992); and Nigel Thrift, *Spatial Formations* (London: Sage, 1996).

19. Such was the importance of rhythm to this articulation that its study seemed to demand the development of a distinctive field, one that Michael Golston calls "rhythmics." See Michael Golston, *Rhythm and Race in Modernist Poetry and Dance* (New York: Columbia University Press, 2008).

20. Alfred North Whitehead, *An Enquiry Concerning the Principles of Natural Knowledge* (New York: Dover, 1982), 198.

21. Henri Bergson, *Time and Free Will: An Essay on the Immediate Data of Consciousness* (Mineola, NY: Dover, [1913] 2001). Bergson's rather acidic treatment of space as a category inhibiting the appreciation of movement, transition, and duration is not always helpful insofar as it fails to acknowledge fully that space and time may be coconstitutive, or that there may be a multiplicity of different kinds of spaces. The legacy of this has been quite profound, especially insofar as Bergson has been reread through Deleuze. Thus, even as perceptive a commentator as Todd May is wont to observe: "If we think spatially, the world is as it seems, exhausted by its identities and distinguished by differences in degree. If we think temporally with Bergson, the world is always more than it seems, always fraught with differences that can actualize themselves in novel and unfamiliar ways." Todd May, *Deleuze* (Cambridge: Cambridge

University Press, 2005), 56. Lefebvre encourages us to modify this juxtaposition of the temporal and spatial. As such, he also encourages us to look for hints in Bergson of such a conception. For instance, in *The Creative Mind*, Bergson makes the following claim: "reality has extension just as it has duration; but this concrete extent is not the infinite and infinitely divisible space the intellect takes as a place in which to build. Concrete space has been extracted from things. They are not in it; it is space which is in them." Henri Bergson, *The Creative Mind: An Introduction to Metaphysics* (New York: Dover, 2007), 77.

22. Bergson, *The Creative Mind*, 69. In *The Dialectic of Duration*, Gaston Bachelard shares this concern: as he puts it, the "creative value of becoming [in Bergson's writing] is limited by the very fact of fundamental continuity" (24). Any sense of continuity is for Bachelard merely the effect or appearance of a "complex of multiple ordering actions which support each other. If we say that we are living in a single, homogenous domain we shall see that time can no longer move on. At the very most, it just hops about. In fact duration always needs alterity for it to appear continuous" (64). For Bachelard, Bergson's emphasis on continuity also has important ethical implications. It underpins "a philosophy of fullness" and "a psychology of plenitude" (23) in which life is "never absolutely and unconditionally at risk" (27). Bachelard argues instead that duration needs to be understood as dialectical and heterogeneous — something whose existence requires active effort. Duration, in other words, must be maintained and activated.

23. Lefebvre, *Critique of Everyday Life*, vol. 2, 342.

24. John Dewey, *Experience and Nature* (New York: Dover, 1958), 51.

25. Bergson, *The Creative Mind*, 69–70.

26. Henri Bergson, *Matter and Memory*, trans. N. M. Paul and W. S. Palmer (London: Zone Books, 1988), 207.

27. For a discussion, see Erin Manning, *Relationscapes: Movement, Art, Philosophy* (Cambridge, MA: MIT Press, 2009).

28. See also Mark Antliff, *Inventing Bergson: Cultural Politics and the Parisian Avant-Garde* (Princeton, NJ: Princeton University Press, 1993), 53.

29. Emile Jaques-Dalcroze, *Rhythm, Music and Education* (London: Chatto and Windus, 1921), 91.

30. Jaques-Dalcroze, *Rhythm, Music and Education*, 63.

31. Jaques-Dalcroze, *Rhythm, Music and Education*, 1.

32. Jaques-Dalcroze, *Rhythm, Music and Education*, vii.

33. Jaques-Dalcroze, *Rhythm, Music and Education*, viii.

34. Jaques-Dalcroze, *Rhythm, Music and Education*, viii, emphasis in original.

35. Jaques-Dalcroze, *Rhythm, Music and Education*, 4–5.

36. Jaques-Dalcroze, *Rhythm, Music and Education*, 4–5.

37. Jaques-Dalcroze, *Rhythm, Music and Education*, 61.

38. Jaques-Dalcroze, *Rhythm, Music and Education*, 93.

39. Jaques-Dalcroze, *Rhythm, Music and Education*, 103.

40. Jaques-Dalcroze, *Rhythm, Music and Education*, 65.

41. Jaques-Dalcroze, *Rhythm, Music and Education*, 78.

42. See also Katherine Everett Gilbert, "Mind and Medium in the Modern Dance," *Journal of Aesthetics and Art Criticism* 1, no. 1 (1941): 106–129.

43. Margaret H'Doubler, *The Dance and Its Place in Education* (New York: Harcourt Brace, 1925), 148. As H'Doubler illustrates, for progressive educators and thinkers Dewey provided a source of intellectual support for the rhythmic exercises devised by Dalcroze. See Patricia Shehan Campbell, "Rhythmic Movement and Public School Music Education: Conservative and Progressive Views of the Formative Years," *Journal of Research in Music Education* 39, no. 1 (1991): 12–22. For a discussion of a figure whose work drew upon both Dewey and Dalcroze, see Fumiko Shiraishi, "Calvin Brainerd Cady: Thought and Feeling in the Study of Music," *Journal of Research in Music Education* 47, no. 2 (1999): 150–162.

44. Lefebvre, *Elements of Rhythmanalysis*.

45. Osip Mandelstam, *The Complete Critical Prose and Letters*, ed. J. G. Harris, trans. J. G. Harris and C. Link (Ann Arbor, MI: Ardis, 1979), 110. In 1919 a National Institute of Rhythmical Education was established in Russia to train teachers, and rhythmic education became compulsory in certain public schools.

46. Mandelstam, *The Complete Critical Prose*, 109–110.

47. See Kurt Meyer, "Rhythms, Streets, Cities," in *Space, Difference, Everyday Life: Reading Henri Lefebvre*, ed. Kanishka Goonewardena et al., 147–160 (London: Routledge, 2008).

48. Lefebvre, *Elements of Rhythmanalysis*, 64, emphasis in original.

49. Lefebvre, *Elements of Rhythmanalysis*, 64.

50. Lefebvre, *Elements of Rhythmanalysis*, 65.

51. Lefebvre, *Elements of Rhythmanalysis*, 67.

52. Lefebvre, *Elements of Rhythmanalysis*, 21.

53. Lefebvre, *Elements of Rhythmanalysis*, 27, emphasis in original.

54. Lefebvre, *Elements of Rhythmanalysis*, 27.

55. Cited in Golston, *Rhythm and Race*, 15.

56. Jaques-Dalcroze, *Rhythm, Music and Education*, 5.

57. Jaques-Dalcroze, *Rhythm, Music and Education*, 96, 97.

58. Jaques-Dalcroze, *Rhythm, Music and Education*, 97.

59. "Dalcroze Explains His Method," *Literary Digest* 78 (1932): 31.

60. Recent commentators have suggested therefore that eurhythmics anticipates much later arguments within philosophy and the neurosciences about the dynamic relations between body, brain, and thinking. See, for example, Jay Seitz, "Dalcroze, the Body, Movement, and Musicality," *Psychology of Music* 33, no. 4 (2005): 419–435; Jay Seitz, "The Bodily Basis of Thought," *New Ideas in Psychology* 18, no. 1 (2000): 23–40; Marja-Leena Juntunen and Leena Hyvönen, "Embodiment in Musical Knowing: How Body Movement Facilitates Learning within Dalcroze Eurhythmics," *British Journal of Musical Education* 21, no. 2 (2004): 199–214; Marja-Leena Juntunen and Leena Hyvönen, "Digging Dalcroze, or, Dissolving the Mind-Body Dualism: Philosophical and Practical Remarks on the Musical Body in Action," *Music Education Research*

3, no. 2 (2001): 203–214; Jessica Phillips-Silver and Laurel Trainor, "Hearing What the Body Feels: Auditory Encoding of Rhythmic Movement," *Cognition* 105 (2007): 533–546.

61. Jaques-Dalcroze, *Rhythm, Music and Education*, viii.

62. Jaques-Dalcroze, *Rhythm, Music and Education*, 257.

63. See Susan Manning, *Ecstasy and the Demon: Feminism and Nationalism in the Dances of Mary Wigman* (Berkeley: University of California Press, 1993).

64. Karl Toepfer, *Empire of Ecstasy: Nudity and Movement in German Body Culture 1910–1935* (Berkeley: University of California Press, 1997), 19.

65. Toepfer, *Empire of Ecstasy*, 19–20. While he undoubtedly mobilizes an ideal of collective rhythmic renewal and education based upon the problematization and pathologizing of a-rhythmic movements, Dalcroze is equally concerned to highlight the potential of eurhythmics for facilitating the development of an expressive individuality. Indeed, once the Nazis came to power, this emphasis on individuality led to the closure of eurhythmics schools in Germany, which had only been reopened in 1927. Prior to that Jaques-Dalcroze had been unpopular in Germany because of his opposition to the First World War. See Irwin Spector, *Rhythm and Life: The Work of Emile Jaques-Dalcroze* (Stuyvesant, NY: Pendragon, 1990).

66. See Dee Reynolds, *Rhythmic Subjects* (Alton, U.K.: Dance Books, 2007).

67. Lefebvre, *Elements of Rhythmanalysis*, 67.

68. Lefebvre, *Elements of Rhythmanalysis*, 68.

69. Lefebvre, *Elements of Rhythmanalysis*, 67.

70. Lefebvre, *Elements of Rhythmanalysis*, 67, emphasis in original.

71. See Meyer, "Rhythms, Streets, Cities."

72. Jo Ann Boydston, ed., *John Dewey: The Later Works 1925–1952* (Carbondale: University of Illinois Press, 1984–1991), 7.

73. Boydston, *John Dewey*, 15.

74. Boydston, *John Dewey*, 160.

75. Boydston, *John Dewey*, 56.

76. Stamatia Portanova, "The Intensity of Dance: Body, Movement and Sensation across the Screen," *Extensions: The Online Journal of Embodied Technology* 2 (2005): 33.

77. Quoted in Richard Beacham, *Adolphe Appia: Artist and Visionary of the Modern Theatre* (Reading: Harwood, 1994), 55.

78. Quoted in George Brandt, ed., *Modern Theories of Drama* (Oxford: Oxford University Press, 1998), 151.

79. Brandt, *Modern Theories of Drama*, 130.

80. Adolphe Appia, *Adolphe Appia: Essays, Scenarios, and Designs*, trans. W. R. Volbach, ed. Richard Beacham (London: UMI Research Press, 1989), 196. As these comments suggest, Appia never quite manages to shake off a sense of the relation between bodies and spaces in terms of an inside and outside. Bodies appear at various points in his writing as discrete objects.

81. Appia, *Adolphe Appia*, 119.

82. Appia, *Adolphe Appia*, 155.

83. Appia, *Adolphe Appia*, 155.

84. The Institute at Hellerau attracted notable cultural figures, including George Bernard Shaw, Constantin Stanislavksy, Max Reinhardt, Serge Rachmaninoff, Paul Claudel, Upton Sinclair, and Serge Diaghilev.

85. Appia, *Adolphe Appia*, 70, emphasis in original.

86. Quoted in Beacham, *Adolphe Appia*, 129.

87. Beacham, *Adolphe Appia*, 58.

88. Beacham, *Adolphe Appia*, 118.

89. Beacham, *Adolphe Appia*, 132.

90. See also Richard Beacham, "'Bearers of the Flame': Music, Dance, Design, and Lighting, Real and Virtual — the Enlightened and Still Luminous Legacies of Hellerau and Dartington," *Performance Research* 11, no. 4 (2006): 81–94.

91. Beacham, *Adolphe Appia*, 132.

92. On the significance of Appia's ideas about lighting for stage design, see Christopher Baugh, *Theatre, Performance and Technology* (Basingstoke: Palgrave Macmillan, 2005).

93. Beacham, *Adolphe Appia*, 95.

94. Beacham, *Adolphe Appia*, 95.

95. Beacham, *Adolphe Appia*, 104.

96. See Gernot Böhme, "Atmosphere as the Fundamental Concept of a New Aesthetics," *Thesis Eleven* 36 (1993): 113–126.

97. Gernot Böhme, "The Art of Stage Set as a Paradigm for Aesthetic Atmospheres," contribution to a colloquium, Cresson, accessed September 28, 2010, www.cresson. archi.fr.

98. See, for instance, Roger Copeland, *Merce Cunningham: The Modernizing of Modern Dance* (London: Routledge, 2004), 147.

99. Beacham, *Adolphe Appia*, 284.

100. Beacham, *Adolphe Appia*, 273.

101. Beacham, *Adolphe Appia*, 281.

102. Beacham, *Adolphe Appia*.

103. Beacham, *Adolphe Appia*, 216. For an account of the afterlife of Hellerau, see Johannes Birringer, *Media and Performance along the Border* (Baltimore, MD: Johns Hopkins University Press, 1998).

104. For a discussion of this kind of practice see Ben Anderson, "Transcending without Transcendence: Utopianism and an Ethos of Hope," *Antipode* 38, no. 4 (2006): 691–710.

105. André Lepecki, *Exhausting Dance: Performance and the Politics of Movement* (London: Routledge, 2006), 130.

106. This becoming present is a kind of rhythmic relation that is never absolutely discontinuous. As William James puts it, in "all this the continuities and the discontinuities are absolutely co-ordinate matters of immediate feeling. The conjunctions are as primordial elements of 'fact' as are the distinctions and disjunctions." To experiment with rhythm as flow by no means precludes a felt sense of discontinuity: it is just

that any such felt sense is contingent upon the affirmation of an ongoing continuous excess in the relations from which experience is composed. See James, *Essays in Radical Empiricism*, 95.

107. Lefebvre, *Elements of Rhythmanalysis*, 44.

Chapter Three. Diagramming Refrains

An earlier version of this chapter was published as Derek P. McCormack, "A Paper with an Interest in Rhythm," *Geoforum* 33, no. 4 (2002): 469–485.

1. Michel Serres, *Genesis*, trans. Geneviève James and James Nielson (Ann Arbor: University of Michigan Press, 1995), 138.

2. Henri Bergson, *The Creative Mind: An Introduction to Metaphysics* (New York: Dover, 2007).

3. See Gabrielle Roth, *Maps to Ecstasy: A Healing Journey for the Untamed Spirit* (Novatarro, CA: New World Library, 1989); Gabrielle Roth, *Sweat Your Prayers: Movement as Spiritual Practice* (New York: Tarcher/Putnam, 1997).

4. This does not prevent Roth from trademarking the practice, a move that makes good business sense in a burgeoning competitive economy of New Age practices.

5. Roth, *Sweat Your Prayers*, 51. By moving in this way, Jordan became the world's highest-paid geography graduate, having majored in the subject at the University of North Carolina. Roth's use of the word "swoosh" also suggests how corporate identity, in this case Nike's, is implicated in the production of everyday kinesthetic vocabularies.

6. Roth, *Sweat Your Prayers*, 83.

7. Roth, *Sweat Your Prayers*, 85

8. Roth, *Sweat Your Prayers*, 114, 119, emphasis added.

9. Roth, *Sweat Your Prayers*, 114.

10. Roth, *Sweat Your Prayers*, 163.

11. Roth, *Sweat Your Prayers*, 158.

12. Roth, *Maps to Ecstasy*, 33.

13. Roth, *Maps to Ecstasy*, 59.

14. Roth, *Maps to Ecstasy*, 59.

15. Roth, *Maps to Ecstasy*, xix.

16. 5Rhythms Global, www.gabrielleroth.com.

17. Roth, *Maps to Ecstasy*, 2.

18. Roth, *Sweat Your Prayers*, 8.

19. Founded in 1962, the Esalen Institute was established in the midst of the emergence of the human potential movement. A range of holistic practices and workshops are offered there under the aegis of "experimental education." See Esalen, www.esalen.org.

20. See Julian Holloway, "Institutional Geographies of the New Age Movement," *Geoforum* 31, no. 4 (2000): 553–565.

21. See José Gil, "Paradoxical Body," TDR/*The Drama Review* 50, no. 4 (2006): 28; see also Nigel Thrift, *Non-representational Theory: Space, Politics, Affect* (London:

Routledge, 2008); Erin Manning, *Politics of Touch: Movement, Sense, Sovereignty* (Minneapolis: University of Minnesota Press, 2007).

22. Gil, "Paradoxical Body," 30.

23. Judith Hamera, *Dancing Communities: Difference and Connection in the Global City* (London: Palgrave Macmillan, 2007), 19. While Hamera's emphasis on relational infrastructures is useful, more problematic is her argument that these can be understood as a "protocol of reading" (20). The relational techniques that feature in this book cannot be reduced to the discursive economies of reading and writing.

24. Gilles Deleuze and Félix Guattari, *A Thousand Plateaus*, trans. Brian Massumi (London: Athlone, 1988), 311.

25. Roth, *Sweat Your Prayers*, 55.

26. Roth, *Maps to Ecstasy*, 24–25.

27. Gregory Bateson, "Some Components of Socialization for Trance," *Ethnos* 3, no. 2 (1975): 152.

28. Gregory Bateson, *Mind and Nature: A Necessary Unity* (New York: E. P. Dutton, 1979), 80.

29. See also Deborah Bird Rose, "Pattern, Connection, Desire: In Honour of Gregory Bateson," *Australian Humanities Review* 35 (June 2005).

30. John Shotter, "Bateson, Double Description, Todes, and Embodiment: Preparing Activities and Their Relation to Abduction," *Journal for the Theory of Social Behaviour* 39 (2009): 226.

31. Bateson, *Mind and Nature*, 142

32. Bateson, *Mind and Nature*, 143.

33. Shotter, "Bateson, Double Description."

34. Gregory Bateson, *Steps to an Ecology of Mind* (London: Paladin, 1973).

35. It might seem that such comments suggest an acidic disdain for and toward subjectivities. This is not necessarily the intention. Following Deleuze and Guattari, and others including James and Dewey, I take subjectivity to be defined in terms of the habits of which it is composed. Some of these habits afford capacities to act and experiment: others don't. Encounters with somatic practices can open up habits for change, but that is not to say that they allow one to dispense with habit — a certain affirmation of habit is necessary in order to maintain a degree of existential consistency in processual subjectivities.

36. Michael Taussig, "Viscerality, Faith and Scepticism: Another Theory of Magic," in *In Near Ruins: Cultural Theory at the End of the Century*, ed. Nicholas Dirks, 221–256 (Minneapolis: University of Minnesota Press, 1998), 226.

37. Bateson, "Some Components of Socialization for Trance," 144.

38. Peggy Phelan, *Unmarked: The Politics of Performance* (London: Routledge, 1997), 17.

39. Roth, *Sweat Your Prayers*, 85–86.

40. William James, *Essays in Radical Empiricism* (Lincoln: University of Nebraska Press, 1996), 238.

41. Bergson, *The Creative Mind*, 141.

42. Bergson, *The Creative Mind*, 141.

43. Bergson, *The Creative Mind*, 169.

44. Erin Manning, *Relationscapes: Movement, Art, Philosophy* (Cambridge, MA: MIT Press, 2009).

45. Gilles Deleuze, *Two Regimes of Madness: Texts and Interviews 1975–1995*, trans. Ames Hodges and Mike Taormina (New York: Semiotext(e), 2007), 381.

46. Bateson, *Steps to an Ecology of Mind*, 86.

47. Deleuze and Guattari, *A Thousand Plateaus*.

48. Deleuze and Guattari, *A Thousand Plateaus*, 323, emphasis in original.

49. Gilles Deleuze and Félix Guattari, *What Is Philosophy?*, trans. Graham Burchell and Hugh Tomlinson (London: Verso, 1994), 19.

50. Deleuze and Guattari, *A Thousand Plateaus*, 313.

51. Deleuze and Guattari, *A Thousand Plateaus*, 313.

52. Deleuze and Guattari, *A Thousand Plateaus*, 313.

53. Deleuze and Guattari, *A Thousand Plateaus*, 313.

54. Deleuze and Guattari, *A Thousand Plateaus*, 313.

55. Deleuze and Guattari, *A Thousand Plateaus*, 317.

56. Deleuze and Guattari, *A Thousand Plateaus*, 336.

57. Deleuze and Guattari, *What Is Philosophy?*, 181, emphasis in original.

58. Roth, *Maps to Ecstasy*, 176.

59. Deleuze and Guattari, *A Thousand Plateaus*, 333.

60. Deleuze and Guattari, *A Thousand Plateaus*, 323, emphasis in original.

61. Deleuze and Guattari, *A Thousand Plateaus*, 329.

62. Neither the music nor the 5 Rhythms teacher dictates this process. As one such teacher puts it, "I choose [the music] moment to moment. I don't plan what kind of music to use. All the time I'm trying to sense what's happening in the group and what needs to happen next. It's almost like helping a butterfly to unfold. I'm sensing what needs to happen next in a group and then picking a track that will support that to happen. The music is really the most powerful tool I have. When we were training, the first six months of teaching we had to teach with no words. We just had to hire a space and put on music and just use music to follow the group and not say anything because that's the most fundamental skill and it's the most powerful tool definitely. So I just choose it moment to moment" (from a personal interview, Bristol, 1999).

63. Deleuze and Guattari, *What Is Philosophy?*, 184.

64. Mark Antliff, *Inventing Bergson: Cultural Politics and the Parisian Avant-Garde* (Princeton, NJ: Princeton University Press, 1993), 53.

65. Wassily Kandinsky, *Point and Line to Plane* (New York: Dover, 1923), 54.

66. Deleuze and Guattari, *What Is Philosophy?*, 184.

67. Kandinsky's interest in dance emerged in the context of and resonated with important rhythmic experiments conducted in the early part of the twentieth century, including those of Dalcroze.

68. Kandinsky, *Point and Line to Plane*, 100.

69. Stephan Harrison, Steve Pile, and Nigel Thrift, eds., *Patterned Ground: Entanglements of Nature and Culture* (London: Reaktion, 2004), 37.

70. D. N. Rodowick, *Reading the Figural, or, Philosophy after the New Media* (Durham, NC: Duke University Press, 2001), 2.

71. See Ronald Bogue, "Minority, Territory, Music," in *An Introduction to the Philosophy of Gilles Deleuze*, ed. Jean Khalfa, 114–132 (London: Continuum, 1999).

72. Gilles Deleuze, *Francis Bacon: The Logic of Sensation*, trans. Daniel Smith (London: Continuum, 2003), 42–43, emphasis in original.

73. Deleuze, *Francis Bacon*, 102.

74. Deleuze, *Francis Bacon*, xi.

75. I borrow this term from the respective writing of Erin Manning, Brian Massumi, and Sher Doruff. See Manning, *Relationscapes*; Brian Massumi, "The Diagram as Technique of Existence," ANY 23 (1998): 42–47; and Sher Doruff, "The Translocal Event and the Polyrhythmic Diagram," PhD diss., Central Saint Martins College of Art and Design, University of London, 2006.

76. Deleuze and Guattari, *A Thousand Plateaus*, 145–146.

77. Gilles Deleuze, *Foucault*, trans. Séan Hand (London: Continuum, 1999), 36.

78. Massumi, "The Diagram as Technique of Existence."

79. See, for example, Tim Ingold, *Lines: A Brief History* (London: Routledge, 2007); and Paul Carter, *Dark Writing: Geography, Performance, Design* (Honolulu: University of Hawai'i Press, 2009).

80. Carter, *Dark Writing*, 15.

81. Deleuze and Guattari, *A Thousand Plateaus*, 282.

82. Louis MacNeice, *Collected Poems* (London: Faber, 1966), 261.

83. Serres, *Genesis*, 138.

84. Catherine Clément, *The Philosophy of Rapture*, trans. Sally O'Driscoll and Deirdre Mahoney (Minneapolis: University of Minnesota Press, 1994), 257.

Chapter Four. Ecologies of Therapeutic Practice

An earlier version of this chapter appeared as Derek P. McCormack, "An Event of Geographical Ethics in Spaces of Affect," *Transactions of the Institute of British Geographers* 28, no. 4 (2003): 488–507.

1. Helen Payne, *Dance Movement Therapy: Theory and Practice* (London: Routledge, 1992), 4.

2. Nikolas Rose, "The Politics of Life Itself," *Theory, Culture and Society* 18, no. 6 (2001): 1–30.

3. Isabelle Stengers, "Introductory Notes on an Ecology of Practices," *Cultural Studies Review* 11, no. 1 (2005): 185. For an alternative way of approaching the relation between therapeutic practice and thinking, particularly in relation to geography, see Liz Bondi, "Making Connections and Thinking through Emotions: Between Geography and Psychotherapy," *Transactions of the Institute of British Geographers* 30, no. 4 (2005): 433–448; David Conradson, "Landscape, Care, and the Relational Self: Therapeutic Encounters in Southern England," *Health and Place* 11, no. 4 (2005): 337–348.

4. Félix Guattari, *Chaosmosis: An Ethico-aesthetic Paradigm*, trans. Paul Bains and Julian Pefanis (Sydney: Power, 1995).

5. See Irmgard Bartenieff, "Dance Therapy: A New Profession or a Rediscovery of an Ancient Role of the Dance," *Dance Scope* 7, no. 6 (1972): 6–18.

6. See Irmgard Bartenieff, Claire Schmais, and Elissa White, "An Interview with Irmgard Bartenieff," *American Journal of Dance Therapy* 4, no. 1 (1981): 5–24.

7. See Payne, *Dance Movement Therapy*; Kristina Stanton-Jones, *An Introduction to Dance Movement Therapy* (London: Routledge, 1992).

8. That is not to say that DMT does not draw upon non-Western traditions. However, in doing so, it often renders these traditions as exotic, authentic others, particularly if they seem to reveal a rhythmic sensibility that has been untrammeled by modernity. See, for instance, France Schott-Billmann, "Primitive Expression: An Anthropological Dance Therapy Method," *Arts in Psychotherapy* 19 (1992): 105–109.

9. Stanton-Jones, *An Introduction to Dance Movement Therapy*, 12.

10. Mark George, "Reanimating the Face: Early Writings by Duchenne and Darwin on the Neurology of Facial Emotion Expression," *Journal of the History of the Neurosciences* 3, no. 1 (1994): 21–33; Paul Ekman, *Emotions in the Human Face: Guidelines for Research and Integration of Findings* (Oxford: Pergamon, 1972).

11. William James, "What Is an Emotion?," *Mind* 9, no. 34 (1884): 191.

12. James, "What Is an Emotion?," 189–190.

13. For an overview of research about the relation between movement and affect that pays particular attention to its influence on DMT, see Irene Rossberg-Gempton and Gary D. Poole, "The Relationship between Body Movement and Affect: From Historical and Current Perspectives," *Arts in Psychotherapy* 19 (1991): 39–46.

14. James, "What Is an Emotion?," 192.

15. Carol Bruno, "Maintaining a Concept of the Dance in Dance/Movement Therapy," *American Journal of Dance Therapy* 12, no. 2 (1990): 111.

16. For an overview of different approaches to the field of movement analysis see Ann Daly, "Movement Analysis: Piecing Together the Puzzle," TDR 32, no. 4 (1988): 40–52.

17. See George Taylor, "François Delsarte: A Codification of Nineteenth-Century Acting," *Theatre Research International* 24, no. 1 (1999): 71–81.

18. See, for instance, Rudolf Laban and Frank Lawrence, *Effort: The Economy of Human Movement* (London: MacDonald and Evans, 1974).

19. In addition, through the work of Irmgard Bartenieff, elements of Laban's system of movement analysis have been developed as part of the systematization of DMT in both the United States and the United Kingdom. See Irmgard Bartenieff, *Body Movement: Coping with the Environment* (Reading: Gordon and Breach Science, 1980).

20. Felicia McCarren, *Dance Pathologies: Performance, Poetics, Medicine* (Stanford, CA: Stanford University Press, 1988).

21. Peggy Phelan, *Unmarked: The Politics of Performance* (London: Routledge, 1997), 95.

22. For instance, some practitioners draw more heavily upon Jungian psychoanalysis in order to explore the relation between movement and imagery. For an overview, see Joan Chodorow, *Dance Therapy and Depth Psychology: The Moving Imagination* (London: Routledge, 1991).

23. Stanton-Jones, *An Introduction to Dance Movement Therapy*, 7.

24. See Lynn Siegal, "Psychoanalytic Dance Therapy: The Bridge between Psyche and Soma," *American Journal of Dance Therapy* 17, no. 2 (1995): 115–128. As Ann Daly

observes, Stern's work on "vitality affects" sits easily with elements of Laban's effort analysis. See Daly, "Movement Analysis"; and Daniel Stern, *The Interpersonal World of the Infant: A View from Psychoanalysis and Developmental Psychology* (New York: Basic Books, 1985).

25. Stanton-Jones, *An Introduction to Dance Movement Therapy*, 3.

26. Michael Henry, *The Genealogy of Psychoanalysis*, trans. Douglas Brick (Stanford, CA: Stanford University Press, 1993).

27. Stanton-Jones, *An Introduction to Dance Movement Therapy*, 7. The extent to which transference and countertransference are used in DMT varies. See, for instance, Siegal, "Psychoanalytic Dance Therapy."

28. I shift from "I" to "You" here, and at other points throughout the book, in order to mobilize a speculative scenario whose consistency is relation-specific rather than person-specific.

29. Alphonso Lingis, *Foreign Bodies* (London: Routledge, 1994), 171.

30. See Brian Massumi, *Parables for the Virtual: Movement, Affect, Sensation* (Durham, NC: Duke University Press, 2002).

31. James, "What Is an Emotion?," 194.

32. Ian Buchanan, "The Problem of the Body in Deleuze and Guattari," *Body and Society* 3, no. 3 (1997): 80.

33. Buchanan, "The Problem of the Body," 83.

34. This does not mean that such work cannot generate important insights. For a good example, see Maristela Moura Silva Lima and Alba Pedreira Vieira, "Ballroom Dance as Therapy for the Elderly in Brazil," *American Journal of Dance Therapy* 29, no. 2 (2007): 129–141.

35. Rom Harré, "An Outline of the Social Constructionist Viewpoint," in *The Social Construction of Emotions*, ed. Rom Harré, 2–14 (Oxford: Blackwell, 1986), 4.

36. Jack Katz, *How Emotions Work* (Chicago: University of Chicago Press, 1999), 4.

37. William Forsythe, in Erin Manning, "Propositions for the Verge: William Forsythe's Choreographic Objects," *Inflexions* 2 (December 2008): 2, www.inflexions.org.

38. Manning, "Propositions," 2.

39. Félix Guattari, "Ritornellos and Existential Affects," in *The Guattari Reader*, ed. Gary Genosko, 158–171 (Oxford: Blackwell, 1996).

40. *Father Ted* was a sitcom that aired initially on British TV station Channel 4, from April 1995 until May 1998. It ran for twenty-five episodes. It centered on the lives of three priests and their housekeeper on a fictional island off the west coast of Ireland (Craggy Island). After a slow start, it gradually generated a cult following. Dermot Morgan, the actor who starred in the title role, died the day after shooting of the last episode finished.

41. Stanton-Jones, *An Introduction to Dance Movement Therapy*, 3. Here Stanton-Jones is making a distinction between codified forms of DMT and any practice that styles itself as a therapeutic practice.

42. Mirroring is a commonly used technique within DMT contexts. The discovery of mirror neurons has generated speculation about the neurobiological basis of mirroring in a therapeutic context. See for instance Cynthia Berrol, "Neuroscience Meets

Dance/Movement Therapy: Mirror Neurons, the Therapeutic Process and Empathy," *Arts in Psychotherapy* 33 (2006): 302–315; Allison Winters, "Emotion, Embodiment, and Mirror Neurons in Dance/Movement Therapy: A Connection across Disciplines," *American Journal of Dance Therapy* 30 (2008): 84–105.

43. Stern, *The Interpersonal World of the Infant*, 142.

44. See Janet Adler, "Who Is the Witness? A Description of Authentic Movement," *Contact Quarterly* 12, no. 1 (1987): 20–29.

45. Shira Musicant, "Authentic Movement: Clinical Considerations," *American Journal of Dance Therapy* 23, no. 1 (2001): 18.

46. Giorgio Agamben, *Remnants of Auschwitz*, trans. Daniel Heller-Roazan (New York: Zone Books, 1999).

47. Paul Gordon, *Face to Face: Therapy as Ethics* (London: Constable, 1999), 97.

48. Ludwig Wittgenstein, *Philosophical Investigations*, trans. G. E. M. Anscombe (Oxford: Wiley-Blackwell, 1978).

49. John Dewey, "Three Prefaces to Books by Alexander," in F. Matthias Alexander, *The Alexander Technique*, 169–184 (New York: Carol Communications, 1989), 178.

50. Dewey, "Three Prefaces to Books by Alexander," 179.

51. Dewey, "Three Prefaces to Books by Alexander," 179.

52. See Michel Foucault, *The Care of the Self: The History of Sexuality*, vol. 3, trans. Robert Hurley (New York: Vintage, 1988).

53. See Richard Shusterman, *Body Consciousness: A Philosophy of Mindfulness and Somaesthetics* (Cambridge: Cambridge University Press, 2008); Cressida J. Heyes, *Self-Transformations: Foucault, Ethics, and Normalized Bodies* (Oxford: Oxford University Press, 2007).

54. See Jean-Jacques Rousseau, *Reveries of a Solitary Walker* (London: Penguin, 1979); Henry David Thoreau, *Walking* (Boston: Beacon, 1994).

55. See Gaston Bachelard, *The Dialectic of Duration*, trans. Mary McAllester Jones (Manchester: Clinamen, 2000), 21.

56. Bachelard, *The Dialectic of Duration*, 21.

57. Guattari, "Ritornellos and Existential Affects," 158.

58. Guattari, "Ritornellos and Existential Affects," 159.

59. See Guattari, *Chaosmosis*.

60. See Guattari, "Ritornellos and Existential Affects," 169.

61. Guattari, "Ritornellos and Existential Affects," 69.

62. Guattari was particularly enthusiastic about family therapy, as demonstrated through his collaboration with Mony Elkaïm. See Mony Elkaïm, "From General Laws to Singularities," *Family Process* 24 (1985): 151–164.

63. Jane Bennett, *The Enchantment of Modern Life: Attachments, Crossings, Ethics* (Princeton, NJ: Princeton University Press, 2001), 152.

64. That is not to say that DMT operates in anything like the political or radical context that framed La Borde during the time Guattari was active there. For a discussion of the use of dance therapy with schizophrenic patients in a short-lived therapeutic community, see Emilio Romero, Alan Hurwitz, and Vicki Carranza, "Dance Therapy in a Therapeutic Community for Schizophrenic Patients," *Arts in Psychotherapy* 10

(1983): 85–92. The origin of these therapeutic communities can be traced, in part, to postwar funding initiatives for mental health services in the United States. Such funding was cut back severely during the late 1970s. See Bruno, "Maintaining a Concept of the Dance in Dance/Movement Therapy."

65. Guattari, *Chaosmosis*, 18.

66. Guattari, *Chaosmosis*, 18.

67. John-David Dewsbury, "Affective Habit Ecologies: Material Dispositions and Immanent Inhabitations," *Performance Research* 17, no. 1 (2012): 81.

68. Stengers, "Introductory Notes on an Ecology of Practices," 195.

Chapter Five. Commentating

1. By football here I mean either soccer or Gaelic football, the two codes I played when growing up in Ireland.

2. See Matthew Fuller, *Media Ecologies: Materialist Energies in Art and Technoculture* (Cambridge, MA: MIT Press, 2005); Nigel Thrift, "Radio," in *Patterned Ground: Entanglements of Nature and Culture*, ed. S. Harrison, S. Pile, and N. Thrift, 269–270 (London: Reaktion, 2004).

3. For discussions of the avant-garde histories of radio, see Douglas Kahn and Gregory Whitehead, eds., *Wireless Imagination: Sound, Radio, and the Avant-Garde* (Cambridge, MA: MIT Press, 1994).

4. Michel Serres, *The Five Senses: A Philosophy of Mingled Bodies*, trans. Margaret Sankey and Peter Cowley (London: Athlone, 2008), 323. It must be added that not everyone experiences team sports in this way.

5. Seamus Heaney, *Seeing Things* (London: Faber and Faber, 1991), 10.

6. Gilles Deleuze and Félix Guattari, *A Thousand Plateaus*, trans. Brian Massumi (London: Athlone, 1988), 311.

7. Quoted in Susan Squier, ed., *Communities of the Air: Radio Century, Radio Culture* (Durham, NC: Duke University Press, 2003), 279.

8. See Jeffrey Sconce, *Haunted Media: Electronic Presence from Telegraphy to Television* (Durham, NC: Duke University Press, 2000); Jay Milutis, *Ether: The Nothing That Connects Everything* (Minneapolis: University of Minnesota Press, 2006).

9. Anthony Enns, "Psychic Radio: Sound Technologies, Ether Bodies, and Spiritual Vibrations," *Senses and Society* 3, no. 2 (2008): 137–152.

10. Paul Carter, *The Sound In Between: Voice, Space, Performance* (Kensington: New South Wales University Press, 1992), 140.

11. Michel Serres, *Genesis*, trans. Geneviève James and James Nielson (Ann Arbor: University of Michigan Press, 1995).

12. Laura Kunreuther, "Technologies of the Voice: FM Radio, Telephone, and the Nepali Diaspora in Kathmandu," *Cultural Anthropology* 21, no. 3 (2006): 326.

13. Teresa Brennan, *The Transmission of Affect* (Ithaca, NY: Cornell University Press, 2004).

14. See Jody Berland, "Locating Listening: Technological Space, Popular Music, Canadian Meditation," in *The Place of Music: Music, Space and the Production of Place*,

ed. Andrew Leyshon, David Matless, and George Revill (New York: Guilford, 1998); Jody Berland, *North of Empire: Essays on the Cultural Technologies of Space* (Durham, NC: Duke University Press, 2009).

15. Simon Frith, "Art versus Technology: The Strange Case of Popular Music," *Media, Culture and Society* 8, no. 3 (2006): 264.

16. See Berland, *North of Empire.*

17. See Abram De Swaan, "Widening Circles of Disidentification: On the Psycho- and Sociogenesis of the Hatred of Distant Strangers — Reflections on Rwanda," *Theory, Culture and Society* 14, no. 2 (1999): 105–122; Darryl Li, "Echoes of Violence: Considerations on Radio and Genocide in Rwanda," *Journal of Genocide Research* 6, no. 1 (2004): 9–27.

18. Danny Kaplan, "The Songs of the Siren: Engineering National Time on Israeli Radio," *Cultural Anthropology* 24, no. 2 (2009): 313. For a discussion of the relation between radio and geopolitics, see Alistair Pinkerton and Klaus Dodds, "Radio Geopolitics: Broadcasting, Listening, and the Struggle for Acoustic Spaces," *Progress in Human Geography* 33, no. 1 (2009): 10–27.

19. Ben Anderson, "Modulating the Excess of Affect: Morale in a State of Total War," in *The Affect Theory Reader*, ed. Melissa Gregg and Gregory Seigworth, 161–185 (London: Duke University Press, 2010).

20. John Tebbutt, "Imaginative Demographics: The Emergence of a Talkback Radio Audience in Australia," *Media, Culture and Society* 28, no. 6 (2006): 869, emphasis in original.

21. Susan Squier, "Wireless Possibilities, Posthuman Possibilities: Brain Radio, Community Radio, Radio Lazarus," in *Communities of the Air: Radio Century, Radio Cultures*, ed. Susan Squier, 275–303 (Durham, NC: Duke University Press, 2004), 294.

22. Jean-Luc Nancy, *Listening*, trans. Charlotte Mandel (New York: Fordham University Press, 2007).

23. For a discussion of this point in relation to music, see Ben Anderson, "A Principle of Hope: Recorded Music, Practices of Listening, and the Immanence of Utopia," *Geografiska Annaler, Series B: Human Geography* 84, nos. 3–4 (2002): 211–227.

24. Henri Lefebvre, *Elements of Rhythmanalysis: Space, Time, and Everyday Life*, trans. Stuart Elden and Gerald Moore (London: Continuum, 2004), 19.

25. Lefebvre, *Elements of Rhythmanalysis*, 46.

26. Quoted in Timothy Taylor, "Music and the Rise of Radio in 1920s America: Technological Imperialism, Socialization, and the Transformation of Intimacy," *Historical Journal of Film, Radio and Television* 22, no. 4 (2002): 437.

27. See Paddy Scannell, *Radio, Television and Modern Life* (Oxford: Blackwell, 1996).

28. Scannell, *Radio, Television and Modern Life*, 84. Such talk differs from much of the rest of radio output insofar as it is not heavily scripted. That is not to say that commentating does not involve preparation — it clearly does. Such preparation is particularly important in the case of preplanned and highly choreographed public events — Richard Dimbleby's television commentary on the coronation of Queen Elizabeth II is a case in point. But insofar as commentary requires preparation, it is to facilitate the impression of a kind of improvised relaying of things as they happen

coupled with the generation of a sense of the atmosphere in which this happening is an active participant. In this respect, radio commentating differs quite significantly from the kind of commentary that evolved, somewhat later, on television.

29. Mike Huggins, "BBC Radio and Sport 1922–1939," *Contemporary British History* 21, no. 4 (2007): 494.

30. Richard Haynes, "There's Many a Slip 'Twixt the Eye and the Lip': An Exploratory History of Football Broadcasts and Running Commentaries on BBC Radio, 1927–1939," *International Review for the Sociology of Sport* 34, no. 2 (1999): 144.

31. Haynes, "There's Many a Slip," 145.

32. Haynes, "There's Many a Slip," 149.

33. Quoted in Huggins, "BBC Radio and Sport," 509.

34. Andrew Crisell, *Understanding Radio* (London: Routledge, 1994), 128.

35. Irving Goffman, *Forms of Talk* (Oxford: Basil Blackwell, 1981).

36. Haynes, "There's Many a Slip," 144.

37. Scannell, *Radio, Television, and Modern Life.*

38. See Huggins, "BBC Radio and Sport."

39. Michael O'Hehir, *My Life and Times* (Dublin: Blackwater, 1996), 8.

40. Mary O'Malley, "A Bit Like Shakespeare," in *Playing the Field: Irish Writers on Sport*, ed. George O'Brien (Dublin: New Island, 2000), 40.

41. Michael Billig, *Banal Nationalism* (London: Sage, 1995); Benedict Anderson, *Imagined Communities: Reflections on the Origin and Spread of Nationalism* (London: Verso, 1983).

42. Arjun Appadurai, *Modernity at Large: Essays on Cultural Globalization* (Minneapolis: University of Minnesota Press, 1996), 103.

43. Richard Barbrook, "Broadcasting and National Identity in Ireland," *Media, Culture and Society* 14, no. 2 (1992): 203–227; Iarfhlaith Watson, "Irish-Language Broadcasting: History, Ideology and Identity," *Media, Culture and Society* 24, no. 6 (2002): 739–757.

44. Quoted in Luke Gibbons, *Transformations in Irish Culture* (Cork: Cork University Press, 1996), 71.

45. Gorham, quoted in Michael McLoone, "Music Hall Dope and British Propaganda? Cultural Identity and Early Broadcasting in Ireland," *Historical Journal of Film, Radio, and Television* 20, no. 3 (2000): 303.

46. See Mike Cronin, "Sport and a Sense of Irishness," *Irish Studies Review* 9 (1994): 1–24; Mike Cronin, "Defenders of the Nation? The Gaelic Athletic Association and Irish Nationalist Identity," *Irish Political Studies* 11, no. 1 (1996): 1–19; W. F. Mandle, *The Gaelic Athletic Association and Irish Nationalist Politics, 1884–1924* (London: Gill and Macmillan, 1987).

47. Alan Bairner, *Sport, Nationalism and Globalization* (Albany: State University of New York Press, 2001), 70.

48. Bairner, *Sport, Nationalism and Globalization*, 70.

49. Raymond Boyle, "From Our Gaelic Fields: Radio, Sport and Nation in Post-partition Ireland," *Media, Culture and Society* 14, no. 4 (1992): 623–636.

50. Gibbons, *Transformations in Irish Culture*, 73.

51. See Kunreuther, "Technologies of the Voice."

52. Mary Robinson, "Foreword," in O'Hehir, *My Life and Times*, vii.

53. Paul Durcan, *Greetings to Our Friends in Brazil* (London: Harvill, 1999), 7.

54. From my transcript from a radio recording of the 2002 All-Ireland football final between Armagh and Kerry. The quote on page 133 is from the same transcript.

55. Ronald Bogue, "Minority, Territory, Music," in *An Introduction to the Philosophy of Gilles Deleuze*, ed. Jean Khalfa, 114–132 (London: Continuum, 1999), 131.

56. Gilles Deleuze and Félix Guattari, *A Thousand Plateaus*, trans. Brian Massumi (London: Athlone, 1988), 308.

57. Brian Massumi, *Parables for the Virtual: Movement, Affect, Sensation* (Durham, NC: Duke University Press, 2002), 76, emphasis in original.

58. Massumi, *Parables for the Virtual*, 76, emphasis in original.

59. Massumi, *Parables for the Virtual*, 84.

60. Brian Massumi, "Introduction," in *A Shock to Thought: Expression after Deleuze and Guattari*, ed. Brian Massumi (London: Routledge, 2002), xvii.

61. This is clear in video footage of his commentating.

62. Michael Serres, *Genesis*, trans. Geneviève James and James Nielson (Ann Arbor: University of Michigan Press, 1995). See also Yves Lomax, *Sounding the Event: Escapades in Dialogue and Matters of Art, Nature and Time* (London: I. B. Tauris, 2005).

63. Serres, *Genesis*, 66.

64. The virtual is not medium specific. As Brian Massumi argues, each "medium, however 'low' technologically, really produces its own virtual reality." See Massumi, *Parables for the Virtual*, 175.

65. Scannell, *Radio, Television, and Modern Life*, 90–91.

66. From the transcript of the 2002 championship game between Meath and Dublin.

67. Lefebvre, *Elements of Rhythmanalysis*, 28.

68. O'Malley, "A Bit Like Shakespeare," 44.

69. From the transcript of the 2002 All-Ireland football final between Armagh and Kerry.

70. For a discussion of the "syncope," see Catherine Clément, *Syncope: The Philosophy of Rapture*, trans. Deirdre M. Mahoney and Sally O'Driscoll (Minneapolis: University of Minnesota Press, 1994).

71. Crisell, *Understanding Radio*, 131.

72. Massumi, *Parables for the Virtual*, 77.

73. MacNeice, quoted in Crisell, *Understanding Radio*, 127.

74. Louis MacNeice, *Collected Poems* (London: Faber, 1966), 158, 159.

75. Neil Corcoran, "The Same Again? Repetition and Refrain in Louis MacNeice," *Cambridge Quarterly* 38, no. 3 (2009): 214.

76. A critical riposte to this might be that the ethics of commentary therefore fails to grasp loss, absence, disappearance, and so on, and celebrates instead a kind of worldly plenitude. Here I think MacNeice is especially perceptive. His poetry is a struggle tensed between the potential of poetry as running commentary and its inevitable failure to capture things in motion, an ethos that "must continue, raiding the

abyss." This ethos is "conscious of sunlight, conscious of death's inveigling touch, not completely conscious but partly — and that is much." MacNeice, *Collected Poems*, 244.

77. Crisell, *Understanding Radio*, 126.

Chapter Six. Moving Images for Moving Bodies

1. The event was organized by Erin Manning, Brian Massumi, and members of Montreal-based SenseLab.

2. From the text of a leaflet produced for the *Projections Series*, Montreal Museum of Modern Art, 2007.

3. "Praise You" captures exactly what Steven Shaviro means when he writes about postcinematic affect: it features a bunch of amateur dancers doing a routine outside a cinema as bemused customers file past.

4. See Jean-Luc Nancy, *Au fond des images* (Paris: Galilée, 2003); Jacques Rancière, *The Future of the Image*, trans. Gregory Eliot (London: Verso, 2007).

5. See, for example, Will Straw, "Music Video in Its Contexts: Popular Music and Post-modernism in the 1990s," *Popular Music* 7, no. 3 (1988): 247–266; Rana Emerson, "'Where My Girls At?': Negotiating Black Womanhood in Music Videos," *Gender and Society* 16, no. 1 (2002): 115–135.

6. See Vivian Sobchack, *Carnal Thoughts: Embodiment and Moving Image Culture* (Berkeley: University of California Press, 2004); Laura Marks, *The Skin of the Film: Intercultural Cinema, Embodiment, and the Senses* (Durham, NC: Duke University Press, 2000); Steven Shaviro, *The Cinematic Body* (Minneapolis: University of Minnesota Press, 1993).

7. Steven Shaviro, "Post-cinematic Affect: On Grace Jones, *Boarding Gate* and *Southland Tales*," *Film-Philosophy* 14, no. 1 (2010): 1–102.

8. See also Jamie Lorimer's analysis in "Moving Image Methodologies for More-Than-Human Geographies," *Cultural Geographies* 17, no. 2 (2010): 237–258.

9. See Nigel Thrift, *Nonrepresentational Theory: Space, Politics, Affect* (London: Routledge, 2008); Ben Anderson, "Affect and Biopower: Towards a Politics of Life," *Transactions of the Institute of British Geographers* 37, no. 1 (2012): 28–43.

10. Henri Bergson, *Matter and Memory*, trans. N. M. Paul and W. S. Palmer (London: Zone Books, 1988), 9.

11. Mark Hansen, *New Philosophy for New Media* (Cambridge, MA: MIT Press, 2006).

12. Gilles Deleuze, *Expressionism in Philosophy: Spinoza*, trans. Martin Joughin (New York: Zone Books, 1990).

13. Brian Massumi, *Parables for the Virtual: Movement, Affect, Sensation* (Durham, NC: Duke University Press, 2002).

14. Gilles Deleuze and Félix Guattari, *A Thousand Plateaus*, trans. Brian Massumi (London: Athlone, 1988); Félix Guattari, *Chaosmosis: An Ethico-aesthetic Paradigm*, trans. Paul Bains and Julian Pefanis (Sydney: Power, 1995); Félix Guattari, "Ritornellos and Existential Affects," in *The Guattari Reader*, ed. Gary Genosko, 158–171 (Oxford: Blackwell, 1996).

15. Guattari, "Ritornellos and Existential Affects."

16. Guattari, "Ritornellos and Existential Affects," 165.

17. See Jill Bennett, "Stigmata and Sense Memory: St. Francis and the Affective Image," *Art History* 24, no. 1 (2001): 1–16.

18. Guattari, *Chaosmosis*, 17.

19. Maurizio Lazzarato, "Struggle, Event, Media," Maurizio Lazzarato, accessed January 6, 2010, www.republicart.net/disc/representations/lazzarato01_en.htm. See also Maurizio Lazzarato, "From Capital-Labour to Capital-Life," *Ephemera* 4, no. 3 (2004): 187–208.

20. Lazzarato, "Struggle, Event, Media."

21. Alberto Toscano, "Vital Strategies: Maurizio Lazzarato and the Metaphysics of Contemporary Capitalism," *Theory, Culture, and Society* 24, no. 6 (2007): 71–91, 83. In particular, Toscano questions the current of optimism running through Lazzarato's work about the potential of cooperation and connection to disclose different possibilities within the immaterial economies of contemporary capitalism.

22. Transcribed from the ad posted on the BMW website, www.expressionofjoy .com, accessed August 1, 2010.

23. See Gabriel Tarde, *The Laws of Imitation*, trans. Elsie Clews Parsons (New York: Henry Holt, 1903).

24. Lazzarato, "Struggle, Event, Media," n.p.

25. Matthew Fuller, *Media Ecologies: Materialist Energies in Art and Technoculture* (Cambridge, MA: MIT Press, 2005).

26. Lazzarato, "Struggle, Event, Media," n.p.

27. J. K. Gibson-Graham, *A Post-capitalist Politics* (Minneapolis: University of Minnesota Press, 2006).

28. On this point, see William Connolly, *Neuropolitics: Thinking, Culture, Speed* (Minneapolis: University of Minnesota Press, 2001); William Connolly, *Pluralism* (Durham, NC: Duke University Press, 2005).

29. Jane Bennett, *The Enchantment of Modern Life: Attachments, Crossings, Ethics* (Princeton, NJ: Princeton University Press, 2001); Jane Bennett, "Commodity Fetishism and Commodity Enchantment," *Theory and Event* 5, no. 1 (2001).

30. Bennett, "Commodity Fetishism and Commodity Enchantment," n.p.

31. Celia Lury, "Marking Time with Nike: The Illusion of the Durable," *Public Culture* 11, no. 3 (1999): 499–526.

32. See, for instance, Simon Frith, Andrew Goodwin, and Laurence Grossberg, eds., *Sound and Vision: The Music Video Reader* (London: Routledge, 1993); Will Straw, "Music Video in Its Contexts: Popular Music and Post-modernism in the 1990s," *Popular Music* 7, no. 3 (1988): 247–266.

33. Joe Gow, "Mood and Meaning in Music Video: The Dynamics of Audiovisual Synergy," *Southern Communications Journal* 59, no. 3 (1994): 255–261.

34. See, for instance, James Ash, "Architectures of Affect: Anticipating and Manipulating the Event in Practices of Videogame Design and Testing," *Environment and Planning D: Society and Space* 28, no. 4 (2010): 653–671.

35. See, for instance, Irene Chien, "This Is Not a Dance," *Film Quarterly* 59, no. 3

(2006): 22–34; Bryan Behrenshausen, "Toward a (Kin)Aesthetic of Video Gaming: The Case of Dance Dance Revolution," *Games and Culture* 2, no. 4 (2007): 335–354.

36. Indeed, the experience of watching these video images echoes an earlier form of image-viewing technology — the "movie-machine" on which "Soundies," three-minute musical films accompanying popular songs, were played. As Amy Herzog notes, the "Soundie required a new kind of image, one not dictated by narrative but by the affectivity of song." Amy Herzog, "Discordant Visions: The Popular Musical Images of the Soundies Jukebox Film," *American Music* 22, no. 1 (2004): 28. Furthermore, "unlike traditional jukeboxes, the design of the Panoram did not allow listeners to choose individual songs. . . . Because the loop was continuous, patrons could only watch and listen to whichever song was next on the reel" (29–30).

37. Derek P. McCormack, "Body-Shopping: Refiguring Geographies of Fitness," *Gender, Place and Culture* 6, no. 2 (1999): 155–177.

38. Tim Luke, "Liberal Society and Cyborg Subjectivity: The Politics of Environments, Bodies, and Nature," *Alternatives* 21, no. 1 (1996): 1–30.

39. Felicia McCarren, *Dancing Machines: Choreographies of the Age of Mechanical Reproduction* (Stanford, CA: Stanford University Press, 2003), 9.

40. See Rudolf Laban and Frank Lawrence, *Effort: The Economy of Human Movement* (London: MacDonald and Evans, 1974).

41. McCarren, *Dancing Machines*, 9.

42. *Master the Treadmill with OK Go*, MP3 file, Capitol, October 23, 2007.

43. Lury, "Marking Time," 500.

44. Berocca, www.berocca.co.uk, accessed June 2010.

45. Friedrich von Borries, *Who's Afraid of Niketown? Nike-Urbanism, Branding, and the City of Tomorrow* (Rotterdam: Episode, 2004).

46. Toscano, "Vital Strategies," 82.

47. Amy Herzog, "Affectivity, Becoming, and the Cinematic Event: Gilles Deleuze and the Futures of Feminist Film Theory," in *Conference Proceedings for Affective Encounters: Rethinking Embodiment in Feminist Media Studies*, ed. Anu Koivunen and Susanna Paasonen, 83–88 (Turku, Finland: University of Turku and the Finnish Society for Cinema Studies, 2001), 87, accessed May 28, 2013, http://www.hum.utu.fi/oppiaineet/mediatutkimus/tutkimus/proceedings_pienennetty.pdf.

48. Jennifer Livett, "'Odd Couples and Double Acts, or Strange but Not Always Queer': Some Male Pairs and the Modern/Postmodern Subject," *Australian Humanities Review* 21, no. 2 (2001); Eve Kosofsky Sedgwick, *Between Men: English Literature and Male Homosocial Desire* (New York: Columbia University Press, 1985).

49. Henri Lefebvre, *Critique of Everyday Life*, vol. 1, trans. John Moore (London: Verso, 2008).

50. Toscano, "Vital Strategies," 86.

51. Toscano, "Vital Strategies," 83.

52. See Lazzarato, "From Capital-Labour to Capital-Life," 207.

53. See also Isabelle Stengers, "Experimenting with Refrains: Subjectivity and the Challenge of Escaping Modern Dualism," *Subjectivity* 22, no. 1 (2008): 38–59.

54. On Cajun dancing, see Charles Stivale, *Disenchanting Les Bon Temps: Identity and Authenticity in Cajun Music and Dance* (Durham, NC: Duke University Press, 2003). On corn, see Gregory Seigworth, "The Affect of Corn," *M/C Journal* 8 (December 2005).

55. Gilles Deleuze, *Difference and Repetition*, trans. Paul Patton (London: Athlone, 1994), 139.

56. Lazzarato, "From Capital-Life to Labour-Life," 207.

57. Lazzarato, "From Capital-Life to Labour-Life," 56.

58. Famously, when describing his relation with Guattari, Deleuze writes: "Together we would like to be the Humpty Dumpty of philosophy, or its Laurel and Hardy. A philosophy-cinema." See Gilles Deleuze, *Two Regimes of Madness: Texts and Interviews 1975–1995*, trans. Ames Hodges and Mike Taormina (New York: Semiotext(e), 2007), 66.

59. Transcribed from *The Flying Deuces*, dir. A. Edward Sutherland (Boris Morros Productions, 1939).

60. Lazzarato, "Struggle, Event, Media," n.p.

Chapter Seven. Choreographing Lived Abstractions

1. This book does not engage directly with the articulations of difference that are invoked here. That is not to say that they are unimportant, or that developing connections between nonrepresentational theories and strands of feminism is not an important project. What I would say, however, is that it is a mistake to automatically cast abstraction as something inimical to difference on the basis of an undifferentiated conception of abstraction. For an excellent discussion of some of the tensions and overlaps between nonrepresentational theories and feminist scholarship, see Rachel Colls, "Feminism, Bodily Difference, and Non-representational Geographies," *Transactions of the Institute of British Geographers* 37, no. 3 (2012): 430–445.

2. For a reading of Descartes that complicates this critique, see Claudia Brodsky Lacour, *Lines of Thought: Discourse, Architectonics, and the Origin of Modern Philosophy* (Durham, NC: Duke University Press, 1996).

3. See, for instance, Gillian Rose, *Feminism and Geography: The Limits of Geographical Knowledge* (Minneapolis: University of Minnesota Press, 1993).

4. For a parallel discussion of the relation between architecture and choreography, see Peter Merriman, "Architecture/Dance: Choreographing and Inhabiting Spaces with Anna and Lawrence Halprin," *Cultural Geographies* 17, no. 4 (2010): 427–449.

5. Henri Lefebvre, *The Production of Space*, trans. Donald Nicholson Smith (Oxford: Blackwell, 1991), 170.

6. Lefebvre, *The Production of Space*, 170, emphasis in original.

7. Lefebvre, *The Production of Space*, 287.

8. Lefebvre, *The Production of Space*, 318.

9. Lefebvre, *The Production of Space*, 308.

10. Lefebvre, *The Production of Space*, 312. This rendering of abstraction as an alienating and technocratic instrumentalism is echoed in the work of other commentators.

It is a version of the critique that can be found, for instance, in Michel de Certeau's writing on the city as an abstraction populated by "a multitude of quantified heroes who lose names and faces as they become the ciphered river of the streets, a mobile language of computations and rationalities that belong to no one." See Michel de Certeau, *The Practice of Everyday Life* (Berkeley: University of California Press, 1984), iii. Equally, it is a version of Paul Virilio's ongoing commentary on the disenchanting and dematerializing effects of modern configurations of technology, perception, and politics. See Paul Virilio, *The Lost Dimension*, trans. Daniel Moshenberg (New York: Semiotext(e), 1991); and Paul Virilio, *Negative Horizon*, trans. Michael Degener (London: Continuum, 2005).

11. Henri Lefebvre, *The Sociology of Marx*, trans. Norbert Guterman (London: Penguin, 1972), 9.

12. Lefebvre, *The Production of Space*, 307.

13. Lefebvre, *The Production of Space*, 308.

14. Lefebvre therefore has little time for forms of artistic expression — such as cubism — that present bodies as a series of planes, surfaces, and lines according to the direction and logic of the geometrical, visual, and phallocentric formants of abstract space. Such work is symptomatic of a more general cultural tendency to "pulverize" bodies into distinct zones and specialized locations, thereby fragmenting their "living unity" both concretely and symbolically. Lefebvre, *The Production of Space*, 310.

15. Lefebvre, *The Production of Space*, 49.

16. Lefebvre, *The Production of Space*, 61.

17. See also Kirsten Simonsen, "Bodies, Sensations, Space and Time: The Contribution from Henri Lefebvre," *Geografiska Annaler* 87 B, no. 1 (2005): 1–14.

18. See Henri Lefebvre, *Critique of Everyday Life*, vol. 2, trans. John Moore (London: Verso, 2008).

19. Lefebvre, *Critique of Everyday Life*, vol. 2, 55–56.

20. Lefebvre, *The Production of Space*, 316.

21. Henri Lefebvre, *Elements of Rhythmanalysis: Space, Time, and Everyday Life*, trans. Stuart Elden and Gerald Moore (London: Continuum, 2004), 6, 27.

22. Lefebvre, *The Production of Space*, 288.

23. Lefebvre, *The Production of Space*, 170.

24. See Richard Feist, "Weyl's Appropriation of Husserl's and Poincaré's Thought," *Synthese* 132, no. 3 (2002): 73–301.

25. Herman Weyl, *Space, Time, Matter*, trans. Henry L. Brose (New York: Cosmino, 2010).

26. Lefebvre, *The Production of Space*, 171.

27. It is worth mentioning here that Lefebvre is not alone in using such ideas to think through the process of genetic differentiation in spacetime. In *Difference and Repetition*, Gilles Deleuze draws a distinction between different kinds of symmetry with respect to the repetition they involve. And in the process, he seems to suggest that geometries can be understood in ways that do not inhibit difference. So, for Deleuze, there is a "static symmetry which is cubic or hexagonal, and a dynamic

symmetry which is pentagonal and appears in a spiral line or in a geometrically pro-gressing pulsation — in short, in a living and mortal 'evolution.'" See Gilles Deleuze, *Difference and Repetition*, trans. Paul Patton (London: Athlone, 1994), 20.

28. Lefebvre, *The Production of Space*, 173.

29. Lefebvre, *The Production of Space*, 173. Here again Lefebvre employs terms that suggest a division between a space internal and external to an already existing body.

30. Lefebvre, *The Production of Space*, 174.

31. Lefebvre, *The Production of Space*, 213.

32. Rudolf Laban, *Choreutics*, annotated and ed. Lisa Ullman (London: MacDonald and Evans, 1966), 10.

33. Colin Counsell has made exactly this point, arguing that Laban's work on choreutics can be seen as the "historical expression of a particular experience of the modern." See Colin Counsell, "The Kinesics of Infinity: Laban, Geometry and the Metaphysics of Dancing Space," *Dance Research* 24, no. 2 (2006): 105.

34. More specifically, Laban's development of a kinesthetic architecture needs to be situated in relation to his earlier choreographic work, in Switzerland but more impor-tantly in Germany, from which his more systematic studies of movement emerged. In this choreographic work, Laban strives toward the kinesthetic expression of organic collectivity. During the 1920s and 1930s, Laban's interest in collective expressive movement (through what he called a "movement choir") became an important ele-ment of an emerging cultural aesthetic of mass choreography, elements of which were harnessed by the Nazi regime. Whether through naïveté or design, Laban appears not to have been particularly critical of how his work could be thus mobilized: his position at the time seemed to be more concerned with achieving a pragmatic ac-commodation with the emerging regime than with distancing himself from it. When Hitler came to power, Laban was the director of movement and dance at the State Opera in Berlin. The end of his contract there was marked by a special performance attended by Goebbels, Göring, and Hitler, "beside whom Laban sat throughout": see Valerie Preston-Dunlop, *Rudolf Laban: An Extraordinary Life* (London: Dance Books, 1998), 181. Following this, Laban was offered and accepted the directorship of the Neue Tanzbühne, an organization created by the Ministry of Propaganda. As things unfolded, neither Laban's work nor his personal politics and aesthetics smoothly or inevitably made the transition from the expressive optimism of Ausdruckstanz to the choreographic imperatives of fascism. Indeed, Laban's eventual departure from Ger-many because of his position vis-à-vis the choreographic politics of interwar Germany has already been well documented and discussed and it is not my aim to discuss it fur-ther here. See Preston-Dunlop, *Rudolf Laban*; John Hodgson, *Mastering Movement: The Life and Work of Rudolf Laban* (London: Methuen, 2001); Isa Partsch-Bergsohn, *Modern Dance in Germany and the United States: Cross Currents and Influences* (Switzerland: Harwood, 1994); Dianne Howe, *Individuality and Expression: The Aesthetics of the New German Dance, 1908–1936* (New York: Peter Lang, 1996). I hope it is clear that such a move is not a gesture of political abdication. Nor is it a reversion to the residual ahis-toricism often taken to characterize concerns with somatic practice.

35. See Preston-Dunlop, *Rudolf Laban*.

36. Laban, *Choreutics*, 111.

37. For an insightful discussion of the basic concepts of Laban's geometrical architecture, see Valerie Preston-Dunlop, "Choreutic Concepts and Practice," *Dance Research* 1, no. 1 (1983): 77–88.

38. Laban's interest in the relation between movement architecture and movement was informed by a period of architectural training in Paris during the late nineteenth century. See Preston-Dunlop, *Rudolf Laban*. Such an interest in the relation between architecture and movement is of course by no means unique to Laban and reflects wider choreographic tendencies, embodied in the modernist spirit of the European avant-garde in the late nineteenth and earlier twentieth centuries, and exemplified, albeit in different ways, in the choreographic experiments of figures like Oscar Schlemmer. See Gerald Siegmund, "Bending towards the Breaking Point: The Deformation of Dance and Mannerist Images of the Body," in *Remembering the Body*, ed. Gabrielle Brandstetter and Hortensia Völckers, 136–170 (Ostfildern-Ruit: Hatje Cantz, 2000).

39. Laban, *Choreutics*, 103–105.

40. Laban, *Choreutics*, 114.

41. Counsell, "The Kinesics of Infinity," 113.

42. Laban's use of the term "effort" must be understood in relation to a range of wider contemporaneous ideas about the psychic topographies of the individual. Growing up in late nineteenth-century Vienna, Laban had encountered the work of Freud and Jung and drew particularly heavily upon the latter's ideas about the four functions of the psyche, in which personality was differentiated along four aspects: thinking-sensing-intuiting-feeling. This schema was in turn based upon the work of Wilhelm Wundt, and his conceptual triad of thinking-feeling-willing. Wundt's ideas, and their subsequent development by Jung in the context of his theories about the four functions of the psyche, were helpful in allowing Laban to develop his ideas about the relation between different factors of movement (time, weight, space, and flow) and the psychic topographies of the individual. For a discussion of this see Vera Malectic, *Body-Space-Expression: The Development of Rudolf Laban's Movement and Dance Concepts* (New York: Mouton de Gruyter, 1987); Mark Franko, "History/Theory: Criticism/Practice," in *Corporealities: Dancing Knowledge, Culture and Power*, ed. Susan Leigh Foster, 25–52 (London: Routledge, 1996).

43. Rudolf Laban, *The Mastery of Movement*, 2nd ed., rev. and enlarged by Lisa Ullmann (London: MacDonald and Evans, 1960), 23.

44. Preston-Dunlop, *Rudolf Laban*, 218–219.

45. For an extensive discussion of their work, see Tim Cresswell, *On the Move: Mobility in the Western World* (New York: Routledge, 2006).

46. Lefebvre, *The Production of Space*, 200, emphasis in original.

47. Laban, *Choreutics*, 3.

48. Laban, *Choreutics*, 5.

49. Indeed, a close parallel can be drawn between Laban's work and that of Maurice Merleau-Ponty. Most basically, both share a concern with attending to the lived body as the grounds of being-in-the-world. Despite the different context in

which it was articulated, Laban's notion of effort can also be seen as a form of kines-thetic intentionality, albeit one with a more purposeful direction — an emergent kinesthetic expression of the relation between the individual and the environment, unfolding through a kinesthetic spatiotemporality in which the four factors of motion are synthesized at each moving movement. For a discussion of the relation between these two figures, see Malectic, *Body-Space-Expression*; Maureen Connolly and Anna Lathrop, "Maurice Merleau-Ponty and Rudolf Laban — an Interactive Appropriation of Parallels and Resonances," *Human Studies* 20 (1997): 27–45.

50. Laban, *Choreutics*, 124.

51. Petra Kuppers, *Disability and Contemporary Performance: Bodies on Edge* (London: Routledge, 2003), 129.

52. Kuppers, *Disability and Contemporary Performance*, 129.

53. This shared concern with the generative relation between moving bodies, abstraction, and space in their respective work is intensified through the emphasis placed by both on the importance of rhythm as a conceptual-empirical and diagnostic matter of concern. Rhythmic movement unfolded simultaneously through what Laban identifies as the four factors of motion — space, time, weight, and flow. Linked with a psychology of effort, these could be used to diagnose and ameliorate individual diffi-culties with movement. See Laban, *Choreutics*, 22.

54. Laban, *Choreutics*, 4.

55. Laban, *Choreutics*, 4. As Lisa Ullmann, in a detailed discussion of Laban's kin-esthetic architecture, observes, "All the directions with which we have so far become acquainted intersect in the centre of our kinesphere. Observing man's natural way of moving, we however see that his movements do not often radiate from the centre of his body, but bypass it. His arms and legs, so to speak, loop around his centre. We therefore distinguish in our considerations of harmony of movement between 'cen-tral' spatial lines meaning those which intersect in the centre of the kinesphere and the body, and 'non central lines,' meaning those which avoid the centre" (Ullman, in Laban, *Choreutics*, 147).

56. Cited in Steven Spiers, "Dancing and Drawing Choreography and Architecture," *Journal of Architecture* 10, no. 4 (2007): 349–364, 352.

57. Patricia Baudoin and Heidi Gilpin, "Proliferation and Perfect Disorder: William Forsythe and the Architecture of Disappearance," Ballet Frankfurt, http://www.hawickert.de/ARTIC1.html (accessed May 31, 2013).

58. Cited in Paul Kaiser, "Dance Geometry (Forsythe)," *Performance Research* 4, no. 2 (1999), http://openendedgroup.com/writings/danceGeometry.html (accessed May 28, 2013).

59. See Erin Manning, "Propositions for the Verge: William Forsythe's Choreo-graphic Objects," *Inflexions* 2 (December 2008), www.inflexions.org.

60. Lefebvre, *The Production of Space*, 397.

61. Lefebvre, *The Production of Space*, 397.

62. William Forsythe, *Improvisation Technologies: A Tool for the Analytical Dance Eye*, CD-ROM (Karlsruhe: ZKM, 1999).

63. Manning, "Propositions for the Verge."

64. Brian Massumi, *Parables for the Virtual: Movement, Affect, Sensation* (Durham, NC: Duke University Press, 2002), 5.

65. Indeed, one of the most influential phenomenological thinkers, Maurice Merleau-Ponty, recognizes as much: "Concrete movement is therefore centripetal whereas abstract movement is centrifugal. The former occurs in the realm of being or of the actual, the latter on the other hand in that of the virtual or the non-existent; the first adheres to a given background, the second throws out its own background." See Maurice Merleau-Ponty, *Phenomenology of Perception*, trans. Colin Smith (London: Routledge, 1962), 111. There are limits to this alignment between Massumi and Merleau-Ponty. For the latter, in particular, the virtual abstract is a space of anticipation that is projected from the actuality of embodiment. For the former, the virtual has an autonomy that resists any such originary incorporation.

66. John Rajchman, *Constructions* (Cambridge, MA: MIT Press, 1998), 65.

67. Alfred North Whitehead, *Adventures of Ideas* (New York: First Free Press, 1967), 69.

68. See Alfred North Whitehead, *Science and the Modern World* (New York: Free Press, 1967); and Alfred North Whitehead, *Process and Reality*, rev. ed. (New York: Free Press, 1978). For Stengers's reading of Whitehead, see Isabelle Stengers, "A Constructivist Reading of *Process and Reality*," *Theory, Culture and Society* 25, no. 4 (2008): 91–110.

69. Stengers, "A Constructivist Reading of *Process and Reality*," 107.

70. Stengers, "A Constructivist Reading of *Process and Reality*," 95–96.

71. Lefebvre, *The Production of Space*, 395.

72. Lefebvre, *The Production of Space*, 396.

73. See also David Cunningham, "The Concept of Metropolis: Philosophy and Urban Form," *Radical Philosophy* 133 (2005): 23.

74. Stengers, "A Constructivist Reading of *Process and Reality*," 96.

Chapter Eight. Promising Participation

1. See Rachel Pain and Sara Kindon, "Participatory Geographies," *Environment and Planning A* 39, no. 12 (2007): 2807–2812; Rachel Pain and Peter Francis, "Reflections on Participatory Research," *Area* 35, no. 1 (2003): 46–54; Duncan Fuller and Kye Askins, "Public Geographies II: Being Organic," *Progress in Human Geography* 34, no. 5 (2010): 654–667.

2. Within the discipline with which I am most familiar — geography — this sense of participation is evident in a range of work. Notable examples include Arun Saldanha, *Psychedelic White: Goa Trance and the Viscosity of Race* (Minneapolis: University of Minnesota Press, 2007), an ethnography of trance in Goa; Hayden Lorimer, "Forces of Nature, Forms of Life: Calibrating Ethology and Phenomenology," in *Taking-Place: Non-representational Theories and Geography*, ed. Ben Anderson and Paul Harrison, 55–78 (Farnham, U.K.: Ashgate, 2010), an account of sensing more-than-human refrains; and Emma Roe, "Material Connectivity, the Immaterial and the Aesthetic of Eating Practices: An Argument for How Genetically Modified Foodstuff Becomes

Inedible," *Environment and Planning A* 38, no. 3 (2006): 465–481, an ethological exploration of the affective qualities of food assemblages. Equally, others are beginning to think through — albeit with different emphases — the question of how this sense of participation might complement and complicate questions of the participatory. See, for example, Peter Kraftl and John Horton, "'The Health Event': Everyday, Affective Politics of Participation," *Geoforum* 38, no. 5 (2007): 1012–1027; and Kye Askins and Rachel Pain, "Contact Zones: Participation, Materiality, and the Messiness of Interaction," *Environment and Planning D: Society and Space* 29, no. 5 (2011): 803–821. Equally, there are various efforts to rework participation via collaborative experiment with artists and performers. For an overview, see Harriet Hawkins, "Dialogues and Doings: Sketching the Relationships between Geography and Art," *Geography Compass* 5, no. 7 (2010): 464–478; and Harriet Hawkins, "Geography and Art, an Expanding Field: Site, the Body and Practice," *Progress in Human Geography* 37, no. 1 (2013): 52–71.

3. Brian Massumi, *Parables for the Virtual: Movement, Affect, Sensation* (Durham, NC: Duke University Press, 2002).

4. Isabelle Stengers, "Experimenting with Refrains: Subjectivity and the Challenge of Escaping Modern Dualism," *Subjectivity* 22, no. 1 (2008): 38–59.

5. Positions represented most forcefully by Derrida and Badiou, respectively.

6. William James, *Pragmatism* (Indianapolis: Hackett, 1981), 29.

7. My thanks to Jane Bennett for forwarding this.

8. From the call for participation to Dancing the Virtual/Danser le Virtual, organized by Senselab and the Workshop for Radical Empiricism, Montreal, 2006.

9. These included Henri Bergson, *The Creative Mind: An Introduction to Metaphysics* (New York: Dover, 2007); Gilles Deleuze, *Difference and Repetition*, trans. Paul Patton (London: Athlone, 1994); José Gil, *Metamorphoses of the Body*, trans. Stephen Muecke (Minneapolis: University of Minnesota Press, 1998); William James, *Essays in Radical Empiricism* (Lincoln: University of Nebraska Press, 1996); Susan Langer, *Philosophy in a New Key* (Cambridge, MA: Harvard University Press, 1941); Alfred North Whitehead, *Symbolism: Its Meaning and Effect* (New York: Fordham University Press, 1958); Alfred North Whitehead, *Adventures of Ideas* (New York: First Free Press, 1967).

10. See Andrew Murphie, "Clone Your Technics: Research Creation, Radical Empiricism and the Constraints of Models," *Inflexions: A Journal for Research-Creation* 1, no. 1 (2008).

11. Gilles Deleuze, *The Fold: Leibniz and the Baroque*, trans. Tom Conley (London: Athlone, 1993); Bernard Cache, *Earth Moves: The Furnishing of Territories* (Cambridge, MA: MIT Press, 1995); Madeline Gins and Arakawa, *Architectural Body* (Tuscaloosa: Alabama University Press, 2002); Greg Lynn, *Animate Form* (Princeton, NJ: Princeton University Press, 1999).

12. See also John-David Dewsbury, "Dancing: The Secret Slowness of the Fast," in *Geographies of Mobilities: Practices, Spaces, Subjects*, ed. Tim Cresswell and Peter Merriman, 51–68 (Farnham, U.K.: Ashgate, 2011); Peter Merriman, "Architecture/ Dance: Choreographing and Inhabiting Spaces with Anna and Lawrence Halprin," *Cultural Geographies* 17, no. 4 (2010): 427–449.

13. Gilles Deleuze, "What Children Say," in *Essays Critical and Clinical*, trans. Daniel Smith and Michael Greco (London: Verso, 1998), 61.

14. Deleuze, "What Children Say," 62.

15. For a discussion of the affective spaces of fathering, see Stuart Aitken, *The Awkward Spaces of Fathering* (Farnham, U.K.: Ashgate, 2009).

16. Deleuze, *Essays Critical and Clinical*, 62.

17. Torsten Hägerstrand, "What about People in Regional Science?" *Papers of the Regional Science Association* 24 (1970): 7–21.

18. David Parkes and Nigel Thrift, *Times, Spaces, and Places: A Chronogeographic Perspective* (Chichester: Wiley, 1980).

19. See, for example, Derek Gregory, *Ideology, Science, and Human Geography* (London: Hutchinson, 1978).

20. Gillian Rose, *Feminism and Geography: The Limits of Geographical Knowledge* (Minneapolis: University of Minnesota Press, 1993).

21. See Alan Latham, "Research, Performance, and Doing Human Geography: Some Reflections on the Diary-Photograph, Diary-Interview Method," *Environment and Planning A* 35, no. 11 (2003): 1993–2017; Tim Schwanen, "Matters of Interest: Artefacts, Spacing and Timing," *Geografiska Annaler* 89 B, no. 1 (2007): 9–22.

22. Nigel Thrift, "Torsten Hägerstrand and Social Theory," *Progress in Human Geography* 29, no. 3 (2005): 337.

23. Thrift, "Torsten Hägerstrand and Social Theory," 338.

24. William Forsythe, "Choreographic Objects," Wexner Center for the Arts, http://synchronousobjects.osu.edu/media/inside.php?p=essay (accessed May 30, 2013).

25. Forsythe, "Choreographic Objects."

26. Deleuze, "What Children Say," 63.

27. Deleuze, "What Children Say," 63.

28. Cache, *Earth Moves.*

29. Cache, *Earth Moves*, 30.

30. Gins and Arakawa, *Architectural Body*, 45.

31. Gins and Arakawa, *Architectural Body*, 45.

32. Gins and Arakawa, *Architectural Body*, 61.

33. Deleuze, "What Children Say," 66–67.

34. Félix Guattari, "Ritornellos and Existential Affects," in *The Guattari Reader*, ed. Gary Genosko, 158–171 (Oxford: Blackwell, 1996).

35. See Marie Huber and Achim Nelke, "Monopoly: The Multiple Career of a Concept," in *Space Time Play: Computer Games, Architecture and Urbanism, the Next Level*, ed. Friedrich von Borries, Steffen P. Walz, and Mattias Böttger, 472–473 (London: Birkhäuser, 2007), 472.

36. Stephen Bottoms and Matthew Ghoulish, *Small Acts of Repair: Performance, Ecology and Goat Island* (London: Routledge, 2007).

37. Gilles Deleuze, *Negotiations: 1972–1900*, trans. Martin Joughin (New York: Columbia University Press, 1995), 161.

38. See William Connolly, *Pluralism* (Durham, NC: Duke University Press, 2005);

and Jane Bennett, *The Enchantment of Modern Life: Attachments, Crossings, Ethics* (Princeton, NJ: Princeton University Press, 2001).

39. See Bennett, *The Enchantment of Modern Life*; and Kathleen Stewart, "Afterword: Worlding Refrains," in *The Affect Theory Reader*, ed. Melissa Gregg and Gregory Seigworth, 339–353 (Durham, NC: Duke University Press, 2010).

40. Franco "Bifo" Berardi, *The Soul at Work: From Alienation to Autonomy*, trans. Francesca Cadel and Giuseppina Mecchia (Los Angeles: Semiotext(e), 2009), 135.

41. Gins and Arakawa, *Architectural Body*, 47.

42. Alfred North Whitehead, *Process and Reality*, rev. ed. (New York: Free Press, 1978), 21.

BIBLIOGRAPHY

Abrahamsson, Sebastian, and Paul Simpson. "The Limits of the Body: Boundaries, Capacities, Thresholds." *Social and Cultural Geography* 12, no. 4 (2011): 331–338.

Adey, Peter. *Mobility*. London: Routledge, 2010.

Adler, Janet. "Who Is the Witness? A Description of Authentic Movement." *Contact Quarterly* 12, no. 1 (1987): 20–29.

Agamben, Giorgio. *Infancy and History: On the Destruction of Experience*. Trans. Lisa Heron. London: Verso, 2007.

———. *The Man without Content*. Trans. Lisa Albert. Stanford, CA: Stanford University Press, 1999.

———. *Remnants of Auschwitz*. Trans. Daniel Heller-Roazan. New York: Zone Books, 1999.

Aitken, Stuart. *The Awkward Spaces of Fathering*. Farnham, U.K.: Ashgate, 2009.

Alexander, F. Matthias. *The Alexander Technique: The Essential Writings of F. Matthias Alexander*. Selected and introduced by Edward Maisal. New York: Carol Communications, 1989.

Amin, Ash. *Land of Strangers*. Cambridge: Polity, 2012.

Anderson, Ben. "Affect and Biopower: Towards a Politics of Life." *Transactions of the Institute of British Geographers* 37, no. 1 (2012): 28–43.

———. "Affective Atmospheres." *Emotion, Space, and Society* 2, no. 2 (2009): 77–81.

———. "Becoming and Being Hopeful: Towards a Theory of Affect." *Environment and Planning D: Society and Space* 24, no. 5 (2006): 733–752.

———. "Modulating the Excess of Affect: Morale in a State of Total War." In *The Affect Theory Reader*, ed. Melissa Gregg and Gregory Seigworth, 161–185. London: Duke University Press, 2010.

———. "A Principle of Hope: Recorded Music, Practices of Listening, and the Immanence of Utopia." *Geografiska Annaler, Series B: Human Geography* 84, nos. 3–4 (2002): 211–227.

———. "Transcending without Transcendence: Utopianism and an Ethos of Hope." *Antipode* 38, no. 4 (2006): 691–710.

Anderson, Ben, and Paul Harrison, eds. *Taking-Place: Non-representational Theories and Geography.* Farnham, U.K.: Ashgate, 2010.

Anderson, Benedict. *Imagined Communities: Reflections on the Origin and Spread of Nationalism.* London: Verso, 1983.

Antliff, Mark. *Inventing Bergson: Cultural Politics and the Parisian Avant-Garde.* Princeton, NJ: Princeton University Press, 1993.

Appadurai, Arjun. *Modernity at Large: Essays on Cultural Globalization.* Minneapolis: University of Minnesota Press, 1996.

Appia, Adolphe. *Adolphe Appia: Essays, Scenarios, and Designs.* Ed. Richard Beacham. Trans. W. R. Volbach. London: UMI Research Press, 1989.

Ash, James. "Architectures of Affect: Anticipating and Manipulating the Event in Practices of Videogame Design and Testing." *Environment and Planning D: Society and Space* 28, no. 4 (2010): 653–671.

Askins, Kye, and Rachel Pain. "Contact Zones: Participation, Materiality, and the Messiness of Interaction." *Environment and Planning D: Society and Space* 29, no. 5 (2011): 803–821.

Bachelard, Gaston. *The Dialectic of Duration.* Trans. Mary McAllester Jones. Manchester: Clinamen, 2000.

Bairner, Alan. *Sport, Nationalism and Globalization.* Albany: State University of New York Press, 2001.

Barbrook, Richard. "Broadcasting and National Identity in Ireland." *Media, Culture and Society* 14, no. 2 (1992): 203–227.

Barnett, Clive. "Political Affects in Public Space: Normative Blind-Spots in Non-representational Ontologies." *Transactions of the Institute of British Geographers* 33, no. 2 (2008): 186–200.

Barry, Andrew. "Political Situations: Knowledge Controversies in Transnational Governance." *Critical Policy Studies* 6, no. 3 (2012): 324–336.

Bartenieff, Irmgard. *Body Movement: Coping with the Environment.* Reading: Gordon and Breach Science, 1980.

———. "Dance Therapy: A New Profession or a Rediscovery of an Ancient Role of the Dance." *Dance Scope* 7, no. 6 (1972): 6–18.

Bartenieff, Irmgard, Claire Schmais, and Elissa White. "An Interview with Irmgard Bartenieff." *American Journal of Dance Therapy* 4, no. 1 (1981): 5–24.

Bateson, Gregory. *Mind and Nature: A Necessary Unity.* New York: E. P. Dutton, 1979.

———. "Some Components of Socialization for Trance." *Ethnos* 3, no. 2 (1975): 143–155.

———. *Steps to an Ecology of Mind.* London: Paladin, 1973.

Bateson, Gregory, and Mary Bateson. *Angels Fear: Towards an Epistemology of the Sacred.* New York: Bantam, 1988.

Baudoin, Patricia, and Heidi Gilpin. "Proliferation and Perfect Disorder: William Forsythe and the Architecture of Disappearance." Ballet Frankfurt. Accessed May 31, 2013, http://www.hawickert.de/ARTIC1.html.

Baugh, Christopher. *Theatre, Performance and Technology*. Basingstoke: Palgrave Macmillan, 2005.

Beacham, Richard. *Adolphe Appia: Artist and Visionary of the Modern Theatre*. Reading: Harwood Academic, 1994.

———. "'Bearers of the Flame': Music, Dance, Design, and Lighting, Real and Virtual — the Enlightened and Still Luminous Legacies of Hellerau and Dartington." *Performance Research* 11, no. 4 (2006): 81–94.

Behrenshausen, Bryan. "Toward a (Kin)Aesthetic of Video Gaming: The Case of Dance Dance Revolution." *Games and Culture* 2, no. 4 (2007): 335–354.

Bennett, Jane. "Commodity Fetishism and Commodity Enchantment." *Theory and Event* 5, no. 1 (2001).

———. *The Enchantment of Modern Life: Attachments, Crossings, and Ethics*. Princeton, NJ: Princeton University Press, 2001.

Bennett, Jill. "Stigmata and Sense Memory: St. Francis and the Affective Image." *Art History* 24, no. 1 (2001): 1–16.

Berardi, Franco "Bifo." *The Soul at Work: From Alienation to Autonomy*. Trans. Francesca Cadel and Giuseppina Mecchia. Los Angeles: Semiotext(e), 2009.

Bergson, Henri. *The Creative Mind: An Introduction to Metaphysics*. New York: Dover, 2007.

———. *Matter and Memory*. Trans. N. M. Paul and W. S. Palmer. London: Zone Books, 1988.

———. *Time and Free Will: An Essay on the Immediate Data of Consciousness*. Mineola, NY: Dover, [1913] 2001.

———. *The Two Sources of Morality and Religion*. Trans. R. Ashley Audra and Cloudesley Brereton, with the assistance of W. Horsfall Carter. Notre Dame, IN: University of Notre Dame Press, 1977.

Berland, Jody. "Locating Listening: Technological Space, Popular Music, Canadian Meditation." In *The Place of Music: Music, Space and the Production of Place*, ed. Andrew Leyshon, David Matless, and George Revill. New York: Guilford, 1998.

———. *North of Empire: Essays on the Cultural Technologies of Space*. Durham, NC: Duke University Press, 2009.

Berlant, Lauren. "On the Case." *Critical Enquiry* 33, no. 4 (2002): 663–671.

Berrol, Cynthia. "Neuroscience Meets Dance/Movement Therapy: Mirror Neurons, the Therapeutic Process and Empathy." *Arts in Psychotherapy* 33 (2006): 302–315.

Billig, Michael. *Banal Nationalism*. London: Sage, 1995.

Bird Rose, Deborah. "Pattern, Connection, Desire: In Honour of Gregory Bateson." *Australian Humanities Review* 35 (June 2005).

Birringer, Johannes. *Media and Performance along the Border*. Baltimore, MD: Johns Hopkins University Press, 1998.

Bishop, Elizabeth. *Complete Poems*. London: Chatto and Windus, 1991.

Bissell, David. "Passenger Mobilities: Affective Atmospheres and the Sociality of Public Transport." *Environment and Planning D: Society and Space* 28, no. 2 (2010): 270–289.

Bissell, David, and Gillian Fuller, eds. *Stillness in a Mobile World*. London: Routledge, 2010.

Blencowe, Claire. *Biopolitical Experience: Foucault, Power, and Positive Critique*. Basingstoke: Palgrave Macmillan, 2011.

Bogue, Ronald. "Minority, Territory, Music." In *An Introduction to the Philosophy of Gilles Deleuze*, ed. Jean Khalfa, 114–132. London: Continuum, 1999.

Böhme, Gernot. "The Art of the Stage Set as a Paradigm for Aesthetic Atmospheres." Contribution to a colloquium. Cresson. Accessed September 28, 2010. www .cresson.archi.fr.

———. "Atmosphere as the Fundamental Concept of a New Aesthetics." *Thesis Eleven* 36 (1993): 113–126.

Bondi, Liz. "Making Connections and Thinking through Emotions: Between Geography and Psychotherapy." *Transactions of the Institute of British Geographers* 30, no. 4 (2005): 433–448.

Borden, Ian. *Skateboarding, Space and the City*. Oxford: Berg, 2001.

Bordogna, Francesca. *William James at the Boundaries: Philosophy, Science, and the Geography of Knowledge*. Chicago: University of Chicago Press, 2008.

Bottoms, Stephen, and Matthew Goulish. *Small Acts of Repair: Performance, Ecology and Goat Island*. London: Routledge, 2007.

Bowman, Isaiah. "Geography in the Creative Experiment." *Geographical Review* 28, no. 1 (1938): 1–19.

Boydston, Jo Ann, ed. *John Dewey: The Later Works 1925–1952*. Carbondale: University of Illinois Press, 1984–1991.

Boyle, Raymond. "From Our Gaelic Fields: Radio, Sport and Nation in Post-partition Ireland." *Media, Culture and Society* 14, no. 4 (1992): 623–636.

Brandt, George, ed. *Modern Theories of Drama*. Oxford: Oxford University Press, 1998.

Brennan, Teresa. *The Transmission of Affect*. Ithaca, NY: Cornell University Press, 2004.

Brodsky Lacour, Claudia. *Lines of Thought: Discourse, Architectonics, and the Origin of Modern Philosophy*. Durham, NC: Duke University Press, 1996.

Brooks Hedstrom, Darlene. "The Geography of the Monastic Cell in Early Egyptian Monastic Literature." *Church History* 78, no. 4 (2009): 756–791.

Bruno, Carol. "Maintaining a Concept of the Dance in Dance/Movement Therapy." *American Journal of Dance Therapy* 12, no. 2 (1990): 101–113.

Buchanan, Ian. "The Problem of the Body in Deleuze and Guattari." *Body and Society* 3, no. 3 (1997): 73–91.

Cache, Bernard. *Earth Moves: The Furnishing of Territories*. Cambridge, MA: MIT Press, 1995.

Carruthers, Mary. *The Craft of Thought: Meditation, Rhetoric, and the Making of Images, 400–1200*. Cambridge: Cambridge University Press, 2000.

Carter, Paul. *Dark Writing: Geography, Performance, Design*. Honolulu: University of Hawai'i Press, 2009.

———. *The Sound In Between: Voice, Space, Performance*. Kensington: New South Wales University Press, 1992.

Chien, Irene. "This Is Not a Dance." *Film Quarterly* 59, no. 3 (2006): 22–34.

Chodorow, Joan. *Dance Therapy and Depth Psychology: The Moving Imagination.* London: Routledge, 1991.

Clément, Catherine. *Syncope: The Philosophy of Rapture.* Trans. Deirdre M. Mahoney and Sally O'Driscoll. Minneapolis: University of Minnesota Press, 1994.

Clough, Patricia, and Jean Halley, eds. *The Affective Turn: Theorizing the Social.* Durham, NC: Duke University Press, 2007.

Colls, Rachel. "Feminism, Bodily Difference and Non-representational Geographies." *Transactions of the Institute of British Geographers* 37, no. 3 (2012): 430–445.

Connolly, Maureen, and Anna Lathrop. "Maurice Merleau-Ponty and Rudolf Laban — an Interactive Appropriation of Parallels and Resonances." *Human Studies* 20 (1997): 27–45.

Connolly, William. "Brain Waves, Transcendental Fields and Techniques of Thought." *Radical Philosophy* 94 (1999): 19–28.

———. *Neuropolitics: Thinking, Culture, Speed.* Minneapolis: University of Minnesota Press, 2001.

———. *Pluralism.* Durham, NC: Duke University Press, 2005.

———. *A World of Becoming.* Durham, NC: Duke University Press, 2011.

Conradson, David. "Landscape, Care and the Relational Self: Therapeutic Encounters in Southern England." *Health and Place* 11, no. 4 (2005): 337–348.

Copeland, Roger. *Merce Cunningham: The Modernizing of Modern Dance.* London: Routledge, 2004.

Corcoran, Neil. "The Same Again? Repetition and Refrain in Louis MacNeice." *Cambridge Quarterly* 38, no. 3 (2009): 214–224.

Counsell, Colin. "The Kinesics of Infinity: Laban, Geometry and the Metaphysics of Dancing Space." *Dance Research* 24, no. 2 (2006): 105–116.

Cresswell, Tim. *On the Move: Mobility in the Western World.* New York: Routledge, 2006.

———. "Review Essay. Nonrepresentational Theory and Me: Notes of an Interested Sceptic." *Environment and Planning D: Society and Space* 30, no. 1 (2012): 96–105.

Crisell, Andrew. *Understanding Radio.* London: Routledge, 1994.

Cronin, Mike. "Defenders of the Nation? The Gaelic Athletic Association and Irish Nationalist Identity." *Irish Political Studies* 11, no. 1 (1996): 1–19.

———. "Sport and a Sense of Irishness." *Irish Studies Review* 9 (1994): 1–24.

Cunningham, David. "The Concept of Metropolis: Philosophy and Urban Form." *Radical Philosophy* 133 (2005): 13–25.

"Dalcroze Explains His Method." *Literary Digest* 78 (1932): 31.

Daly, Ann. "Movement Analysis: Piecing Together the Puzzle." TDR/*The Drama Review* 32, no. 4 (1988): 40–52.

de Certeau, Michel. *The Practice of Everyday Life.* Berkeley: University of California Press, 1984.

Deleuze, Gilles. *Cinema 1: The Movement-Image.* Trans. Hugh Tomlinson and Barbara Habberjam. London: Athlone, 1986.

———. *Cinema 2: The Time-Image.* Trans. Hugh Tomlinson and Robert Galeta. London: Athlone, 1989.

———. *Difference and Repetition.* Trans. Paul Patton. London: Athlone, 1994.

———. *Essays Critical and Clinical.* Trans. Daniel Smith and Michael Greco. London: Verso, 1998.

———. *Expressionism in Philosophy: Spinoza.* Trans. Martin Joughin. New York: Zone Books, 1990.

———. *The Fold: Leibniz and the Baroque.* Trans. Tom Conley. London: Athlone, 1993.

———. *Foucault.* Trans. Séan Hand. London: Continuum, 1999.

———. *Francis Bacon: The Logic of Sensation.* Trans. Daniel Smith. London: Continuum, 2003.

———. *Negotiations: 1972–1900.* Trans. Martin Joughin. New York: Columbia University Press, 1995.

———. *Two Regimes of Madness: Texts and Interviews 1975–1995.* Trans. Ames Hodges and Mike Taormina. New York: Semiotext(e), 2007.

Deleuze, Gilles, and Félix Guattari. *A Thousand Plateaus.* Trans. Brian Massumi. London: Athlone, 1988.

———. *What Is Philosophy?* Trans. Graham Burchell and Hugh Tomlinson. London: Verso, 1994.

De Swaan, Abram. "Widening Circles of Disidentification: On the Psycho- and Sociogenesis of the Hatred of Distant Strangers — Reflections on Rwanda." *Theory, Culture and Society* 14, no. 2 (1999): 105–122.

Dewey, John. *Art as Experience.* New York: Minton Balch, 1958.

———. "The Need for a Recovery of Philosophy." In *The Philosophy of John Dewey,* ed. John McDermott, 59–97. Chicago: University of Chicago Press, 1981.

———. "Three Prefaces to Books by Alexander." In F. Matthias Alexander, *The Alexander Technique,* 169–184. New York: Carol Communications, 1989.

Dewsbury, John-David. "Affective Habit Ecologies: Material Dispositions and Immanent Inhabitations." *Performance Research* 17, no. 1 (2012): 74–82.

———. "Dancing: The Secret Slowness of the Fast." In *Geographies of Mobilities: Practices, Spaces, Subjects,* ed. Tim Cresswell and Peter Merriman, 51–68. Farnham, U.K.: Ashgate, 2011.

———. "Performativity and the Event: Enacting a Philosophy of Difference." *Environment and Planning D: Society and Space* 18, no. 4 (2000): 473–496.

———. "Witnessing Space: 'Knowledge without Contemplation.'" *Environment and Planning A* 35, no. 11 (2003): 1907–1932.

Dewsbury, John-David, and Simon Naylor. "Practising Geographical Knowledge: Fields, Bodies and Dissemination." *Area* 34, no. 3 (2003): 253–260.

Doruff, Sher. "The Translocal Event and the Polyrhythmic Diagram." PhD diss., Central Saint Martins College of Art and Design, University of London, October 2006.

Durcan, Paul. *Greetings to Our Friends in Brazil.* London: Harvill, 1999.

Edensor, Tim, ed. *Geographies of Rhythm.* Farnham, U.K.: Ashgate, 2010.

Ekman, Paul. *Emotions in the Human Face: Guidelines for Research and Integration of Findings.* Oxford: Pergamon, 1972.

Eksteins, Modris. *Rites of Spring: The Great War and the Birth of the Modern Age.* New York: First Mariner Books, 2000.

Elkaïm, Mony. "From General Laws to Singularities." *Family Process* 24 (1985): 151–164.

Emerson, Rana. "'Where My Girls At?': Negotiating Black Womanhood in Music Videos." *Gender and Society* 16, no. 1 (2002): 115–135.

Enns, Anthony. "Psychic Radio: Sound Technologies, Ether Bodies, and Spiritual Vibrations." *Senses and Society* 3, no. 2 (2008): 137–152.

Everett Gilbert, Katherine. "Mind and Medium in the Modern Dance." *Journal of Aesthetics and Art Criticism* 1, no. 1 (1941): 106–129.

Feist, Richard. "Weyl's Appropriation of Husserl's and Poincaré's Thought." *Synthese* 132, no. 3 (2002): 73–301.

Forsythe, William. "Choreographic Objects." Wexner Center for the Arts. Accessed May 30, 2013, http://synchronousobjects.osu.edu/media/inside.php?p=essay.

———. *Improvisation Technologies: A Tool for the Analytical Dance Eye.* CD-ROM. Karlsruhe: ZKM, 1999.

Foucault, Michel. *The Care of the Self: The History of Sexuality,* vol. 3. Trans. Robert Hurley. New York: Vintage, 1988.

———. *Ethics, Subjectivity and Truth: Essential Works of Foucault 1954–1984.* Ed. Paul Rabinow. London: Penguin, 1997.

———. "Technologies of the Self." In *The Essential Works of Michel Foucault, 1954–1984,* vol. 1, ed. Paul Rabinow and Nikolas Rose, 145–169. New York: New York University Press, 2003.

Franko, Mark. "History/Theory: Criticism/Practice." In *Corporealities: Dancing Knowledge, Culture and Power,* ed. Susan Leigh Foster, 25–52. London: Routledge, 1996.

Friel, Brian. *Dancing at Lughnasa.* London: Faber, 1990.

Frith, Simon. "Art versus Technology: The Strange Case of Popular Music." *Media, Culture and Society* 8, no. 3 (2006): 263–279.

Frith, Simon, Andrew Goodwin, and Laurence Grossberg, eds. *Sound and Vision: The Music Video Reader.* London: Routledge, 1993.

Fuller, Duncan, and Kye Askins. "Public Geographies II: Being Organic." *Progress in Human Geography* 34, no. 5 (2010): 654–667.

Fuller, Matthew. *Media Ecologies: Materialist Energies in Art and Technoculture.* Cambridge, MA: MIT Press, 2005.

George, Mark. "Reanimating the Face: Early Writings by Duchenne and Darwin on the Neurology of Facial Emotion Expression." *Journal of the History of the Neurosciences* 3, no. 1 (1994): 21–33.

Gibbons, Luke. *Transformations in Irish Culture.* Cork: Cork University Press, 1996.

Gibson-Graham, J. K. *A Post-capitalist Politics.* Minneapolis: University of Minnesota Press, 2006.

Gil, José. *Metamorphoses of the Body.* Trans. Stephen Muecke. Minneapolis: University of Minnesota Press, 1998.

———. "Paradoxical Body." *TDR/The Drama Review* 50, no. 4 (2006): 21–35.

Gins, Madeline, and Shusaku Arakawa. *Architectural Body*. Tuscaloosa: Alabama University Press, 2002.

Goffey, Andrew. "Abstract Experience." *Theory, Culture and Society* 25, no. 4 (2008): 15–30.

Goffman, Irving. *Forms of Talk*. Oxford: Basil Blackwell, 1981.

Golston, Michael. *Rhythm and Race in Modernist Poetry and Dance*. New York: Columbia University Press, 2008.

Gordon, Paul. *Face to Face: Therapy as Ethics*. London: Constable, 1999.

Gow, Joe. "Mood and Meaning in Music Video: The Dynamics of Audiovisual Synergy." *Southern Communications Journal* 59, no. 3 (1994): 255–261.

Gregg, Melissa, and Gregory Seigworth, eds. *The Affect Theory Reader*. Durham, NC: Duke University Press, 2010.

Gregory, Derek. *Ideology, Science, and Human Geography*. London: Hutchinson, 1978.

Grossberg, Lawrence. *Cultural Studies in the Future Tense*. Durham, NC: Duke University Press, 2010.

Grosz, Elizabeth. *Chaos, Territory, Art: Deleuze and the Framing of the Earth*. New York: Columbia University Press, 2010.

Guattari, Félix. *Chaosmosis: An Ethico-aesthetic Paradigm*. Trans. Paul Bains and Julian Pefanis. Sydney: Power, 1995.

———. "Ritornellos and Existential Affects." In *The Guattari Reader*, ed. Gary Genosko, 158–171. Oxford: Blackwell, 1996.

Hägerstrand, Torsten. "What about People in Regional Science?" *Papers of the Regional Science Association* 24 (1970): 7–21.

Hamera, Judith. *Dancing Communities: Difference and Connection in the Global City*. London: Palgrave Macmillan, 2007.

Hansen, Mark. *Bodies in Code: Interfaces with Digital Media*. London: Routledge, 2006.

———. *New Philosophy for New Media*. Cambridge, MA: MIT Press, 2006.

Harré, Rom. "An Outline of the Social Constructionist Viewpoint." In *The Social Construction of Emotions*, ed. Rom Harré, 2–14. Oxford: Blackwell, 1986.

Harrison, Paul. "'How Shall I Say It . . . ?': Relating the Nonrelational." *Environment and Planning A* 39, no. 1 (2007): 590–608.

Harrison, Stephan, Steve Pile, and Nigel Thrift, eds. *Patterned Ground: Entanglements of Nature and Culture*. London: Reaktion, 2004.

Hawkins, Harriet. "Dialogues and Doings: Sketching the Relationships between Geography and Art." *Geography Compass* 5, no. 7 (2010): 464–478.

———. "Geography and Art, an Expanding Field: Site, the Body and Practice." *Progress in Human Geography* 37, no. 1 (2013): 52–71.

Haynes, Richard. "There's Many a Slip 'Twixt the Eye and the Lip': An Exploratory History of Football Broadcasts and Running Commentaries on BBC Radio, 1927–1939." *International Review for the Sociology of Sport* 34, no. 2 (1999): 143–156.

H'Doubler, Margaret. *The Dance and Its Place in Education*. New York: Harcourt Brace, 1925.

Heaney, Seamus. *Seeing Things*. London: Faber and Faber, 1991.

Henry, Michael. *The Genealogy of Psychoanalysis*. Trans. Douglas Brick. Stanford, CA: Stanford University Press, 1993.

Herzog, Amy. "Affectivity, Becoming, and the Cinematic Event: Gilles Deleuze and the Futures of Feminist Film Theory." In *Conference Proceedings for Affective Encounters: Rethinking Embodiment in Feminist Media Studies*, ed. Anu Koivunen and Susanna Paasonen, 83–88. Turku, Finland: University of Turku and the Finnish Society for Cinema Studies, 2001. Accessed May 28, 2013, http://www.hum.utu.fi/oppiaineet/mediatutkimus/tutkimus/proceedings_pienennetty.pdf.

———. "Discordant Visions: The Popular Musical Images of the Soundies Jukebox Film." *American Music* 22, no. 1 (2004): 27–39.

Heyes, Cressida J. *Self-Transformations: Foucault, Ethics, and Normalized Bodies*. Oxford: Oxford University Press, 2007.

Highmore, Ben. "Homework." *Cultural Studies* 18, no. 2 (2004): 306–327.

Hinchliffe, Steve, Matthew Kearnes, Monica Degen, and Sarah Whatmore. "Urban Wild Things: A Cosmopolitical Experiment." *Environment and Planning D: Society and Space* 23, no. 5 (2005): 643–658.

Hodgson, John. *Mastering Movement: The Life and Work of Rudolf Laban*. London: Methuen, 2001.

Holloway, Julian. "Institutional Geographies of the New Age Movement." *Geoforum* 31, no. 4 (2000): 553–565.

Horn, Walter. "On the Origins of the Medieval Cloister." *Gesta* 12, nos. 1–2 (1973): 13–52.

Howe, Dianne. *Individuality and Expression: The Aesthetics of the New German Dance, 1908–1936*. New York: Peter Lang, 1996.

Huber, Marie, and Achim Nelke. "Monopoly: The Multiple Career of a Concept." In *Space Time Play: Computer Games, Architecture and Urbanism, the Next Level*, ed. Friedrich von Borries, Steffen P. Walz, and Mattias Böttger, 472–473. London: Birkhäuser, 2007.

Huggins, Mike. "BBC Radio and Sport 1922–1939." *Contemporary British History* 21, no. 4 (2007): 491–515.

Ingold, Tim. *Lines: A Brief History*. London: Routledge, 2007.

Irwin, Robert. *Being and Circumstance*. San Francisco: Lapis, 1985.

James, William. "The Energies of Men." *Science N.S.* 25, no. 635 (1907): 321–332.

———. *Essays in Radical Empiricism*. Lincoln: University of Nebraska Press, 1996.

———. *A Pluralistic Universe*. Lincoln: University of Nebraska Press, 1996.

———. *Pragmatism*. Indianapolis: Hackett, 1981.

———. *The Principles of Psychology*, vol. 1. New York: Dover, 1950.

———. "What Is an Emotion?" *Mind* 9, no. 34 (1884): 188–205.

———. "What Pragmatism Means." In *The Writings of William James*, ed. John McDermott. New York: Modern Library, 1968.

Jaques-Dalcroze, Emile. *Rhythm, Music and Education*. London: Chatto and Windus, 1921.

Jarzombek, Mark. "Corridor Spaces." *Critical Inquiry* 36 (summer 2010): 728–770.

Juntunen, Marja-Leena, and Leena Hyvönen. "Digging Dalcroze, or, Dissolving the Mind-Body Dualism: Philosophical and Practical Remarks on the Musical Body in Action." *Music Education Research* 3, no. 2 (2001): 203–214.

———. "Embodiment in Musical Knowing: How Body Movement Facilitates Learning within Dalcroze Eurhythmics." *British Journal of Musical Education* 21, no. 2 (2004): 199–214.

Jupp, Eleanor. "The Feeling of Participation: Everyday Spaces and Urban Change." *Geoforum* 39, no. 1 (2008): 331–343.

Kahn, Douglas, and Gregory Whitehead, eds. *Wireless Imagination: Sound, Radio, and the Avant-Garde*. Cambridge, MA: MIT Press, 1994.

Kaiser, Paul. "Dance Geometry (Forsythe)." *Performance Research* 4, no. 2 (1999). Accessed May 28, 2013, http://openendedgroup.com/writings/danceGeometry .html.

Kandinsky, Wassily. *Point and Line to Plane*. New York: Dover, 1923.

Kaplan, Danny. "The Songs of the Siren: Engineering National Time on Israeli Radio." *Cultural Anthropology* 24, no. 2 (2009): 313–345.

Katz, Jack. *How Emotions Work*. Chicago: University of Chicago Press, 1999.

Kaye, Nick. *Site Specific Art: Performance, Place, and Documentation*. London: Routledge, 2000.

Kiberd, Declan. "Dancing at Lughnasa." *Irish Review* 27 (2001): 18–23.

Kochhar-Lindgren, Kanta. *Hearing Difference: The Third Ear in Experimental, Deaf, and Multicultural Theater*. Washington, DC: Gallaudet University Press, 2006.

Kosnoski, Jason. "Artful Discussion: John Dewey's Classroom as a Model of Deliberative Association." *Political Theory* 33, no. 5 (2005): 654–677.

Kosofsky Sedgwick, Eve. *Between Men: English Literature and Male Homosocial Desire*. New York: Columbia University Press, 1985.

Kraftl, Peter, and John Horton. "'The Health Event': Everyday, Affective Politics of Participation." *Geoforum* 38, no. 5 (2007): 1012–1027.

Kunreuther, Laura. "Technologies of the Voice: FM Radio, Telephone, and the Nepali Diaspora in Kathmandu." *Cultural Anthropology* 21, no. 3 (2006): 323–353.

Kuppers, Petra. *Disability and Contemporary Performance: Bodies on Edge*. London: Routledge, 2003.

———. "Landscaping: Spacings." *Women and Performance: A Journal of Feminist Theory* 13, no. 2 (2003): 41–56.

Laban, Rudolf. *Choreutics*. Annotated and ed. Lisa Ullman. London: MacDonald and Evans, 1966.

———. *The Mastery of Movement*, 2nd ed. Rev. and enlarged Lisa Ullmann. London: MacDonald and Evans, 1960.

Laban, Rudolf, and Frank Lawrence. *Effort: The Economy of Human Movement*. London: MacDonald and Evans, 1974.

Langer, Susan. *Philosophy in a New Key*. Cambridge, MA: Harvard University Press, 1941.

Last, Angela. "Experimental Geographies." *Geography Compass* 6, no. 12 (2012): 706–724.

Latham, Alan. "Research, Performance, and Doing Human Geography: Some

Reflections on the Diary-Photograph, Diary-Interview Method." *Environment and Planning A* 35, no. 11 (2003): 1993–2017.

Latour, Bruno. "How to Talk about the Body: The Normative Dimension of Science Studies." *Body and Society* 10, nos. 2–3 (2004): 205–229.

——. *Pandora's Hope*. Cambridge, MA: Harvard University Press, 2002.

Laurier, Eric, and Chris Philo. "Possible Geographies: A Passing Encounter in a Café." *Area* 38, no. 4 (2006): 353–363.

Lazzarato, Maurizio. "From Capital-Labour to Capital-Life." *Ephemera* 4, no. 3 (2004): 187–208.

——. "Struggle, Event, Media." Maurizio Lazzarato. Accessed January 6, 2010, www.republicart.net/disc/representations/lazzarato01_en.htm.

Lefebvre, Henri. *Critique of Everyday Life*, vol. 1. Trans. John Moore. London: Verso, 2008.

——. *Critique of Everyday Life*, vol. 2. Trans. John Moore. London: Verso, 2008.

——. *Critique of Everyday Life*, vol. 3. Trans. Gregory Elliot. London: Verso, 2008.

——. *Elements of Rhythmanalysis: Space, Time, and Everyday Life*. Trans. Stuart Elden and Gerald Moore. London: Continuum, 2004.

——. *The Production of Space*. Trans. Donald Nicholson Smith. Oxford: Blackwell, 1991.

——. *The Sociology of Marx*. Trans. Norbert Guterman. London: Penguin, 1972.

Lepecki, André. *Exhausting Dance: Performance and the Politics of Movement*. London: Routledge, 2006.

Li, Darryl. "Echoes of Violence: Considerations on Radio and Genocide in Rwanda." *Journal of Genocide Research* 6, no. 1 (2004): 9–27.

Lingis, Alphonso. *Foreign Bodies*. London: Routledge, 1994.

Livett, Jennifer. "'Odd Couples and Double Acts, or Strange but Not Always Queer': Some Male Pairs and the Modern/Postmodern Subject." *Australian Humanities Review* 21, no. 2 (2001).

Lomax, Yves. *Sounding the Event: Escapades in Dialogue and Matters of Art, Nature and Time*. London: I. B. Tauris, 2005.

Lorimer, Hayden. "Forces of Nature, Forms of Life: Calibrating Ethology and Phenomenology." In *Taking-Place: Non-representational Theories and Geography*, ed. Ben Anderson and Paul Harrison, 55–78. Farnham, U.K.: Ashgate, 2010.

——. "The Geographical Fieldcourse as Active Archive." *Cultural Geographies* 10, no. 3 (2003): 278–308.

——. "Progress in Cultural Geography: Non-representational Conditions and Concerns." *Progress in Human Geography* 32, no. 4 (2008): 551–559.

Lorimer, Jamie. "Moving Image Methodologies for More-Than-Human Geographies." *Cultural Geographies* 17, no. 2 (2010): 237–258.

Luke, Tim. "Liberal Society and Cyborg Subjectivity: The Politics of Environments, Bodies, and Nature." *Alternatives* 21, no. 1 (1996): 1–30.

Lury, Celia. "Marking Time with Nike: The Illusion of the Durable." *Public Culture* 11, no. 3 (1999): 499–526.

Lynn, Greg. *Animate Form*. Princeton, NJ: Princeton University Press, 1999.

MacNeice, Louis. *Collected Poems*. London: Faber, 1966.

Malectic, Vera. *Body-Space-Expression: The Development of Rudolf Laban's Movement and Dance Concepts*. New York: Mouton de Gruyter, 1987.

Mandelstam, Osip. *The Complete Critical Prose and Letters*. Ed. J. G. Harris. Trans. J. G. Harris and C. Link. Ann Arbor, MI: Ardis, 1979.

Mandle, W. F. *The Gaelic Athletic Association and Irish Nationalist Politics, 1884–1924*. London: Gill and Macmillan, 1987.

Manning, Erin. *Politics of Touch: Movement, Sense, Sovereignty*. Minneapolis: University of Minnesota Press, 2007.

———. "Propositions for the Verge: William Forsythe's Choreographic Objects." *Inflexions* 2 (December 2008). www.inflexions.org.

———. *Relationscapes: Movement, Art, Philosophy*. Cambridge, MA: MIT Press, 2009.

Manning, Susan. *Ecstasy and the Demon: Feminism and Nationalism in the Dances of Mary Wigman*. Berkeley: University of California Press, 1993.

Manvell, Roger. *On the Air: A Study of Broadcasting in Sound and Television*. London: Andre Deutsch, 1953.

Marks, Laura. *The Skin of the Film: Intercultural Cinema, Embodiment, and the Senses*. Durham, NC: Duke University Press, 2000.

Massey, Doreen. *For Space*. London: Sage, 2005.

Massumi, Brian. "The Diagram as Technique of Existence." ANY 23 (1998): 42–47.

———. "Introduction." In *A Shock to Thought: Expression after Deleuze and Guattari*, ed. Brian Massumi, xiii–xxxix. London: Routledge, 2002.

———. *Parables for the Virtual: Movement, Affect, Sensation*. Durham, NC: Duke University Press, 2002.

———. "Urban Appointment: A Possible Rendez-Vous with the City." In *Making Art out of Databases*, ed. Joke Brouwer and Arjen Mulder, 28–55. Rotterdam: v2 Organisatie/Dutch Architecture Institute, 2003.

May, Jon, and Nigel Thrift, eds. *TimeSpace: Geographies of Temporality*. New York: Routledge, 2001.

May, Todd. *Deleuze*. Cambridge: Cambridge University Press, 2005.

McCarren, Felicia. *Dance Pathologies: Performance, Poetics, Medicine*. Stanford, CA: Stanford University Press, 1988.

———. *Dancing Machines: Choreographies of the Age of Mechanical Reproduction*. Stanford, CA: Stanford University Press, 2003.

McCloud, Mary. "Introduction." In *The Pragmatist Imagination: Thinking about Things in the Making*, ed. Joan Ockman, 170–175. Princeton, NJ: Princeton Architectural Press, 2000.

McCormack, Derek P. "Body-Shopping: Refiguring Geographies of Fitness." *Gender, Place and Culture* 6, no. 2 (1999): 155–177.

———. "Diagramming Practice and Performance." *Environment and Planning D: Society and Space* 23, no. 1 (2005): 119–147.

———. "Drawing Out the Lines of the Event." *Cultural Geographies* 11, no. 2 (2004): 212–220.

———. "Engineering Affective Atmospheres: On the Moving Geographies of the 1897 Andrée Expedition." *Cultural Geographies* 15, no. 4 (2008): 413–430.

———. "An Event of Geographical Ethics in Spaces of Affect." *Transactions of the Institute of British Geographers* 28, no. 4 (2003): 488–507.

———. "A Paper with an Interest in Rhythm." *Geoforum* 33, no. 4 (2002): 469–485.

McLoone, Michael. "Music Hall Dope and British Propaganda? Cultural Identity and Early Broadcasting in Ireland." *Historical Journal of Film, Radio, and Television* 20, no. 3 (2000): 301–315.

McMullan, Anna. "'In Touch with Some Otherness': Gender, Authority and the Body in 'Dancing at Lughnasa.'" *Irish University Review* 29, no. 1 (1999): 90–100.

Merleau-Ponty, Maurice. *Phenomenology of Perception.* Trans. Colin Smith. London: Routledge, 1962.

Merriman, Peter. "Architecture/Dance: Choreographing and Inhabiting Spaces with Anna and Lawrence Halprin." *Cultural Geographies* 17, no. 4 (2010): 427–449.

Meyer, Kurt. "Rhythms, Streets, Cities." In *Space, Difference, Everyday Life: Reading Henri Lefebvre,* ed. Kanishka Goonewardena et al., 147–160. London: Routledge, 2008.

Milutis, Jay. *Ether: The Nothing That Connects Everything.* Minneapolis: University of Minnesota Press, 2006.

Mullarkey, John. *Post-continental Philosophy.* London: Athlone, 2006.

Murphie, Andrew. "Clone Your Technics: Research Creation, Radical Empiricism and the Constraints of Models." *Inflexions: A Journal for Research-Creation* 1, no. 1 (2008).

Musicant, Shira. "Authentic Movement: Clinical Considerations." *American Journal of Dance Therapy* 23, no. 1 (2001): 11–28.

Nancy, Jean-Luc. *Au fond des images.* Paris: Galilée, 2003.

———. *Listening.* Trans. Charlotte Mandel. New York: Fordham University Press, 2007.

Navarro-Yashin, Yael. *The Make-Believe Space: Affective Geography in a Postwar Polity.* Durham, NC: Duke University Press, 2012.

O'Hehir, Michael. *My Life and Times.* Dublin: Blackwater, 1996.

O'Malley, Mary. "A Bit Like Shakespeare." In *Playing the Field: Irish Writers on Sport,* ed. George O'Brien, 37–49. Dublin: New Island, 2000.

Osborne, Peter. "The Reproach of Abstraction." *Radical Philosophy* 127 (2004): 21–28.

Pain, Rachel, and Peter Francis. "Reflections on Participatory Research." *Area* 35, no. 1 (2003): 46–54.

Pain, Rachel, and Sara Kindon. "Participatory Geographies." *Environment and Planning A* 39, no. 12 (2007): 2807–2812.

Parkes, David, and Nigel Thrift. *Times, Spaces, and Places: A Chronogeographic Perspective.* Chichester: Wiley, 1980.

Partsch-Bergsohn, Isa. *Modern Dance in Germany and the United States: Cross Currents and Influences.* Switzerland: Harwood, 1994.

Payne, Helen. *Dance Movement Therapy: Theory and Practice.* London: Routledge, 1992.

Pearson, Mike, and Michael Shanks. *Theatre/Archaeology.* London: Routledge, 2001.

Peirce, Charles Sanders. *The Collected Papers of Charles S. Peirce*, 8 vols. Ed. Charles Hartshorne, Paul Weiss, and Arthur Burks. Cambridge, MA: Harvard University Press, 1931–1958.

Perec, George. *Species of Spaces and Other Pieces*. London: Penguin, 1999.

Phelan, Peggy. *Unmarked: The Politics of Performance*. London: Routledge, 1997.

Phillips-Silver, Jessica, and Laurel Trainor. "Hearing What the Body Feels: Auditory Encoding of Rhythmic Movement." *Cognition* 105 (2007): 533–546.

Pinkerton, Alistair, and Klaus Dodds. "Radio Geopolitics: Broadcasting, Listening, and the Struggle for Acoustic Spaces." *Progress in Human Geography* 33, no. 1 (2009): 10–27.

Portanova, Stamatia. "The Intensity of Dance: Body, Movement and Sensation across the Screen." *Extensions: The Online Journal of Embodied Technology* 2 (2005): 33–44.

Powell, Richard. "Becoming a Geographical Scientist: Oral Histories of Arctic Fieldwork." *Transactions of the Institute of British Geographers* 33, no. 4 (2008): 548–565.

Powell, Richard, and Alex Vasudevan. "Geographies of Experiment." *Environment and Planning A* 39, no. 8 (2007): 1790–1793.

Preston-Dunlop, Valerie. "Choreutic Concepts and Practice." *Dance Research* 1, no. 1 (1983): 77–88.

———. *Rudolf Laban: An Extraordinary Life*. London: Dance Books, 1998.

Pryke, Michael, Gillian Rose, and Sarah Whatmore, eds. *Using Social Theory: Thinking through Research*. London: Sage, 2003.

Rabinbach, Anson. *The Human Motor: Energy, Fatigue and the Origins of Modernity*. Berkeley: University of California Press, 1992.

Rajchman, John. *Constructions*. Cambridge, MA: MIT Press, 1998.

Rancière, Jacques. *The Future of the Image*. Trans. Gregory Eliot. London: Verso, 2007.

Reynolds, Dee. *Rhythmic Subjects*. Alton, U.K.: Dance Books, 2007.

Robinson, Mary. "Foreword." In Micheal Ó Hehir, *My Life and Times*, vii. Dublin: Blackwater, 1996.

Rodowick, D. N. *Reading the Figural, or, Philosophy after the New Media*. Durham, NC: Duke University Press, 2001.

Roe, Emma. "Material Connectivity, the Immaterial and the Aesthetic of Eating Practices: An Argument for How Genetically Modified Foodstuff Becomes Inedible." *Environment and Planning A* 38, no. 3 (2006): 465–481.

Rogers, Clark. "Dalcroze Eurhythmics." *Southern Communication Journal* 35, no. 3 (1970): 225–226.

Romero, Emilio, Alan Hurwitz, and Vicki Carranza. "Dance Therapy in a Therapeutic Community for Schizophrenic Patients." *Arts in Psychotherapy* 10 (1983): 85–92.

Rose, Gillian. *Feminism and Geography: The Limits of Geographical Knowledge*. Minneapolis: University of Minnesota Press, 1993.

Rose, Nikolas. "The Politics of Life Itself." *Theory, Culture and Society* 18, no. 6 (2001): 1–30.

Rossberg-Gempton, Irene, and Gary D. Poole. "The Relationship between Body Movement and Affect: From Historical and Current Perspectives." *Arts in Psychotherapy* 19 (1991): 39–46.

Roth, Gabrielle. *Maps to Ecstasy: A Healing Journey for the Untamed Spirit.* Novatarro, CA: New World Library, 1989.

———. *Sweat Your Prayers: Movement as Spiritual Practice.* New York: Tarcher/Putnam, 1997.

Rousseau, Jean-Jacques. *Reveries of a Solitary Walker.* London: Penguin, 1979.

Saldanha, Arun. *Psychedelic White: Goa Trance and the Viscosity of Race.* Minneapolis: University of Minnesota Press, 2007.

Scannell, Paddy. *Radio, Television and Modern Life.* Oxford: Blackwell, 1996.

Schott-Billmann, France. "Primitive Expression: An Anthropological Dance Therapy Method." *Arts in Psychotherapy* 19 (1992): 105–109.

Schwanen, Tim. "Matters of Interest: Artefacts, Spacing and Timing." *Geografiska Annaler* 89 B, no. 1 (2007): 9–22.

Schwartz, Hillel. "Torque: The New Kinaesthetic of the Twentieth Century." In *Incorporations*, ed. Jonathan Crary and Sandford Kwinter, 71–126. New York: Zone Books, 1991.

Sconce, Jeffrey. *Haunted Media: Electronic Presence from Telegraphy to Television.* Durham, NC: Duke University Press, 2000.

Seigworth, Gregory. "The Affect of Corn." *M/C Journal* 8 (December 2005).

Seigworth, Gregory, and Michael Gardiner. "Rethinking Everyday Life: And Then Nothing Turns Itself Inside Out." *Cultural Studies* 18, nos. 2–3 (2004): 139–159.

Seitz, Jay. "The Bodily Basis of Thought." *New Ideas in Psychology* 18, no. 1 (2000): 23–40.

———. "Dalcroze, the Body, Movement, and Musicality." *Psychology of Music* 33, no. 4 (2005): 419–435.

Serres, Michel. *The Five Senses: A Philosophy of Mingled Bodies.* Trans. Margaret Sankey and Peter Cowley. London: Athlone, 2008.

———. *Genesis.* Trans. Geneviève James and James Nielson. Ann Arbor: University of Michigan Press, 1995.

Shaviro, Steven. *The Cinematic Body.* Minneapolis: University of Minnesota Press, 1993.

———. "Post-cinematic Affect: On Grace Jones, *Boarding Gate* and *Southland Tales.*" *Film-Philosophy* 14, no. 1 (2010): 1–102.

Shehan Campbell, Patricia. "Rhythmic Movement and Public School Music Education: Conservative and Progressive Views of the Formative Years." *Journal of Research in Music Education* 39, no. 1 (1991): 12–22.

Shiraishi, Fumiko. "Calvin Brainerd Cady: Thought and Feeling in the Study of Music." *Journal of Research in Music Education* 47, no. 2 (1999): 150–162.

Shotter, John. "Bateson, Double Description, Todes, and Embodiment: Preparing Activities and Their Relation to Abduction." *Journal for the Theory of Social Behaviour* 39 (2009): 219–245.

Shouse, Elizabeth. "Feeling, Emotion, Affect." *M/C Journal* 8, no. 6 (2005).

Shusterman, Richard. *Body Consciousness: A Philosophy of Mindfulness and Somaesthetics.* Cambridge: Cambridge University Press, 2008.

Siegal, Lynn. "Psychoanalytic Dance Therapy: The Bridge between Psyche and Soma." *American Journal of Dance Therapy* 17, no. 2 (1995): 115–128.

Siegmund, Gerald. "Bending towards the Breaking Point: The De-formation of Dance and Mannerist Images of the Body." In *Remembering the Body*, ed. Gabrielle Brandstetter and Hortensia Völckers, 136–170. Ostfildern-Ruit: Hatje Cantz, 2000.

Silva Lima, Maristela Moura, and Alba Pedreira Vieira. "Ballroom Dance as Therapy for the Elderly in Brazil." *American Journal of Dance Therapy* 29, no. 2 (2007): 129–141.

Simonsen, Kirsten. "Bodies, Sensations, Space and Time: The Contribution from Henri Lefebvre." *Geografiska Annaler* 87 B, no. 1 (2005): 1–14.

Simpson, Paul. "Chronic Everyday Life: Rhythmanalysing Street Performance." *Social and Cultural Geography* 9, no. 7 (2008): 807–829.

Sobchack, Vivian. *Carnal Thoughts: Embodiment and Moving Image Culture*. Berkeley: University of California Press, 2004.

Spector, Irwin. *Rhythm and Life: The Work of Emile Jaques-Dalcroze*. Stuyvesant, NY: Pendragon, 1990.

Spiers, Steven. "Dancing and Drawing Choreography and Architecture." *Journal of Architecture* 10, no. 4 (2007): 349–364.

Squier, Susan, ed. *Communities of the Air: Radio Century, Radio Culture*. Durham, NC: Duke University Press, 2003.

———. "Wireless Possibilities, Posthuman Possibilities: Brain Radio, Community Radio, Radio Lazarus." In *Communities of the Air: Radio Century, Radio Cultures*, ed. Susan Squier, 275–303. Durham, NC: Duke University Press, 2004.

Stanton-Jones, Kristina. *An Introduction to Dance Movement Therapy*. London: Routledge, 1992.

Steegmuller, Francis. *Cocteau: A Biography*. London: Macmillan, 1970.

Stengers, Isabelle. "A Constructivist Reading of *Process and Reality*." *Theory, Culture and Society* 25, no. 4 (2008): 91–110.

———. "Experimenting with Refrains: Subjectivity and the Challenge of Escaping Modern Dualism." *Subjectivity* 22, no. 1 (2008): 38–59.

———. "Introductory Notes on an Ecology of Practices." *Cultural Studies Review* 11, no. 1 (2005): 183–196.

Stern, Daniel. *The Interpersonal World of the Infant: A View from Psychoanalysis and Developmental Psychology*. New York: Basic Books, 1985.

Stewart, Kathleen. "Afterword: Worlding Refrains." In *The Affect Theory Reader*, ed. Melissa Gregg and Gregory Seigworth, 339–353. Durham, NC: Duke University Press, 2010.

———. "Atmospheric Attunements." *Environment and Planning D: Society and Space* 39, no. 3 (2011): 445–453.

———. *Ordinary Affects*. Durham, NC: Duke University Press, 2007.

Stivale, Charles. *Disenchanting les Bon Temps: Identity and Authenticity in Cajun Music and Dance*. Durham, NC: Duke University Press, 2003.

Straw, Will. "Music Video in Its Contexts: Popular Music and Post-modernism in the 1990s." *Popular Music* 7, no. 3 (1988): 247–266.

Swanton, Dan. "Flesh, Metal, Road: Tracing the Machinic Geographies of Race." *Environment and Planning D: Society and Space* 28, no. 3 (2010): 447–446.

Tarde, Gabriel. *The Laws of Imitation.* Trans. Elsie Clews Parsons. New York: Henry Holt, 1903.

Taussig, Michael. "Viscerality, Faith and Scepticism: Another Theory of Magic." In *In Near Ruins: Cultural Theory at the End of the Century*, ed. Nicholas Dirks, 221–256. Minneapolis: University of Minnesota Press, 1998.

Taylor, George. "François Delsarte: A Codification of Nineteenth-Century Acting." *Theatre Research International* 24, no. 1 (1999): 71–81.

Taylor, Timothy. "Music and the Rise of Radio in 1920s America: Technological Imperialism, Socialization, and the Transformation of Intimacy." *Historical Journal of Film, Radio and Television* 22, no. 4 (2002): 425–443.

Tebbutt, John. "Imaginative Demographics: The Emergence of a Talkback Radio Audience in Australia." *Media, Culture and Society* 28, no. 6 (2006): 857–882.

Thoreau, Henry David. *Walking.* Boston: Beacon, 1994.

Thrift, Nigel. "Afterwords." *Environment and Planning D: Society and Space* 18, no. 3 (2000): 213–255.

———. *Non-representational Theory: Space, Politics, Affect.* London: Routledge, 2008.

———. "Radio." In *Patterned Ground: Entanglements of Nature and Culture*, ed. S. Harrison, S. Pile, and N. Thrift, 269–270. London: Reaktion, 2004.

———. "Space." *Theory, Culture and Society* 23, nos. 2–3 (2006): 21–35.

———. *Spatial Formations.* London: Sage, 1996.

———. "Torsten Hägerstrand and Social Theory." *Progress in Human Geography* 29, no. 3 (2005): 337–340.

Toepfer, Karl. *Empire of Ecstasy: Nudity and Movement in German Body Culture 1910–1935.* Berkeley: University of California Press, 1997.

Toscano, Alberto. "The Culture of Abstraction." *Theory, Culture and Society* 25, no. 4 (2008): 57–75.

———. "The Open Secret of Real Abstraction." *Rethinking Marxism* 20, no. 2 (2008): 273–287.

———. "Vital Strategies: Maurizio Lazzarato and the Metaphysics of Contemporary Capitalism." *Theory, Culture and Society* 24, no. 6 (2007): 71–91.

Urry, John. *Mobilities.* Cambridge, MA: Polity, 2007.

Vasudevan, Alexander. "Symptomatic Acts, Experimental Embodiments: Theatres of Scientific Protest in Interwar Germany." *Environment and Planning A* 39, no. 8 (2007): 1812–1837.

Virilio, Paul. *The Lost Dimension.* Trans. Daniel Moshenberg. New York: Semiotext(e), 1991.

———. *Negative Horizon.* Trans. Michael Degener. London: Continuum, 2005.

Virno, Paolo. "The Two Masks of Materialism." *Pli* 12 (2001): 167–173.

von Borries, Friedrich. *Who's Afraid of Niketown? Nike-Urbanism, Branding, and the City of Tomorrow.* Rotterdam: Episode, 2004.

Watson, Iarfhlaith. "Irish-Language Broadcasting: History, Ideology and Identity." *Media, Culture and Society* 24, no. 6 (2002): 739–757.

Weyl, Herman. *Space, Time, Matter.* Trans. Henry L. Brose. New York: Cosmino, 2010.

Whitehead, Alfred North. *Adventures of Ideas.* New York: First Free Press, 1967.

———. *The Concept of Nature.* New York: Prometheus Books, 2004.

———. *An Enquiry Concerning the Principles of Natural Knowledge.* New York: Dover, 1982.

———. *Process and Reality*, rev. ed. New York: Free Press, 1978.

———. *Science and the Modern World.* New York: Free Press, 1967.

———. *Symbolism: Its Meaning and Effect.* New York: Fordham University Press, 1958.

Williams, Raymond. *Keywords.* London: Flamingo, 1984.

Winters, Allison. "Emotion, Embodiment, and Mirror Neurons in Dance/Movement Therapy: A Connection across Disciplines." *American Journal of Dance Therapy* 30 (2008): 84–105.

Wittgenstein, Ludwig. *Philosophical Investigations.* Trans. G. E. M. Anscombe. Oxford: Wiley-Blackwell, 1978.

Wylie, John. "Landscape, Absence and the Geographies of Love." *Transactions of the Institute of British Geographers* 34, no. 3 (2009): 275–289.

———. "Smoothlands: Fragments/Landscapes/Fragments." *Cultural Geographies* 13, no. 3 (2006): 458–465.

INDEX

Stones, Alan, 197

Structure of feeling, 43, 144, 151, 164; kinesthetic, 173, 175; modernity as, 21

Subjectivity, 92, 156; affect and, 112; Guattari
on, 112–116, 147, 191; habit and, 223n35;
milieu and, 194; resingularizing of, 93,
113, 115

Suggestion, 28

Surfaces of variation, 200, 205

Swanton, Dan, 208n6

Symmetry, 170–172, 237n27

Syncope, 138

Taking place, Dewey and, 41

Tarde, Gabriel, 149, 161

Taylor, F. W., 176

Tebbut, John, 123

Techniques of relation, 106–110

Techniques of thinking, 29

Television, 135, 147–149, 152–153

Temperament, as rhythmic, 51

Territory, 8, 80–81, 84, 113, 121, 133, 199

Tessenow, Heinrich, 56

Therapeutic interventions, 105–106, 112–113,
115

Therapeutic objects, 103–105

Threshold of consistency, 139, 157, 161

Thrift, Nigel, xi, 9, 22, 195

Throwing a paddy, 105–106

Time and motion studies, 166, 176

Time geography, 194–195

Tissue of experience, 14, 204

Toepfer, Karl, 52

Toscano, Alberto, 148, 234n21

Trace-forms (movement as), 174, 182

Transversality, 114; of affect, 112, 115; of affective spacetimes, 8, 203; becomings, 116;
lines, 87, 179; movements, 171; refrains, 84,
104; relations, 14, 103; rhythm, 86

Treadmill, 154–157, 159–160, 162

Turbulence, 20, 42; affective, 33, 35

Ullmann, Lisa, 240n55

Utopianism, 45, 52, 56, 61

Value, xii, 15–16, 21, 144, 148, 150, 155–156,
164, 166, 191, 204; diagramming, 201–202;
universes of, 115, 193

Video games, 153

Virtual, 34–36, 82, 93, 116, 183, 200; commentating and, 136

Voice, 39, 47, 121–126, 129, 131, 133–134, 139

Voluminous space, 121, 124, 135

von Borries, Friedrich, 156

Walking, 36, 47, 48, 193

Way Out West (Laurel and Hardy), 158, 161

Weyl, Hermann, 170–171

Whitehead, Alfred North, 26, 43, 210n12; on
abstraction, 184–185; on rhythm, 43

Wilford, Andrew, 197

Williams, Raymond, 22

Witnessing, 108–110, 140

Wittgenstein, Ludwig, 110

Worldly arrangements, 204

Writing, 11, 77

Wundt, Wilhelm, 239n42

Wylie, John, 212n33